POPULISM

POPULISM

WHAT EVERYONE NEEDS TO KNOW®

PAUL D. KENNY

OXFORD
UNIVERSITY PRESS

Oxford University Press is a department of the University of Oxford. It furthers the University's objective of excellence in research, scholarship, and education by publishing worldwide. Oxford is a registered trade mark of Oxford University Press in the UK and certain other countries.

"What Everyone Needs to Know®" is a registered trademark of Oxford University Press.

Published in the United States of America by Oxford University Press
198 Madison Avenue, New York, NY 10016, United States of America.

CIP data is on file at the Library of Congress

ISBN 978–0–19–775833–5 (pbk.)
ISBN 978–0–19–775832–8 (hbk.)

DOI: 10.1093/wentk/9780197758328.001.0001

Paperback printed by Sheridan Books, Inc., United States of America
Hardback printed by Bridgeport National Bindery, Inc., United States of America

The manufacturer's authorized representative in the EU for product safety is Oxford University Press España S.A., Parque Empresarial San Fernando de Henares, Avenida de Castilla, 2 – 28830 Madrid (www.oup.es/en or product.safety@oup.com). OUP España S.A. also acts as importer into Spain of products made by the manufacturer.

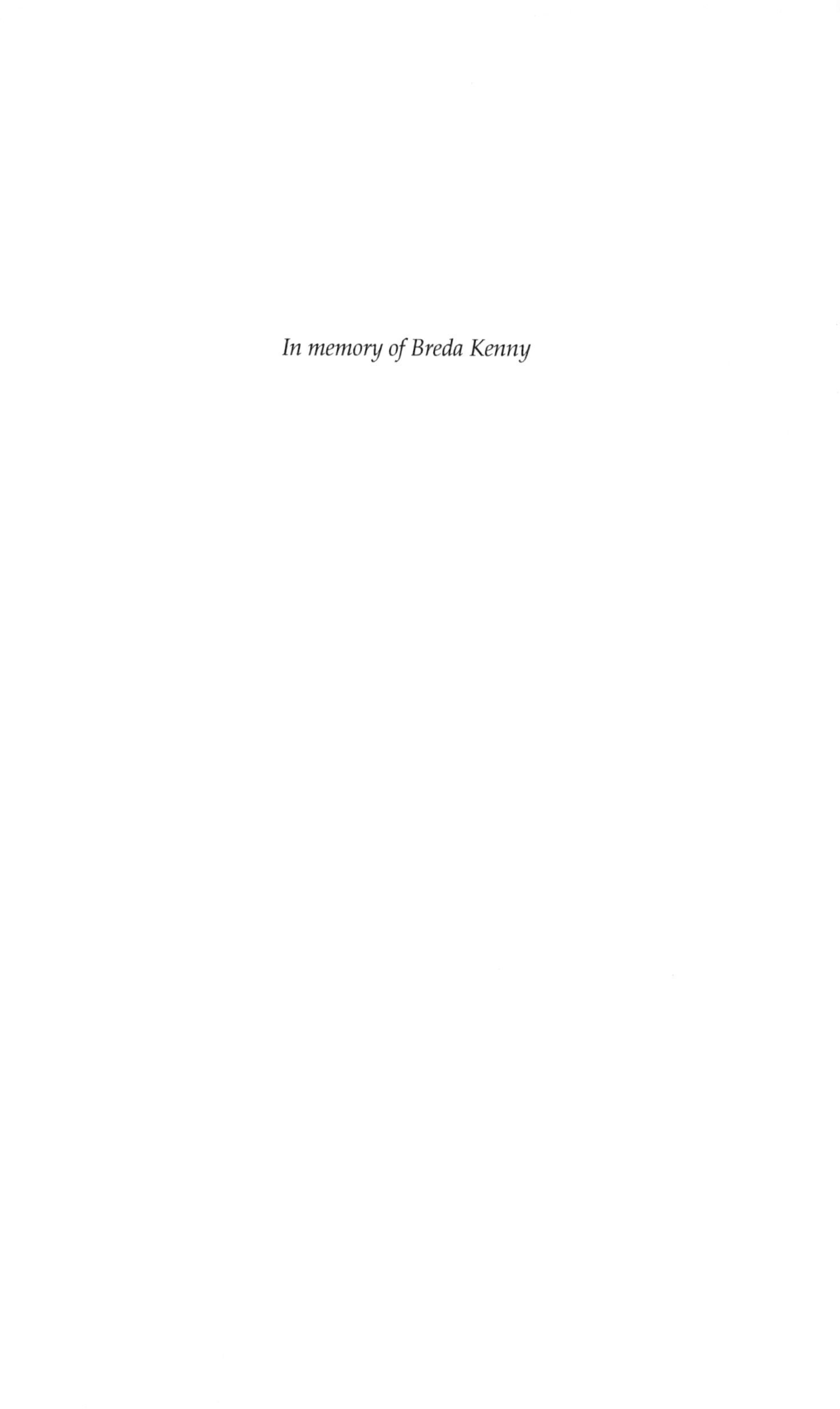

In memory of Breda Kenny

ACKNOWLEDGMENTS

Sadly, while I was writing this book, I lost my mother, Breda, to the cancer she had fought for many years. I thank my family, especially Paul, Rachel, Maurice, Andrew, Kate, Declan, and Patrick for their support over those difficult months. I know mum would have been proud to see this book in print. I am sorry I couldn't complete it in time for that to happen, but I dedicate it to her memory.

I'm grateful too to my commissioning editor at Oxford University Press, Dave McBride, who saw the potential in this project, and showed great patience through my delays in completing it. I also thank the rest of the team at the press for helping to see it to fruition.

CONTENTS

1

INTRODUCTION

Can it happen here, again?

From early in the morning of January 6, 2021, supporters of President Donald J. Trump began congregating on the National Mall in Washington, DC. "Be there. Will be wild!" Trump had tweeted the night before. By noon, the crowd had swelled to some 25,000. As Trump took to the stage, delivering one of his trademark speeches—disjointed, rambling, but laced with venom—the atmosphere was charged, infused with anger and resentment. In addition to their standard issue *Make America Great Again*© baseball caps, Trump partisans showed up sporting an assortment of merchandise from *QAnon*—a bizarre conspiracy theory popular among Trump's supporters. They brandished religious paraphernalia and Confederate and Gadsden flags—the latter flag with its "Don't tread on me" motto. Some carried mock gallows, a chilling portent of the violence to come. And then there were those in combat gear—militant, armed, prepared for something darker, something far beyond the bounds of even the usual rambunctious MAGA rally.

Refusing to accept that he had lost the November 6, 2020, election to Joe Biden fair and square, Trump had spent the ensuing two months propagating the "Big Lie" of a vast Democratic Party–Deep State–International Communist conspiracy to steal the election by fraud. By the turn of the year, all of Trump's legal challenges to the result had failed. As the day on which Vice President Mike Pence was set to formally tally the votes of the Electoral College, January 6 was billed by Trump as the last chance for his supporters to prevent the catastrophe of a Biden administration. Catastrophe, however, was exactly what they brought on. Over two thousand Trump supporters, some of whom were armed with Tasers, baseball bats, pepper spray, and other weapons, stormed the Capitol building, halting the formal vote count, and coming dangerously close to taking the vice president and members of Congress hostage.

Trump's failure to calm, never mind police, his overzealous followers on January 6 led many political opponents, journalists, and scholars to label him a dictator and a fascist. Impeached for an unprecedented second time, Trump's brash but brief career in politics appeared to be done. Yet, four years later, Trump won the popular vote and earned himself a second non-consecutive term in office—a feat achieved only once before in American history. As I complete the writing of this book in mid-2025, Trump has used the early months of his second term to concentrate power in the executive branch to an unprecedented degree. Yet his popularity with his base remains undiminished. How do we explain the extraordinary resilience of Trump's support? Have Americans voted for dictatorship as many commentators fear? If so, how did America, the world's longest-standing mass democracy, fall so far?

Populism, I'll argue in this book, provides answers to these questions and others like them. Trump is not the first leader to rise to power through democratic means only to endanger the very system that brought him there. Populists across the world have followed a pattern: Power, once attained, is centralized. Lawmaking authority, once dispersed among legislatures and parliaments, is drawn inward, toward the executive—to the president's office or the prime minister's desk. The judiciary, once independent, is brought to heel. The press, once free, is silenced. And in some cases, the opposition itself is not only weakened but destroyed. The names are familiar. Hugo Chávez in Venezuela. Alberto Fujimori in Peru. Recep Tayyip Erdoğan in Türkiye. Viktor Orbán in Hungary. Each took office through free and fair elections. Each, once in power, moved swiftly to undermine the institutions that constrained them. Nor is this pattern new. In January 1933, Adolf Hitler, head of Germany's most popular political party, legally assumed office as chancellor. Two months later, with the passage of the Enabling Act, German democracy was all but finished.

Yet despite this troubling record, to equate populism with dictatorship—or worse, with fascism—is a mistake. Trump is no fascist. Unlike Hitler or Mussolini, he has never stood at the head of a "militia party"—the defining characteristic of fascism as a political movement. Even the events of January 6, chaotic and violent as they were, do not change the fundamental fact: Violence has not played a central role in Trump's rise to power. Indeed, in the course of his 2024 re-election campaign, the only major act of violence was one directed at him—an assassination attempt. To be sure, Trump sought to subvert the 2020 election. He attempted to pressure officials, to have unfavorable ballots quashed, to cast doubt on the legitimacy of the vote. But he failed. He left office. As he himself phrased it, he accepted defeat without conceding. He tested the boundaries of dictatorship, but he did not cross them.[1]

Populism, dictatorship, and fascism are not interchangeable concepts. They should not be treated as such and the over-used contradictions in terms, "populist authoritarianism" and "authoritarian populism," should be dispensed with altogether. As its Latin etymological roots imply, populism has something to do with "the people"—the *populus*—in a way that authoritarian political systems do not. Populism's dependence on mass support marks it off as something different from dictatorship. Because of this need for popular backing, according to political theorist, Jan-Werner Müller, "Populism is only thinkable in the context of representative democracy." Unlike fascism, populism is a form of democracy not dictatorship.[2]

Indeed, populism is in some respects a corrective to democratic decay. Populism is not merely an ideology but a political movement—one that arises from the frustrations of those who believe, often with good reason, that the institutions meant to serve them serve others instead. Critics of Trump—the journalists who catalogued every breach of decorum, the diplomats who warned of the damage done to the rules-based international order—often fail to grasp this essential fact: that for his supporters, such breaches are not defects but proof that he is doing the job they elected him to do. The old order works for the elite; it does not work for them. And so, when liberal elites warn of the dangers of his presidency, their warnings are received not as alarms but as self-preservation, as the dominant defending their privileges.

But populism contains within it a paradox. Because while it is true that populists, more than almost any other political actors, govern according to the perceived will of their supporters, they also, inevitably, seek to consolidate their power in ways that undermine democracy. The same institutions they rail against as obstacles become, once they are in control, tools of their own dominance. Huey Long, the populist governor of Depression-era Louisiana who had promised to break the power of the corporations, soon demanded absolute fealty from his state legislature, punishing any who refused with political exile. Juan Perón, president of Argentina from 1946 to 1955, who had built his movement on the rhetoric of social justice, stacked the courts with loyalists who would ensure he never faced real opposition. And Trump, who presented himself as the great disruptor, attacked the legitimacy of elections themselves the moment they no longer served him.

Populists push the institutions of democracy to their limits. They test every rule. And while it is true that some rules are written to serve those already in power, it is equally true that other rules are essential to democracy itself. Without the institutions that allow today's opposition to become tomorrow's government. Populism is not dictatorship, but it is a threat to democracy.

Why is populism a threat to democracy?

To appreciate why populism is a threat to democracy, we first need to understand what democracy itself means. In the simplest terms, democracy is a system where a nation's leaders can be removed through free and fair elections. If they cannot, the system is authoritarian. Ultimately, democracy is a process, not an outcome. It does not guarantee economic equality, justice, or participation—only the ability to remove those in power. As long as voters can throw a government out, democracy remains intact. Democracy, then, is not about virtue or good governance—it is about accountability. This minimalist definition may seem cynical, even cold. But it is precise. Determining whether a state is democratic or not means asking one simple question: Is the government chosen, and replaceable, through elections that are free and fair?

A frequent criticism of this minimalist approach is that democracy cannot be reduced to the mere fact of periodic elections. While this is of course true, it is also a straw man fallacy. Elections per se are not enough; they must be real contests. Russia and China hold elections, yet neither is democratic because their leaders cannot realistically lose. Free and fair elections require more than the casting of ballots—they demand freedom of speech, of assembly, and an independent judiciary. Without these, the opposition cannot organize, and elections become empty rituals. Consider Hungary. Orbán's grip on the press makes true opposition almost impossible. Erdoğan's opposition in Türkiye sees its influence marginalized by one of the most disproportional electoral systems in the world. In Russia, Putin's control of the state's legal apparatus has made opposition a virtual death sentence—ask the widow of Alexei Navalny. These regimes hold elections, but without competition, without the chance of loss, they are not democracies.

In what sense then, are populist regimes a threat to democracy? The answer to this question lies in populism's defining characteristic: *its opposition to the institutional status quo*. When the prevailing institutions are democratic, as they largely are today, populism poses a threat to this form of government. In other words, even if populist rule is not authoritarian by definition, it usually undermines rather than enhances democracy. What does it mean to weaken democracy but not to destroy it, to approach the threshold of dictatorship, but not to cross it?

Let me answer this by returning to the Trump case. The shambolic nature of the Capitol Riot and Trump's reluctant concession shouldn't disguise the fact that the two-month period following his election defeat was one of the most fraught episodes for American democracy since the Civil War more than 150 years earlier. Irrespective of the events of January 6, the actions Trump took in the months leading up to it made clear his willingness to bend or break the law to stay in power.

We now have evidence that his disavowal of the results on election night was no ill-tempered outburst but a premeditated act of deception. Exploiting the fact that Biden supporters were more likely to use mail-in ballots, which took longer to be counted than Trump's predominantly in-person votes, no matter the early tally, Trump planned to declare himself the winner and let Biden challenge him for the crown. When this bluff failed, Trump then pressured government officials to "find" him the votes he needed to beat Biden; he removed officials who resisted his efforts, replacing them with loyalists; he publicly and privately browbeat Pence to discard the legally certified results of the election; Trump even considered using the US military to confiscate ballot boxes that tilted Biden's way. Well before the 2020 election season, Trump had sought to use the justice system to prosecute his political opponents. Although he could do little to silence media criticism due to

America's entrenched protections for free speech, he strove to undermine the credibility of the press, dismissing negative commentary as "fake news."[3]

This is what populists do. They weaken press freedoms, they politicize the justice system, and they manipulate electoral rules to tilt the playing field to their advantage. Pursued together, these tactics all make it a little harder for the opposition to win an election. In short, populists weaken the institutions that sustain democracy. Yet populists rarely complete the turn to full dictatorship. We even have an estimate of how unusual this is—occurring in only about 10 to 20 percent of the cases in which populists have been elected to office. Under populism, as opposed to dictatorship, defeat remains possible. This distinction between populism and authoritarianism matters. We already have words for leaders who cannot be voted out: dictator, tyrant, despot. Populist should not be one of them.[4]

The evidence on this point is clear. Populists erode the institutional constraints on their authority, but in most cases, they remain subject to the ultimate political sanction: losing elections. In the United States, Trump's machinations to find a legal loophole to hold on to power were publicly exposed and he lost support because of them. Even with a sympathetic Supreme Court, Trump's challenges to the 2020 election were unceremoniously thrown out. Several Republican senators defected from the Trump camp, voting for his impeachment. Or consider the case of Poland. The Law and Justice Party (PiS) came to power in 2015 and quickly set about silencing the press and eroding the judiciary's independence. Critics labeled PiS's leader, Jarosław Kaczyński, a de facto dictator, but ultimately his party lost power at the 2023 elections. Similarly, in the Philippines, President Rodrigo Duterte tried and failed to amend the constitution to permit his re-election, and then tried and failed again to secure the succession of his longtime aide, Bong Go, as president. Duterte had to settle for the consolation prize of having his estranged daughter become vice president to rival Bong Bong Marcos—son of the late dictator Ferdinand

Marcos—instead. Such electoral defeats do not happen in dictatorships.

This doesn't mean that we should be complacent about the threat of populism. The survival of American democracy in 2021 had nothing to do with Trump's personal commitment to democratic values. Nor was it due to the "strength" of American institutions per se. Rather, it was that as late as November 2020, Trump and his inner circle still had a limited understanding of how most of America's governmental institutions worked. And so, they were unable to find a way to fundamentally undermine them.

But Trump has learned. Rules, like those set out in the Constitution, are subject to interpretation. Successfully bending or breaking such rules depends on having control over their interpreters and enforcers. In other words, it is the personnel who matter, rather than the institutions—laws, rules, and regulations—per se. Trump's chaotic personnel strategy during his first term meant that he lacked authority over the interpreters and enforcers of critical institutions when the decisive moment came. With the benefit of experience, however, it is conceivable that Trump's second term could pose a greater threat to one of the world's oldest democracies. If the early days of his return to office are any indication, Trump has grasped that this time his control over personnel needs to penetrate deeper into the government bureaucracy. As Trump put it on the campaign trail in 2024, "We had great people, but I had some people that I would not have chosen for a second time," he said. "Now, I know everybody. Now, I am truly experienced." The massive layoffs in the federal bureaucracy reflect not just an ideological commitment to small government or efficiency, but to establishing fuller control over the levers of the state.[5]

It is also important to stress here that even if populist leaders pose a danger to democracy, it does not follow that their supporters are themselves authoritarians. Populist supporters are frustrated with, and resentful of, an institutional status quo they believe is unfair. We'll see that there is often good reason for these feelings. In the West, while highly educated employees in knowledge sectors have become increasingly well off, those left in lower-skilled sectors of the economy, like manufacturing and services, have seen their welfare stagnate or even decline. The main beneficiaries of the twentieth-century economy—working-class white men—have experienced a double blow, with legislative efforts to improve educational, health, and financial equity concentrating on minorities and women.

In developing countries, where populists have historically fared even better than in the West, large swaths of the population are resentful of rampant corruption, misgovernance, and ethnic favoritism. Even where economic growth rates are high, this seems only to feather the nest of the politically connected. As political outsiders, populists are the only ones who can credibly promise to challenge the iniquities of an unfair institutional status quo, even if in the process they put at risk the pluralism necessary for democracy to work. Most voters turn to populists, not *because* they threaten democracy, but *despite* it.

Moreover, before we rush to condemn populism as a halfway house on the road to dictatorship, we have to recall that populism's opposition to minority-protecting institutions is contingent on these institutions *being* the status quo. Casting our gaze a bit wider, we'll see that this isn't always the case. In the—albeit unusual—instances in which the political system is not democratic, but people are allowed to mobilize and protest, populism can advance the cause of democratization. In fact, because of the challenges of political organization under authoritarianism, populism may be the best hope for democratic reform. Yet such cases are rare because most dictatorships repress any kind of spontaneous political activity. Dictators who fail to prevent or put down such popular mobilization find themselves, like the Soviet Union's Mikhail Gorbachev or Egypt's Hosni Mubarak, on the wrong side of a revolutionary regime change. Moreover, the democratic quality of populist protest movements does not seem to survive the transition to power. The likes of Zimbabwe's Robert Mugabe, Indonesia's Sukarno, and Russia's Boris Yeltsin are all too common—each of these one-time democratizers eventually perpetrated coups of their own to remain in power. What these cases best illustrate, perhaps, is that closing institutions to the popular will often produces a populist reaction that can be as bad or worse than the original. All democrats should take note.

What is in this book?

After many years of relative neglect, research on populism has exploded over the last two decades. There is a huge volume of research out there, so much so that it is difficult even for specialists to keep up. Also, as this body of research has grown in methodological sophistication, it has become increasingly challenging for general readers to know which of the many conflicting results they should believe. This first goal of this book is to summarize and interpret in non-technical language a vast literature that extends across political science, economics, sociology, psychology, and history. I can't cite every relevant piece of research, but in the further reading at the end of this book, I list most of the major contributions, then refer those interested to more detailed reviews of specific topics where they are available. The book should be a useful primer for general readers and students of politics, but my hope is that those with a deeper knowledge of the topic will also gain something from my overview of the field.

The book's second aim is more ambitious. It sets out a new research agenda for populism studies in the years to come. After so much ink has already been spilled on populism, it would be fair to ask whether there is anything new to be said on the topic. I believe there is, and this book will outline why I hold this view. I put forward a new approach to understanding populism, which both helps to integrate the best-supported findings of existing research and leads to a novel theory of the causes and consequences of populism that can be tested and refined in future research.

To understand the paradox of populism, we first need to know what it means. In Chapter 2, I'll take a critical look at the three most common ways of defining populism, before setting out a new alternative in Chapter 3. The *ideational* approach argues that populism is a "thin-centered" political ideology, which views politics as an existential struggle between a "pure people" and a "corrupt elite." For many scholars, this populist worldview is expressed in public *discourse* and personal *attitudes*, but for others who adopt a *cultural-stylistic* view, populism refers to a broader style of the "low" people versus the "high" elite that includes a leader's image and behavior. An alternative definition, usually labeled the *political-strategic* approach, concentrates on how populist movements are organized. Populism in this sense is a political movement that rejects structured political parties in favor of the direct mobilization of the masses by a charismatic leader. A third option, which I call the *constitutional* approach, argues that populism is an "anti-pluralist" or "illiberal" way of governing that dismisses the rights of the opposition and minorities, and that erodes institutional limits on executive power.

In Chapter 3, I argue that these seemingly distinct approaches to defining populism can be reconciled; keeping what is most useful and minimalizing what is problematic about them. What I call the *institutional* approach defines populism as *a politics of popular opposition to the institutional status quo*. Like the ideational approach, the institutional approach concurs that there is no populism without the people—popular sentiment is at the heart of populism. However, it views populism not in terms of an opposition between the *people* and *elites*, but between the *people* and *institutions*.

In this sense, populism captures the sense that society's rules of the game are rigged against regular people. Elites are often the beneficiaries of this rigged system; but so too in the populist worldview are immigrants and other minorities—those at the bottom, rather than the top, of the economic pyramid. Resentment of the institutional status quo is likely to be expressed in the speech of political leaders and in the attitudes and opinions of voters. Ultimately, however, ideas (or ideologies) are insufficient to fully grasp the meaning of populism.

Critically, populism is a type of political movement that is anti-institutional not just in terms of its discourse but also in its organization. Consistent with the strategic approach noted above, populist movements eschew the use of deeply institutionalized political parties. Populist supporters are not the only ones to feel *the system* is unfair. But populism is distinct from radical (socialist), revolutionary (communist), and reactionary (fascist) movements in that its organizing structure combines non-violent mass popular participation *and* charismatic leadership in a way that these alternatives do not. While populist movements sometimes initially take the form of amorphous popular protests, like America's Occupy Wall Street, France's Gilets Jaunes, and Spain's Indignados, for them to endure and capture power, they rely on having charismatic leaders who serve as a focal point to unite an otherwise diffuse and disorganized body of support that opposes an unfair institutional status quo.

Finally, the anti-institutionalism at the heart of populism extends to the impact of populist government. As the constitutional approach suggests, populist leaders in power typically erode constraints on the executive and weaken protections for minorities—institutions that are central to democracy. Populist supporters are not, as some scholars propose, soft authoritarians. Rather they see themselves as genuine democrats, in the sense of believing in the legitimacy of rule by the majority. The problem, as we'll see, is that in undermining the institutions that preserve the rights of minorities to contest political power, populism risks veering into dictatorship. We should remember, however, that this latter effect is contingent on the status quo itself being a liberal democratic one, the implication being that populism's defining quality is not antiliberalism but anti-institutionalism.

With this analysis of the meaning of populism out of the way, we can move on to the more interesting questions of its causes and consequences. Most explanations for the recent surge in populism—especially in the West—are concerned with what is called the "demand side." That is, they ask, why do people *want* populism? Although there is some consensus on the factors associated with populist success, there is a curious disconnect between theories of populism as either a pro-people and anti-elite ideology or as popular illiberalism, and the empirical research that has accumulated to date.

One branch of research suggests that populists do best in times of economic hardship. Yet it is unclear why the response to such crises is populism per se, rather than simply a turn to another regular non-populist party. Another body of results show that populist voters seem to be more motivated by nationalist, racist, and misogynistic beliefs. In this case, scholars argue that if white working-class men formed Trump's core base of support, this was more because they were white and male than because they were working class. However, unless populism is equated with nativism, based on existing approaches it is unclear why ethnocentric, anti-immigrant, racist, and chauvinistic beliefs would draw voters to populism per se.

I argue that conceiving of populism as popular anti-institutionalism allows us to better understand variation in support for populism over time and place. Prolonged or severe economic decline leaves many voters not just disenchanted with the ruling party, but with government institutions in general. In this context of institutional distrust, those bodies of rules that attend to the rights and needs of minorities, whether asylum seekers or domestic minorities, become the objects of majority resentment. Institutional distrust can also be directed outward at international organizations like the European

Union and the World Trade Organization, which seem to primarily benefit the politically connected.

Understanding populism in terms of an opposition to the institutional status quo also provides a better explanation for populism in less developed countries. The typical economic and cultural explanations for populism in the West travel poorly to Latin America and Asia—regions, incidentally, where populism has been especially successful. Institutional resentment in these places stems primarily from endemic corruption, nepotism, and inefficiency. In the Philippines and El Salvador, rampant crime and abuse of power, not economics, drove the penal populism of Rodrigo Duterte and Nayib Bukele. In both cases, the enemy was a rigged system that served the connected few while leaving the rest in precarity. Populists, as outsiders, are seen as the only ones willing to blow up a corrupt status quo.

Understanding voter preferences is vital to explaining the rise of populism. Yet, it's common knowledge that "demand" provides only one side of any marketplace. In my most recent book, *Why Populism? Political Strategy from Ancient Greece to the Present*, I argued that popular resentments and disappointments alone cannot explain the rise of populism. We need also to pay attention to the "supply side" of the problem. This means we need an explanation for the choices that voters have in the first place. Doing away with institutionalized parties, populism is a low-cost political strategy that can provide a quick and cheap means to winning power for the political outsider. Communicating directly with voters through the mass media technology of the day, populists avoid the costs of building up complex political party machines.

Yet this low-cost personalistic strategy is only likely to be effective under certain conditions. Changes over time and across the world in media technology and society (e.g., the post-industrial transition) affect the costs and benefits of the populist strategy relative to its alternatives. In the West, the decline in civil society over recent decades, especially in terms of union and church membership, has made the programmatic party building strategy more expensive and more challenging. Analogously, clientelism, or vote buying, becomes much more expensive with economic development and population growth. Even in places like Indonesia and the Philippines, where the practice is common in local elections, it is of declining importance in national ones. Across the world, the costs of direct communication with the masses through new technologies like social media have fallen dramatically. The result is that populism has become increasingly cost effective relative to alternative strategies.

Let me reiterate here that populism—in the sense of a popular opposition to the status quo—goes beyond rhetoric. If populism was merely a type of people-oriented speech, it could be easily and cheaply replicated by all political leaders. The result would be that voters couldn't tell the real populist—the one who will upend the institutional status quo—from the fake. Thus, drawing on the theoretical apparatus of economics, if leaders want to effectively signal their opposition to the institutional status quo, that signal must be *costly*. As the name implies, a costly signal is one that cannot be cheaply replicated. A ballistic missile test sends a far more convincing message to potential enemies than a speech—even one laced with "fire and fury." Populists signal their commitment to challenging the institutional status quo by forgoing the advantages of a well-organized political party. Cutting out the middlemen of a political party, populist leaders deny themselves an important means of getting out the vote, but in doing so they tell voters that they will not be bound by the same old insider deals of the smoke-filled party room.

I concluded *Why Populism?* with the proposition that a full explanation for populism required bringing the demand and supply sides into equilibrium. This means solving a puzzle that has been largely ignored to date. When people feel that the political system is unfair and unresponsive, the typical reaction is apathy and disengagement. People frustrated with the status quo don't mobilize—they do nothing. Indeed, declining voter turnout is a common precursor to populism. Again, in economic terms, it is a classic collective action problem. People want change but they cannot coordinate to bring it about. Few people are willing to put in the effort to achieve a goal, if others can reap the benefits without contributing themselves. For each individual person, no matter their personal grievances or desires, inaction is the rational choice.

This problem can be overcome by the offer of selective material rewards to participants (as in clientelism) or by the social pressures inherent in programmatic parties. However, the sustained mobilization of a mass of people who reject the usual means of political organization—the party—poses an enormous problem. Existing accounts fail to explain how this collective action dilemma is overcome. Neither frustration with "the elite" nor resentment of minorities is sufficient to explain why people vote *at all*, never mind for a populist. What, all of a sudden, makes the disaffected get up off the couch and vote for populists like Trump?

The answer is charismatic leadership. While many scholars continue to argue that charisma is merely coincidental to populism, I believe it is essential. Charismatic leaders are uniquely able to mobilize masses of supporters without the use of an organized political machine. Drawing on new social and evolutionary psychological research on charisma, I argue that three features of charismatic leadership explain why it provides a solution to the collective action problem and why *identity* is so important to populist mobilization. Charisma, as contemporary research shows, is not so much a set of personality traits as a quality that *followers* attribute to a leader. I argue that people believe a leader to have charismatic authority when they (1) identify as part of a group, (2) feel their group is under threat, and (3) perceive the leader as the savior of their group. I outline my charisma-based institutional theory of populism in Chapter 3 and then examine evidence on the demand and supply sides in Chapters 4 and 5, respectively.

The next part of the book returns to the relationship between populism and democracy. What happens when populists gain power? For many scholars, especially those who take a constitutional approach, populism is inherently illiberal. Purporting to be the authentic voice of the people, any opposition to the populist project is cast as illegitimate. The result is the deep erosion of democratic institutions. Yet by focusing on the most egregious cases—Erdoğan's Türkiye, Chávez's Venezuela, Orbán's Hungary—this approach neglects the enormous variation in the degree to which populists can effectively personalize power. It leaves unexplained *how* some populists manage this feat while most other fail.

To address this puzzle, I again stress the role of institutions. The critical fact, I argue, is not merely (or even) that populists are *ideologically* opposed to institutions, but that the uninstitutionalized structure of populist movements provides leaders both the *opportunity* and the *incentive* to erode vertical and horizontal constraints on their authority. As personalistic leaders who rely more on the direct support of the masses, populists' independence from party has two perverse effects. One effect, as much scholarship has argued, is to push populist governments to undermine pluralist institutions and edge toward dictatorship. The other, paradoxical as it may seem, is to make populist government more responsive to public opinion and, in its way, more democratic. These two effects are intertwined but not in the way that is usually assumed.

Chapter 6 deals with the latter effect first: the connection between populist policy and democracy. Contrary to an early wave of research focused on Latin America, which argued that populism was characterized by reckless fiscal and monetary policies, over a broader set of cases there is no evidence of a distinct populist policy with respect to the domestic economy. Or for that matter, with respect to immigration, crime, or most other issues. What we see instead is that populist policy is characteristically *heterodox*, running against the status quo. In some cases, like Chávez's Venezuela, this has meant a turn to the socialist left; in others, like Javier Milei's Argentina, it has gone to the libertarian right. In some, like Orbán's Hungary, it has meant immigration restriction; in others, like Bukele's El Salvador, it has meant a crackdown on crime. What is consistent is that populists *follow* the policy preferences of their base, even if that means violating existing institutional rules. Economic logic, international treaties, and even domestic statutes are secondary to public opinion. In this way, populism caters to the demands of the popular majority—or at least, to the winning plurality that has put a populist into office.

The second effect, and the subject of Chapter 7, is the way in which populist leaders undermine the usual horizontal institutional checks and balances—judicial autonomy, legislative oversight, etc.—on their personal authority. It is far from clear that this process reflects a popular decline in support for democracy. Rather, it seems to result instead from populists' ability and willingness to exploit popular resentment of pluralist, or minority-protecting, institutions to grab power for themselves. In a minority of cases, such as Russia, populists break free of vertical constraints on their power also, so eroding the ability of the opposition to contest elections that they cross the threshold to dictatorship.

Chapter 8 examines the question of what comes *after* populism. Populism rarely provides the basis for stable democracy. At best, it has underpinned the formation of clientelist party systems, like the one that emerged in Jacksonian America. But the corruption these systems foster only tends to breed new forms of mass resentment. Populism's anti-institutionalism means that it undermines, rather than fosters, the establishment of programmatic political parties. The social and technological changes of recent decades have made mass party building extraordinarily difficult. As a result, the legacy of populist government today tends to be even more pernicious. In many instances, a kind of serial populism has developed. In places as diverse as Italy, France, Guatemala, and Greece, there have been long periods in which one populist leader follows another. Once released, it has become ever more difficult to put the populist genie back into the bottle. I end the chapter and the book with some speculations on the future of populism and offer some thoughts on how we might respond.

Notes

1. "militia party," John Foot, *Blood and Power: The Rise and Fall of Italian Fascism* (London: Bloomsbury, 2022), 108. Fascism, like populism, is a disputed concept. While some define it as an ideology, like Foot, I see it more as a practice—a uniquely violent one at that. I will say more on this in Chapter 7.
2. "Populism is only," Jan-Werner Müller, *What Is Populism?* (University of Pennsylvania Press, 2016), 77.
3. Final Report of the Select Committee to Investigate the January 6th Attack on the United States Capitol, https://www.govinfo.gov/collection/january-6th-committee-final-report?path=/gpo/January%206th%20Committee%20Final%20Report%20and%20Supporting%20Materials%20Collection/Final%20Report/%7B%22pageSize%22%3A%2250%22%2C%22offset%22%3A%220%22%7D; for more on Trump's alleged involvement in election malfeasance in 2020–21, see "Government's Motion for Immunity Determinations, US vs. Donald Trump, available at *MSNBC*, October 3, 2024, https://www.msnbc.com/top-stories/latest/trump-presidential-immunity-jack-smith-redacted-motion-document-pdf-rcna173714.
4. The 10–20 percent figure comes from Alexander Baturo, Paul Kenny, and Evren Balta, "Leaders' Experience and the Transition from Populism to Dictatorship," *Democratization* (2024), 1–24, https://doi.org/10.1080/13510347.2024.2391482.
5. Emily Bazelon and Mattathias Schwartz, "Why Legal Experts Are Worried about a Second Trump Presidency," *New York Times Magazine*, October 3, 2024, https://www.nytimes.com/2024/10/03/magazine/trump-justice-department-rivals.html; "We had great," Nancy Cook, Joshua Green, and Mario Parker. "Trump on Taxes, Tariffs, Jerome Powell and More," *Bloomberg*, July 16, 2024, rhttps://www.bloomberg.com/features/2024-trump-interview/.

2

THE MEANING OF POPULISM

What does populism mean (literally)?

Amid the uproar over Donald Trump's most provocative remarks in the 2016 campaign, Barack Obama objected to the common habit of calling him a populist. "I'm not prepared to concede the notion that some of the rhetoric that's been popping up is populist," Obama said. He didn't believe that a candidate who has "worked against economic opportunity for workers and ordinary people" could possibly be a populist. Someone doesn't "suddenly become a populist because they say something controversial in order to win votes," he continued. "Somebody who labels 'us versus them' or engaged in rhetoric about how we're going to look after ourselves and take it to the other guy, that's not the definition of populism." That kind of divisiveness, he said, is just "nativism, or xenophobia, or worse." Obama claimed the populist mantle for himself because of his more progressive policies on healthcare, education, and inequality. Was Obama right? Was he the populist—and not Trump? Yes and no. He was right to argue that mere "us versus them" rhetoric does not define populism. However, his own assumption—that a commitment to progressive policies makes one a populist—is equally flawed.[1]

One of the first things to note about populism is that it has no single *true* definition. Populism is not a concept like a quark, the number zero, or gravity that has a fixed, objective meaning. Populism is instead an inherently imprecise, socially constructed notion like democracy, about which reasonable people—including the former president and I—will legitimately disagree. This ambiguity is to be expected given that populism comfortably meets the three criteria of what philosophers call an "essentially contested concept." What does this mean?[2]

First, any definition of populism requires the use of terms such as "the people," whose meanings are also contested; second, populism is a moral concept like justice, meaning that it implies a value judgment of the ideas or actions that are being labeled; and third, there is no definitive measurement of populism or set of rules that determines how to identify it when we see it. As a result, there is no objective way to determine the superiority of one definition of populism over another. When Peter Wiles wrote in the 1960s with tongue half in cheek of the problem of defining populism, "to each his own definition according to the academic axe he grinds," he wasn't necessarily wrong. The definition we adopt depends on what purpose we have in mind for the concept.[3]

This doesn't imply that we are free to adopt a definition of populism at random or just to skirt the problem and avoid defining the concept altogether. Whatever definition we choose, it should refer to some common core idea. Fortunately, when it comes to populism, it turns out that there is nearly universal agreement on at least one point, and that is something on which we can build a working definition. Populism refers to a way of doing or thinking about politics in which *the people* figure prominently. With its linguistic roots in the Latin word *populus*, populism literally means something like "a practice, system, or doctrine of *the people*."[4]

Accepting the primacy that populism places on the role of the people is a good starting point, but as readers will probably anticipate, there is much less consensus on *how* the people matter, or even on *who* the people are. This chapter examines the three most common approaches to defining populism, each of which views the people's role in a different way. While each has its strengths, they all fall short in key ways. In the next chapter, I present a new alternative.

The first approach claims that the people matter at the level of *ideas*. For many political theorists, populism is an ideology—or a set of interlinked beliefs about the political, economic, and social world. This approach puts populism alongside other ideologies like conservatism, socialism, and liberalism. There are subtly different variants of the "ideational approach" to populism, which I'll discuss in more detail in the next section, but the predominant interpretation places the people in an existential conflict with an elite that includes the rich, the well-educated, and the politically powerful. In this sense, populism is a political ideology of the bottom versus the top.

A second way that the people could matter to populism is in the collective political actions that they take. In this view, populism is defined by the personalistic mobilization of politically detached or alienated voters against the establishment. Central to what is called the "strategic approach" to populism is the role of the leader in channeling mass opposition to the status quo. Populism bypasses traditional political parties and the civil society organizations—such as churches and unions—that typically support them. This direct connection between charismatic leaders and loosely organized followers sets populism apart from other forms of democratic politics.

A third view, which I label the "constitutional approach," focuses on the majoritarian, anti-pluralist logic inherent in the concept of a singular *people*. Equating the majority with the people, populism implies an intolerance of difference or an opposition to the ideas and practice of pluralism. In this case, the opposite pole of the people is not usually the establishment, but a foreign, ethnic, criminal, or undesirable minority "other" that threatens the body politic. Rather than the people looking resentfully up at the elite, in this version of populism, the people themselves are looking down, or at least askance.

Although this approach refers to political beliefs and even rhetoric, it is more commonly analyzed by examining what populists *do* once in power. Acting in the name of the people, populist leaders subvert those liberal democratic institutions, from courts to the mainstream media, that protect the rights of minorities.

Despite their differences, I believe the strongest elements of the ideational, political-strategic, and constitutional approaches can be integrated into an alternative framework I call the *institutional approach*. In Chapter 3, I argue that populism is best understood as an anti-institutional form of mass politics, evident in both ideas and actions. This perspective provides a foundation for analyzing populism's causes and consequences. However, before turning to this new conceptualization, we must first assess the strengths and shortcomings of the dominant approaches to populism in use today.

Is populism an ideology?

Ideologies are not just abstract theories; they are the blueprints that shape the political, economic, and social order. They define how power is structured and, just as crucially, how it ought to be structured. Some ideologies, like conservatism, exist to defend the status quo, to justify the distribution of power and wealth as natural, inevitable, even just. Others, like Leninism, seek not to justify but to overthrow—to tear down the old order and build a new one in its place.

At its broadest, populism is said to be an ideology that asserts that the people—the *populus*—should rule. This idea, the assertion of popular sovereignty, gives populism a seemingly universal reach. Some scholars see this as its greatest strength. Argentine political theorist Ernesto Laclau famously argued that "the people" is an "empty signifier," a vessel waiting to be filled with whatever meaning a political leader chooses. Laclau and his followers believed that populism's natural trajectory would be economic—that class conflict would drive a populism of the left. History, however, has proven otherwise. A right-wing populism, one based not on class but on national or ethnic divisions, has proved just as potent—if not more so.[5]

For critics, to leave populism at the vague level of popular sovereignty is to define it so broadly that it becomes meaningless—like having a master key that fits no particular lock. Under this approach, it's unclear what wouldn't count as populism. Since appeals to "the people" can be dressed up in almost any garb, nearly every democratic politician—along with a fair number of autocrats—suddenly qualifies as a populist, at least in some dimly lit sense. By this logic, anyone who dares acknowledge the existence of voters becomes a demagogue in disguise. If a politician declares that "most of politics isn't about politics"—that it is, instead, about "people" rather than "meetings, resolutions, or speeches"—does this make him a populist? What if that politician were Tony Blair, the very model of mainstream centrism? This approach ultimately forces us into a hopeless game of political taxonomy, where identifying "real" populism becomes an act of personal judgment, as scientific as tea-leaf reading. It may provide ample fodder for theorists and armchair philosophers, but if our goal is to apply scientific standards to explain populism's causes and consequences, we are left with little more than a shapeless fog and a great deal of academic hand-waving.[6]

A potentially more productive way to differentiate populism from sister concepts like democracy is to focus on what the people allegedly *oppose*. Some scholars have argued that populism is an "anti-elite" ideology in a way that democracy by itself is not. Writing in the context of the anti-communist crusade of demagogic Wisconsin Senator Joseph McCarthy during the 1950s, sociologist Edward Shils argued that populism is distinct from mere democracy in that it is an "ideology of popular resentment" that sets the common people against the "ruling class." In another early comparative analysis, political theorist Margaret Canovan wrote that "populism in modern democratic societies is best seen as an appeal to 'the people' against both the established structure of power and the dominant ideas and values of the society."[7]

Along these lines, political scientist Pierre Ostiguy has more recently argued that populism is a political program that mobilizes "the low" against "the high," with these terms defined more culturally than socioeconomically. In this case, as proposed by Benjamin Moffitt, the populist worldview is expressed not just in public discourse but in a broader populist low-brow "style." In a similar vein, Paul Taggart has argued that populism is based on the opposition between a "heartland" that represents a "virtuous and united people" and an alien technocratic establishment. The authoritative *Oxford English Dictionary* (*OED*) defines populism simply as "the policies or principles of any of various political parties which seek to represent the interests of *ordinary* people."[8]

Even with these supposed clarifications, however, the distinction between populism and democracy is hard to sustain. For Aristotle, the rule of the common or ordinary people over the elite was not some accidental feature of democracy—it was the very thing that set it apart from oligarchy and monarchy. The word itself, *democracy,* is practically a Greek etymology lesson in anti-elitism: *kratos* (rule) by the *demos* (common people). Deeply immersed in classical political theory, America's founders consciously distinguished their *republican* form of government from *democracy.* Alexander Hamilton, John Adams, and James Madison all saw democracy as a dangerous free-for-all—the unchecked rule of the mob. Democracy is not what such elites saw as being in their best interest.

Nor is this anti-elitist interpretation of democracy the exclusive property of classical or conservative thinkers. It runs so deep in socialist political thought that one would struggle to find a left-wing movement that doesn't, by this standard, qualify as populist. Worse still, if mere opposition to the political establishment is the litmus test, then virtually every opposition party, protest movement, and eccentric independent candidate suddenly becomes a populist by default. Put another way: If populists are different because they seek to represent *ordinary* people, as the OED supposes, we're left to ask, are there any democratic parties that *don't* do this? When Margaret Thatcher declared to her Conservative Party colleagues after her selection as leader in 1976 that "we are a party of *ordinary people* with ordinary hopes and beliefs," did this make her and her party populist? And if your preferred party doesn't qualify as populist, does that mean you yourself aren't an *ordinary* person? The entire exercise starts to resemble a political version of *Through the Looking-Glass*, where everyone is a populist and yet, somehow, no one is.[9]

Other scholars have sought a way out of this conceptual thicket by proposing that populism is a "thin" political ideology in contrast to "thick" ideologies such as conservatism or socialism. In an influential 2004 article, political scientist Cas Mudde defined populism as "a thin-centered ideology that separates society into two homogenous and antagonistic groups: 'the pure people' and 'the corrupt elite,' and argues that politics should be an expression of the *volonté générale* (general will) of the people." According to Michael Freeden, an expert on political ideology, a "thin ideology" is "one that, like mainstream ones, has an identifiable morphology but, unlike mainstream ones, a restricted one." Put a bit more simply, thin-centered ideologies differ from thick ones in that they do not offer a vision for how society should be ordered; they are instead either single-issue programs (e.g., environmentalism), or must be associated with other more complete ideologies (e.g., conservatism). In this "thin" sense, populism refers to the people-centric and anti-elite content of speech and style rather than to a form of political mobilization or a program for government. Hence the need for qualifiers like "right wing populism" and "left wing populism."[10]

According to this approach, populism is effective as a thin political ideology because of the way it combines with other "host" ideologies like socialism, neoliberalism, or nationalism. This minimalist interpretation of populism has been applied with success to a wide range of populist movements. Around the turn of the twenty-first century, scholars of Latin American politics focused on the "inclusive" populism of economically left of center leaders like Venezuela's Hugo Chávez and Bolivia's Evo Morales. Before this, there had been a brief period when populism in Latin America was associated with neoliberal economic policy, with reformers like Argentina's Carlos Menem and Colombia's Alvaro Uribe being its poster boys. Today, at least in Western Europe, it is most common to equate populism with nativism or xenophobia, collapsing the composite notion of the "populist radical right" into populism *tout court*. Leaders like Austria's Jörg Haider, the Netherlands' Geert Wilders, and France's Marine Le Pen have all come close to taking power on the back of widespread anti-immigrant sentiment. All these movements appear to fit well within the "thin" ideational approach, combining people-centric and anti-elite discourse with other more substantive policies.

However, even if we concede, for argument's sake, that a "thin" populist ideology exists in the realm of political philosophy, the moment we try to pin it down empirically—in the terms of social science or history—it becomes problematic. The first issue is simply how to measure populism. One method has been to examine the speech of political leaders for evidence of the classic populist trope of "the people versus the elite." For proponents of this discursive approach, when a politician says they stand for the people against the elite, they are said to be populist. When Hugo Chávez said, "I am not an individual—I am the people," he was precisely verbalizing the populist credo. But how often must a politician invoke "the people" to be counted as populist? Maybe a single speech appealing to the people against the elite is not enough to categorize a politician as a populist, but where is the cut off? Two, three, twenty?

Given that politicians are notorious for tailoring their message to their audience, which speeches or writings should we use to make our classification? When Trump tweeted in

January 2016 that "I am for the people and the people are for me," or when he wrote in a *Wall Street Journal* op-ed in April that year that "the only antidote to decades of ruinous rule by a small handful of elites is a bold infusion of popular will. . . . On every major issue affecting this country, the people are right and the governing elite are wrong," or at his acceptance of the Republican Party nomination in July 2016 when he pronounced, "These are people who . . . no longer have a voice. I am your voice," it seems that he should be clearly categorized as a populist. Remarkably, however, for Mudde, the best-known proponent of understanding populism as a people-centric and anti-elite ideology, Trump "does not claim to follow the wisdom of the people" and so cannot be a populist. This latter objection seems to shift the conceptual goalposts somewhat, but it is illustrative of how subjective discourse analysis can be.[11]

In any case, it is doubtful that speech alone provides a sufficient basis to identify populism. In practice, every politician has a strong incentive to wrap themselves in the language of "the people," regardless of what they really think behind closed doors. The examples of Thatcher and Blair are hardly outliers. Once mass democracy had taken hold—at least for men, if not for all adults—only the most politically tone-deaf reactionary would dare tell the rabble to leave governance to their betters. As the sociologist Robert Michels observed in 1911, a conservative candidate who bluntly informed voters they were unfit for politics and "ought to be deprived of the suffrage, would be a man of incomparable sincerity, but politically insane." If people-centric rhetoric is a reliable vote-winner, any politician with a functioning survival instinct will adopt it, whatever their private convictions. Few understood this better than Senator McCarthy, a man who made an entire career out of cynical opportunism. As he once confided to a friend, "If you want to get anywhere in politics, you've got to feed the public what they want to hear and not what you believe."[12]

I would also argue that even if anti-elite and pro-people rhetoric once served as a useful marker to distinguish populists from non-populists, that ship has long since sailed. Scholarly research on the subject has seeped so thoroughly into mainstream political strategy that it is now almost impossible to tell the so-called authentic populists from the well-rehearsed mimics. Trump's frequent references to "the people" were often inserted by his political strategist, Steve Bannon. Others have clearly learned the lesson. As an exercise, I ask my students to categorize politicians as populist or not based on their speeches. Time and again, they classify mainstream figures like Kamala Harris and Rishi Sunak as populists—after all, they, too, claim to represent the people's best interests. And who can blame my students? If populism is simply a matter of talking about "the people" in glowing terms, then every politician worth their consultant's fee must be a populist, at least on the campaign trail.

Nor is this problem of mimicry limited to democratic competitors. In fact, so de rigueur have appeals to "the people" become that even the heads of authoritarian regimes—from China's Xi Jinping to Saudi Arabia's Mohammad Bin Salman—have mastered the art of so-called populist discourse. The strongman of old, who ruled by divine right or brute force, has been replaced by the modern autocrat, like Viktor Orbán—nodding solemnly to the will of the people while tightening the screws. If populism is defined solely by speech, then we must conclude that nearly every political party, from the most liberal democracy to the most closed dictatorship, is populist. Or, if that seems absurd, we need to find another way to separate the true believers from the opportunistic copycats.

A common rejoinder to this objection is that when the likes of Blair or Thatcher or Xi appeal to the people, they don't *really* mean it. This is a textbook case of the "no true Scotsman" fallacy. It works like this: Your sociology professor, eager to display his worldly wisdom, announces that no Scotsman puts sugar on his porridge. You pause, then point out that your Edinburgh-born roommate douses his porridge in sugar every morning. "Ah," the professor replies smugly, "but *no true Scotsman* would do such a thing." This kind of logic leaves us in an impossible position when it comes to identifying populists. Are figures like Trump and Orbán genuine tribunes of the people, or are they merely skilled impersonators? How do they differ from Thatcher and her ilk? Since sincerity is a notoriously tricky thing to measure—politicians being what they are—we are left either mind-reading or guessing.

What seems to be happening here is that the conclusion has already been reached: Certain figures *are* populists, and certain figures *aren't*. The supposed analysis of their discourse is then reverse-engineered to match the prior intuition. In the end, we are not so much studying populism as sorting politicians into preordained moral categories—an exercise that often tells us more about the analyst than the analyzed.

The usefulness of a social scientific concept isn't just a matter of how neatly it sorts the world into categories—whether a given leader is or isn't a populist—but also what kind of meaningful explanations it allows us to build. The most researched hypothesis emerging from the ideational approach is that there is a widely held set of beliefs called "populist attitudes" that explain why people support populist politicians.

Populist attitudes are said to include three components, which draw on the parts of Mudde's ideational definition of populism. They are "people-centrism," "anti-elitism," and a "Manichaean outlook." People-centrism refers to the view that the people are the host of positive values in society, and although not explicitly classist or nativist in orientation, it reflects a belief in folk values rather than in learned expertise. Anti-elitism is a belief that the problems with society are due to the machinations of political, economic, and/or cultural elites. The last component, a Manichaean outlook, describes the belief that politics is an existential struggle between the *good* people and the *bad* elite. People who hold these populist values or attitudes are said to agree with statements such as "the people, not the politicians, should make our most important policy decisions."[13]

A series of early studies found correlations between such populist attitudes and prior or expected support for populist leaders in several different countries, suggesting that the ideational approach to populism was genuinely capturing what was going on, at least in Western Europe. Despite this initial promise, however, recent research has cast a good deal of doubt on the reliability of this approach.[14]

First, there are questions about how populist attitudes should be measured. Not only are the various components of populist attitudes disputed but so is the approach taken to aggregate them. It makes an enormous difference simply whether the scores on each component are added or multiplied. Second, a growing body of work shows that the kinds of populist attitudes that appear to be correlated with support for populist candidates in Western Europe do not travel well to Asia, the Middle East, or even Eastern Europe. Third, it seems that populist attitudes primarily capture a preference for political outsiders, as they are unrelated to support for populists in power. Fourth, given that adherents of the ideational approach argue that populism is a "thin" ideology that attaches to other "host" ideologies and beliefs, it is perhaps unsurprising that it is these additional attitudes that seem to be doing much of the heavy lifting. When views about immigrants, minorities, or conspiratorial thinking are elicited in additional survey questions, populist attitudes as such usually become statistically insignificant.[15]

All this research suggests that early studies vastly overestimated the effect of so-called populist attitudes, largely because they failed to account for related beliefs, policy preferences, and various measurement issues. Recent studies lend weight to this interpretation by using what is known as a *conjoint experiment*—a method designed to isolate the role populism actually plays in shaping political preferences.

In these experiments, survey respondents are asked to evaluate the campaign messages of pairs of fictional candidates. Researchers then test whether support changes when two otherwise identical messages—same policies, same promises—differ only in the addition of a populist flourish. The results? The populist rhetoric makes no difference. People who approve of an anti-immigrant (or pro-immigrant) candidate are just as likely to support them whether or not they pepper their speeches with talk of the "true people" and the "corrupt elite." In other words, populism in its so-called thin ideological sense is so devoid of content that it is the *other* ideologies it attaches to that actually do the work: socialism for supporters of Chávez, nativism for Wilders's voters, and so on. As an independent force, populism doesn't seem to push people one way or the other—it merely embellishes the message. As Michael Freeden wryly put it, as an ideology, populism is not just thin; it is "emaciated."[16]

It is certainly plausible that support for populist leaders has deep psychological roots in personality traits or more immediate causes in political attitudes. The problem is that the evidence is neither convincing nor consistent. Yes, personality traits, populist attitudes, and political values often show correlations with each other and with support for populist movements—these things sometimes travel together. But as the experimental research mentioned earlier makes clear, correlation is not causation, and the missing piece of the puzzle is any solid proof that populist attitudes actually *cause* support for populist leaders.

This shouldn't come as a great surprise. Demonstrating that one set of thoughts or ideas causes another is an extraordinarily difficult task. The brain is not a hydraulic machine where one lever predictably moves another. To the extent that we see correlations between populist beliefs and support for populist leaders, we must seriously consider the possibility that the behavior causes the attitudes, not the other way around. People may vote for populists for reasons they themselves don't fully grasp—self-interest, frustration, or a general desire to shake things up—and only afterward construct justifications for their choices, both for themselves and for survey researchers eager to map their motives.[17]

The ideational approach is surely correct in asserting that populism refers to a kind of politics in which the disaffection of the popular classes matters. It is probably also right in noting that populist leaders claim to speak on behalf of "the people." But words are cheap. As we'll see in the next section, populists have a far more convincing way of signaling their opposition to the institutional status quo than mere rhetoric.

Is populism a political strategy?

Already by 1971, Lawrence Goodwyn, one of the foremost scholars of the American Populist era of the 1880s and 1890s, lamented that the focus of scholarship "has been chiefly upon the word, not the deed." That is, scholars were increasingly assuming that populism was driven by the speeches and writings of populist thinkers rather than by the material circumstances and behaviors of the farmers, workers, and political leaders who comprised the movement. Instead of thinking of populism as something that political leaders or their followers *believed* or *said*, Goodwyn was arguing that we think of it in terms of the marginal position of its supporters with respect to the political and economic establishment, and the tactics and strategies that the movement's leaders deployed to mobilize them. What made the Populists of the 1890s significant was that they directly rallied these neglected and unorganized voters. In short, populism referred to a way of doing, rather than speaking or thinking about, politics.[18]

If politics is, at its core, the art of winning, keeping, and exercising power, then the "strategic approach" views populism not as an ideology but as a toolkit—a set of actions geared toward those goals. As political scientist Kurt Weyland puts it, "Populism revolves around personalistic, usually charismatic leadership sustained by (quasi-) direct, unmediated, and uninstitutionalized connections to a heterogeneous, amorphous, and largely unorganized mass of followers." In other words, populist leaders thrive not through institutions but in spite of them, relying on direct appeals to the crowd rather than the machinery of party organization. Populist movements share this lack of structure with inchoate social movements in general, but there is an important difference.[19]

Whereas protest movements like Occupy Wall Street often fizzle out or, in some cases, morph into bureaucratic institutions—environmental activism, for instance, eventually hardening into formal Green parties—the more politically effective populist movements follow a different trajectory. Their defining feature is not organizational longevity but the dominance of a charismatic leader. As sociologist Oliver Nachtwey observes of one of the most prominent recent populist movements, Spain's Indignados, what began as a radical, anti-austerity mass protest in the public square was eventually absorbed into a political party, Podemos. Despite its rhetoric of grassroots participation, the party soon revolved around a single figure—Pablo Iglesias—becoming, in Nachtwey's words, "a model of charismatic populism." The Indignados experience showed that while crowds can create momentum, it takes a leader to capture power.[20]

Though not as commonly invoked as ideational definitions, the strategic approach to populism has deep roots in political science and sociology, stretching back to the late nineteenth and early twentieth centuries—most notably to the work of German sociologist Max Weber. Weber famously distinguished between three forms of political authority: the bureaucratic-rational, the traditional-patrimonial, and the charismatic. While the modern bureaucratic form of authority relies on the application of impartial rules for its legitimacy, and patrimonial authority is based on historically sanctified hierarchical relationships between a leader and his dependents, charismatic authority is a different beast. It depends not on institutions or tradition but on the almost mystical belief that a leader possesses extraordinary qualities—qualities seen as self-evident by their followers but often invisible to their critics.

In an effort to explain the rise of contentious mass politics across Latin America in the mid-twentieth century, in the late 1960s a group of scholars turned to Weber's framework for answers. Rather than embracing the discourse-theoretical approach to populism, they took a historical-sociological route, focusing on the material conditions that fueled its rise. One of the best developed arguments came from Italian sociologist Gino Germani, who saw populism as the byproduct of late industrialization and urban migration. These twin upheavals disrupted Latin America's oligarchic political systems, creating a rapidly expanding yet impoverished urban working class—precisely the kind of political orphan that populist leaders thrive on. The region's ruling elites, content in their old hierarchies, largely ignored this growing mass, failing to realize that political vacuums do not remain empty for long. This neglect opened the space for populists to mobilize newly available and unattached masses, with charismatic leaders like Brazil's Getúlio Vargas, Argentina's Juan Perón, Colombia's Jorge Eliécer Gaitán, and Ecuador's José Maria Velasco Ibarra coming to the fore.[21]

For these leaders, populism was less an ideology than a strategy—a way to bypass the political establishment and forge a direct connection with an atomized and restless base in an era of rapid structural upheaval. Their movements were fiercely anti-oligarchic and highly nationalistic, yet ideologically fluid, blending policies from both the left and the right as needed. Take Brazil's two-time populist president, Getúlio Vargas. Before earning the title "the father of the poor" for his attention to the politically neglected masses, he had no qualms about brutally suppressing the country's leftist leaders and their followers. Likewise, Argentina's Juan Perón alternately courted and crushed radical factions, depending entirely on their usefulness to him at any given moment.

What tied these movements together—and set them apart from others—was not ideology, but organization. Populism, scholars of the period argued, was not so much a political doctrine as a method: a leader-centric, anti-establishment mass politics where institutions were obstacles to be overcome rather than pillars to be built upon. However, as with early ideational approaches, these first-wave sociological studies suffered from a crucial blind spot: They failed to clearly define what wasn't populism. Populists mobilized against the establishment—but so does any opposition party worth its salt. Populists were charismatic leaders—but so too were fascists, monarchs, and the occasional messianic cult leader. The result? A concept still mired in ambiguity.

The real value of the strategic approach to populism didn't fully emerge until the 1980s, when Greek sociologist Nicos Mouzelis introduced a more systematic comparative perspective. Mouzelis framed populism not as a mere style or ideology but as a *mode of incorporation*—a way in which political leaders and parties link themselves to voters. Mouzelis argued that political leaders "incorporate" or bring the people into the political system. Drawing explicitly on Weber's distinction between bureaucratic, patrimonial, and charismatic forms of authority, Mouzelis maintained that political incorporation tends to occur in one of three ways: through programmatic incorporation, clientelistic incorporation, or populist incorporation. With this step, Mouzelis not only gave populism a distinct conceptual identity but also placed it within a broader taxonomy of political behavior—transforming it from a nebulous catch-all into something that could actually be analyzed, compared, and explained.[22]

Programmatic, clientelistic, and populist incorporation yield three main types of political organization: programmatic parties, clientelistic parties, and populist movements.

Programmatic or bureaucratic parties are characterized by rules and procedures governing the distribution of authority within the organization and a range of institutionalized relationships with supporters externally. Civil society organizations like unions, churches, and nationalist associations provide an enduring link between parties and voters. Parties like the Social Democratic Party (SPD) in Germany and the Conservative Party in the United Kingdom are some classic examples.

In contrast, clientelistic parties engage in a quid pro quo with supporters in which votes are exchanged for material benefits. Voters are given jobs, favors, and even cash in return for their support. This was the way in which the earliest political parties in the United States expanded, most infamously with the Tammany Hall machine of New York City, and it has been the most common approach to building political support in new democracies ever since.

In contrast to programmatic or clientelistic parties, populist movements are ones in which the links between the leadership and its followers are weakly organized. Populist leaders aim to establish direct, or unmediated, ties with voters. Weyland writes that populist leaders often establish a "direct, quasi-personal relationship [between them and supporters that] bypasses established intermediary organizations" such as parties. Mouzelis similarly notes, "As a rule, populist leaders are hostile to strongly institutionalized intermediary levels, whether clientelist or bureaucratic. The emphasis on the leader's charisma, on the necessity for direct, nonmediated rapport between the leader and 'his people' as well as the relatively sudden process of political incorporation all lead to a fluidity of organizational forms." The supporters of a populist movement delegate authority to a leader rather than to an institution. Just as Messiahs have disciples, charismatic leaders have *followers*. While some populists do build or capture political parties, others remain independents or lead groups with only the most ephemeral organizations. I prefer the term "movement" to "party" for populists precisely because of this fluidity.[23]

Some critics of the strategic approach argue that it is too restrictive, that it describes only a few instances in mid-twentieth-century Latin America. Populism in this strategic sense, critics maintain, could only be the product of late industrialization and the rapid urbanization and the social disruption that it caused. With the political systems of most of Western Europe and North America still dominated by deeply institutionalized, bureaucratic parties at the time these original theories were penned, populism in the strategic sense seemed to have little relevance outside of late democratizing polities in the global south.

However, this line of critique takes the sociological innovators of the strategic approach too literally. There is no reason that different social or economic shocks—other than late industrialization and urbanization—could not have similar effects. Much of my early research used this approach in explaining the success of populism in Asia, while others have demonstrated its applicability to post–Cold War Latin America and Eastern Europe. Understood more broadly, the populist strategy can be successful in a range of contexts that make other forms of political mobilization—namely, programmatic or clientelistic party mobilization—more challenging or more costly.

Moreover, even where political parties have long been established, as in Western Europe and North America—as we'll see in Chapter 5—the post-industrial disappearance of unions and churches, along with the economic shocks of the Global Financial Crisis and the COVID-19 pandemic, has weakened programmatic political parties and created openings for populist outsiders to appeal to increasingly unattached voters.

Another common critique of the strategic approach is that politicians like France's Marine Le Pen and Austria's Jörg Haider cannot be classified as populists due to the presumed institutionalization of their parties. However, while populism in the strategic sense is anti-institutional, this doesn't mean that populist movements are completely devoid of organization. The distinctive characteristic of the populist strategy is its personalistic structure. As Weber wrote, "Charismatic authority does not imply an amorphous condition; it indicates rather a definite social structure with a staff and an apparatus of services and material means that is adapted to the mission of the leader." Charismatic authority entails the personalization of political authority; no rules, whether bureaucratic or traditional, constrain the leader's will. In this sense, populist parties or organizations can exist but they are weakly institutionalized in not being based on the application of formal regulations. It's not that populist movements lack procedures or positions altogether; rather, the leader's personal authority overrides them, bending institutional norms to their whims. What matters is not the system, but who gets to interpret it.[24]

Nazi Germany offers a chilling example of this dynamic. Its bureaucratic structure was a maze of overlapping responsibilities and competing chains of command, deliberately designed so that, in the end, only Hitler himself could determine which policies applied or who had the authority to carry them out. This ambiguity created a system in which subordinates, uncertain of the exact rules but certain of the leader's will, engaged in what historian Ian Kershaw famously described as "working towards the Führer"—anticipating his desires and shaping policy accordingly, often with catastrophic consequences.[25]

As recent experience has shown, even well-established parties—once thought to be sturdy pillars of institutional politics—are not immune to hostile takeovers by populist leaders. The Republican Party in the United States is a case in point. More broadly, political scientist Kurt Weyland observes that populists have a knack for hollowing out party institutions, bending them to "the leader's personal will." A party's age, its bureaucratic structures, or even the presence of positions like a party whip may give the illusion of stability, but in practice, they offer little resistance to a leader who holds the power to hire, fire, and replace personnel in the party organization at will. As we'll see later on, control the man, control the rules. This is the populist party leader's creed.[26]

Overall, I find the strategic approach to populism both robust and useful, and my research to date has been grounded in it. As we'll see, it lends itself well to empirical analysis of both the causes and consequences of populism. But no framework is without its blind spots. By stripping populism of any ideological content, the strategic approach gains broad applicability—but at a cost. It has little to say about why populists say the things they do, or why their supporters seem so willing to believe them. Populist rhetoric follows recognizable patterns, and it's unlikely this is mere coincidence. The strategic approach explains well why populists, as outsiders, rail against the establishment—that much is predictable. But it struggles to account for something equally consistent: why so many populists, across different times and places, also champion nationalist or nativist causes. Why does anti-institutionalism so often march hand in hand with identity politics? On this, the strategic approach has little to say.

The strategic approach sidesteps another crucial question—not why voters support populists but why they vote at all. The puzzle of why people vote—given the negligible impact their single ballot has—has long troubled political scientists. But this problem is exacerbated when it comes to voting for populists in a way that preceding scholarship has neglected. A core claim of the strategic approach is that populist voters are not embedded in traditional party networks—they are, in effect, unattached political free agents, unbound by institutional loyalties and therefore *available* for populist mobilization. But in most cases, we know that political disengagement leads to apathy and abstention, not sudden activism. Without party institutions to provide structure, populist mobilization runs headlong into a classic collective action problem: How do you coordinate a movement without an organization? The strategic approach, for all its strengths, remains silent on this question. I attempt to address these gaps in the *institutional approach* I set out in Chapter 3.

Is populism illiberal?

A third approach, taken up primarily by political theorists and constitutional law scholars, has been to focus on populism's supposed illiberalism or anti-pluralism. According to what I label here as the "constitutional approach," the populist is a politician who champions the people in some way but also signals that they do not view normal political disagreement as legitimate. The majority *is* the people and the preferences of minorities, whether based on class, religion, race, or mere political preference, are of little concern. Populists assert an equivalence between their base and the will of the people. In *What Is Populism?* Jan-Werner Müller writes that populists don't even claim to be "the 99 percent"; rather, they claim to be "the 100 percent."[27]

This approach to populism has implications at the level of ideas or discourse. Trump's statement on the 2016 campaign trail that "the only important thing is the unification of the people—because the other people don't mean anything" was textbook populism according to this approach. However, an advantage of the constitutional approach over the ideational one is that we don't have to rely on speech alone to classify populists. Rather, the actions of leaders and the policy preferences and voting behavior of the electorate provide additional sources of evidence. Simply, those elected leaders and their supporters who seek to erode institutional pluralism and undermine minority rights are populist.[28]

This approach captures well the identity-based populism common to much of the contemporary world. Trump's efforts to round up, intern, and deport undocumented immigrants is a poignant example. In Eastern Europe, Hungary's Orbán, Poland's Jarosław Kaczyński, and Slovakia's Robert Fico all came to embrace an anti-immigrant ethnonationalism more reminiscent of the interwar period than the supposedly globalized twenty-first century. India's Narendra Modi has operationalized Hindu Nationalism in a raft of discriminatory legislation, including an amendment to the citizenship law, which allows immigrants from Afghanistan, Bangladesh, and Pakistan to obtain Indian nationality, but only if they are Hindu, Sikh, Buddhist, Jain, Parsi, or Christian; in other words, as long as they are anything but Muslim. Importantly, this majoritarian idea of the people also captures the radical left-wing populism of the likes of Hugo Chávez, who repeatedly disobeyed or discarded those institutions that protected the interests of minorities as he and his supporters saw them.

Beyond the level of anti-minority policies, populists' illiberalism extends to the erosion of any institutional constraints on their own power. That is, populists oppose pluralism, not just in a sociological sense of denying the rights of ethnic minorities, but in the sense of attacking the division of powers—executive, legislative, judicial—common to democratic regimes. Although almost everyone agrees that populism is something different from authoritarianism, it is nevertheless the case that populists weaken formal and informal limits on the executive branch's control over government. The division of powers between presidents and legislatures, or between upper and lower houses of parliament, and the existence of an autonomous judiciary all serve to protect the rights of minorities. Populists chafe against these constraints and, as we'll see in Chapter 7, erode them in practice.

Building on the observation that populism is distinct from dictatorship, but that it still damages democracy, several scholars working in this approach have characterized populism as a regime type that sits somewhere between democracy and dictatorship; hence the coining of novel synonyms for populism like "illiberal democracy" and "anti-pluralism." What these neologisms aim to capture is the idea that populism combines the majoritarian, mass mobilization aspect of democracy with an aversion to the procedural protections for minorities that are characteristic of liberalism. As long-time CNN pundit Fareed Zakaria put it in a seminal *Foreign Affairs* article in 1997, "Today the two strands of liberal democracy, interwoven in the Western political fabric, are coming apart in the rest of the world. Democracy is flourishing; constitutional liberalism is not." When Hungary's Viktor Orbán stated in a 2016 speech "that a democracy is not necessarily liberal. Just because something is not liberal, it still can be a democracy," he sought to draw out this distinction between the "democratic" will of the majority from the typical array of "liberal" institutions that work to contain it. For those working in the constitutional approach, Orbán's politics precisely capture the notion of populism as democracy without liberalism.[29]

Why might this kind of politics work? Are people being hoodwinked into voting for closet dictators or is there a logic to this sort of anti-pluralist mass politics? There is support for the idea that people are turning to such illiberal leaders with their eyes open. Liberalism, in the populist imagination, is the ruling ideology of the elite. It provides not for individual freedom, as liberals themselves might insist, but for procedural limits on the people's will. This view is not without substance. Technocratic bodies like central banks and health regulators often seem to have more power than elected representatives, undermining the principles of democracy. Populism promises to set the people loose from these institutional shackles. There is evidence that populist voters have a "majoritarian" view of democracy, preferring a system that satisfies the popular will over pluralist guarantees for minorities.[30]

There are, however, two issues with *defining* populism as a kind of anti-pluralist or illiberal democracy. First, on closer inspection, Orbán's very notion of "illiberal democracy" turns out to be a contradiction in terms. For sure, the unfettered majoritarianism he describes resembles democracy in one important respect—the people get to cast a vote in an election. But both in theory and in practice, it is impossible to have even a minimalist, plebiscitarian democracy without some degree of liberalism.

Contrary to the modern Anglo-American connotation of liberalism as respect for *individual* rights that was pioneered by John Stuart Mill, John Dewey, and other late nineteenth- and early twentieth-century thinkers, for the classical liberals of the late eighteenth and early nineteenth centuries, liberalism meant freedom of belief and expression for political and religious *minorities*. Unless a minority is free to speak and organize, it can never become a majority. Minorities would be at perpetual risk of harm. In the wake of the bloody purges of the French Revolution, the celebrated liberal Franco-Swiss political philosopher, Benjamin Constant, observed, "Everyone in turn finds himself in the minority. . . . To grant the majority unlimited power is to offer to the people *en masse* the slaughter of the people piecemeal." Understood in the sense of political protections for minorities, liberalism is inseparable from democracy. As political scientists Armin Schafer and Michael Zurn curtly put it, "liberal democracy" is a pleonasm. There is no other kind of democracy. What many scholars working in the constitutional approach are thus describing when looking at democracy-without-liberalism is not populism but dictatorship. The cases most commonly invoked in studies using this approach—regimes like that of Orbán, Chávez, and Erdoğan—have already crossed the threshold into authoritarianism before many of these analyses of supposed populist rule begin. Seeking to eliminate the opposition altogether is a feature of fascism, not populism.[31]

Second, insisting on an equivalence between populism and anti-pluralism means having to rule out movements like the original Populist Party as being populist. The same would probably be true of numerous populist parties of the new left in Europe like the British Labour Party under Jeremy Corbyn, Syriza under Alexis Tsipras in Greece, and Podemos under Iglesias in Spain. These movements do advocate primarily for the interests of a broad middle and working class as opposed to the rich, but this is hardly exclusionary in the sense that anti-pluralist notion of populism implies. Moreover, although populists often make use of identity politics in mobilizing support, it seems problematic to insist on this as a definitional quality of populism. None of the above groups stressed this kind of anti-minority identity politics in the conventional sense—in fact, the reverse was more likely to be true.

The constitutional approach descriptively captures a lot of what many populists do. It rightly stresses the populist tendency to degrade the institutions of democracy, not least those that preserve the rights of minorities. However, if we see populism as a mass political movement that opposes the institutional status quo, the relationship between populism and democracy becomes contingent on the nature of the status quo. When the status quo is democratic, populism invites violations of the rights of minorities and thereby imperils democracy. The constitutional approach is correct for this set of cases. But as I'll describe in more detail in Chapter 8, populist movements—including the original Populist Party itself—sometimes oppose an unrepresentative status quo. In these cases, populism can even be democracy enhancing. This is even more true when the status quo is authoritarian—as it was under many colonial regimes. These cases of democratizing populism are unusual, but they should nevertheless inform how we define the term.

Who are the populists?

Much as the ideational, political-strategic, and constitutional approaches appear to describe distinct phenomena, they each capture one dimension of a politics in which *the people* figure prominently. Even though each approach stresses a different way in which the people matter (ideology, organization, or policies), there is a remarkable consensus on what semantic scholars call the *extension* of the concept—the cases in the world to which it applies. Indeed, one recent edited volume on populism makes this clear, acknowledging that even though contributors to the volume couldn't agree on a single definition of populism, they accepted that all the cases under investigation were populist.[32]

There are certainly marginal cases, political leaders who make rhetorical appeals to the people in opposition to the establishment, but whose parties are too deeply institutionalized to be classified as populist in a strategic sense; Brazil's Lula da Silva, leader of the Workers' Party (PT), being perhaps the best example. Conversely, leaders like Emmanuel Macron, a charismatic leader who directly mobilized support without the use of a political party, remains too personally committed to liberal norms to be considered populist from the constitutional standpoint. Yet, overall, the picture is one of consensus rather than disagreement.

Just how much overlap is there? To get a sense of this, we need to briefly examine how these different approaches go about classifying, or "coding," whether leaders and their movements are populist. There are two main methods of determining whether a party or leader is populist, deriving from the ideational and strategic approaches, respectively.[33]

For those working in the ideational approach, categorizing a leader or party as populist typically entails examining the content of public discourse for evidence of people-centric and anti-elite rhetoric. One method of doing this entails using a small number of leaders' speeches, which are then human coded to determine their main sentiment. While this "holistic grading" approach has strong face validity, it risks introducing bias in the selection of leaders and speeches that are chosen for analysis. Another approach, which minimizes the issue of selection bias, is to examine party manifestos. However, these documents are not always available (as was the case for the Republican Party in the run-up to Trump's 2020 campaign), and it seems likely that the "discourse" of political parties and leaders might be very different in an official document like a manifesto compared to a campaign speech. A third approach, which also deals better with issues of selection bias, is to rely on a much broader sample of public discourse. Quantitative text analysis methods examine bodies of speech, social media, and party publications that can include millions of words for elements of populist discourse. Researchers can search for instances of words like "the people" and "enemies" that might be expected of populists. However, it's not clear that this data-intensive approach properly captures the sentiment of the discourse, while deeper sentiment analysis is more costly and has yet to be applied on a large cross-national sample.

Based on the strategic approach, populists are classified as distinct from the leaders of programmatic and clientelistic parties based on how their movements are organized. Recall that while programmatic parties are rule-based organizations that link to supporters through mass membership and allied civil society organizations like unions and churches, clientelistic parties are factional coalitions of political elites who control blocs of voters through the distribution of patronage such as government jobs or cash.

The strategic approach requires asking how the party is organized "externally" with respect to its support base, and "internally" in terms of the relationship between the leader and other politicians within the party or movement. On the external side, this means answering the following questions: Does the movement have a formal mass membership? Is it closely aligned with unions, churches, or other groups? Does it rely on distributing patronage to win votes? Or does it depend on mass communication, from mass rallies to television to social media, to link with its supporters?

On the internal side, it investigates how populist movements are organized: Was the party created by the current leader? How is the leader selected and replaced? Does the movement have a formal membership with voting rights? Are election campaigns centered on the personality of the leader, as opposed to a party or an issue? The more leader-centric the organization and the more it depends on mass communication rather than bureaucratic or clientelistic linkages with supporters, the more it is a populist movement. This approach too is imperfect, requiring subject assessments of party structures and processes, although intercoder reliability seems acceptable.[34]

How do these different approaches compare? Although we lack a complete database of all populists who have contested political office around the globe, we can get a sense of the overlap in classification by comparing two of the most comprehensive datasets of populist leaders according to the strategic and ideational approaches. In a 2017 book, *Populism and Patronage*, I assembled a dataset of political leaders in power in Asia, Europe, and the Americas between 1980 and 2000, based on a strategic definition of populism. Over the years, I have extended the coverage of that database, so that it now has global coverage from 1900 to 2022.

Using the ideational approach, in 2023, Manuel Funke and his coauthors conducted a review of the primary literature to build a dataset of populists in office from 1900 to 2020. Not all of the source materials use the same approach to measurement; some are based on the analysis of speech, while others take a more subjective and high-level approach. Nevertheless, when compared to smaller datasets that systematically apply the same measurement approach, the classifications are very similar. Because this dataset is based on the secondary literature, it omits the relatively less studied cases of populism in Africa and the Middle East. Nevertheless, this remains the most comprehensive dataset based on the ideational approach.

There are some important differences in coding procedure. The strategic approach relies on examining how political movements are structured during elections *prior* to assuming office with a view to distinguishing populist movements from both programmatic and clientelistic parties. In this approach, populist leaders must come to power through reasonably free and fair elections. Simply being a charismatic, personalistic leader, therefore, is not enough to qualify as a populist. This approach rules out the possibility of the leader of a successful coup d'état becoming a populist unless he subsequently wins elections that are reasonably free and fair. The latter approach

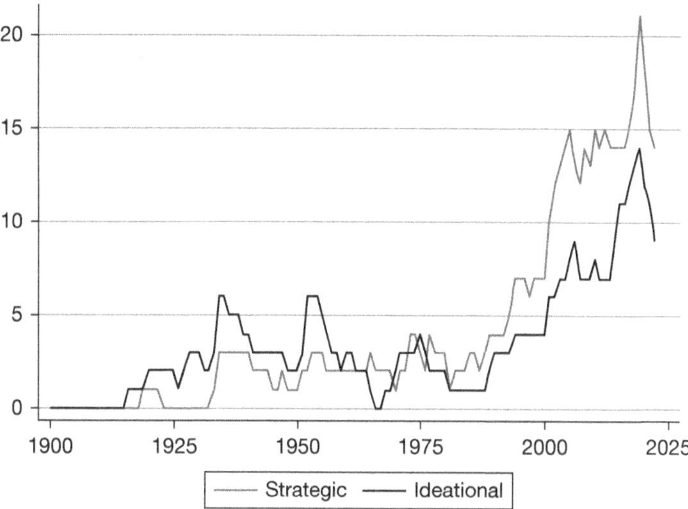

Figure 2.1 Populist Leaders in Office, 1900–2022

was followed by Brazil's Vargas, for example. In contrast, the ideational approach allows for incumbents to turn populist through rhetoric alone without ever winning an election.

Figure 2.1 provides a comparison of my strategic dataset with that of the Funke et al. ideational dataset (for comparability, Africa and the Middle East have been excluded). The degree of overlap strongly suggests that both the ideational and strategic definitions of populism are capturing essentially the same phenomenon. Regardless of the operational definition used, each illustrates the growing prevalence of populist leaders in office over time. This is certainly encouraging. It suggests, at least, that there is less at stake in the definition wars than many scholars believe. Might it be, despite the persistence of the so-called definition war over populism, that we're all really talking about the same thing? If so, how might these diverse approaches be reconciled?

One way of marrying these approaches is to simply combine two or more of them together in a compound definition. For example, political scientist Kenneth Roberts combines the ideational and strategic aspects of populism, defining it as "the top-down political mobilization of mass constituencies by personalistic leaders who challenge elite groups on behalf of an ill-defined pueblo, or 'the people.'" To Roberts's definition, we might add something from the constitutional approach regarding populism's hostile view of pluralist or liberal democracy. We could then visualize a Venn diagram in which the ideational, strategic, and constitutional approaches have areas of overlap—the truly populist movements would be those at the intersection of all three approaches. Populism in this sense would refer to a personalistic, plebiscitarian movement, whose discourse valorizes the people and denigrates the elite, and has an antithetical relationship with liberal democracy.[35]

Although in practical terms, we can be quite sure that those movements that satisfy all parts of such a composite definition are populist, it is not a very satisfactory approach to building a concept. Although the ideational, strategic, and constitutional manifestations of populism run together, such an "additive" concept doesn't provide a compelling internally coherent rationale for *why* they do; what semanticists call the *intension* of the concept is poorly developed. What has been missing until now, in other words, is a conceptualization of populism that logically works at these various levels simultaneously. Developing one is the goal of Chapter 3.

Notes

1. "I'm not prepared," quoted in David Von Drehle, "Barack Obama Reveals His Populist Blindspot," *Time*, June 30, 2016, https://time.com/4389939/barack-obama-donald-trump-populism/.
2. W. B. Gallie, "Essentially Contested Concepts," *Proceedings of the Aristotelian Society* 56 (1955): 167–198.
3. "to each his," Peter Wiles, "A Syndrome Not a Doctrine," in Ghita Ionescu and Ernest Gellner, eds., *Populism: Its Meaning and National Characteristics* (Macmillan, 1969), 166.
4. "a practice, system" Paul D. Kenny, *Populism in Southeast Asia* (Cambridge University Press, 2019), 8.
5. Ernesto Laclau, *On Populist Reason* (Verso, 2005).

6. "Most of politics," Tony Blair's speech to the Labour Party Conference, 27 Sept., 2006, *The Guardian*, https://www.theguardian.com/politics/2006/sep/26/labourconference.labour3.
7. "ideology of popular resentment," Edward Shils, *The Torment of Secrecy: The Background and Consequences of American Security Policies* (Melbourne: W. Heinemann, 1956), 133; "populism in modern," Margaret Canovan, "Trust the People! Populism and the Two Faces of Democracy," *Political Studies* 47, no. 1 (1999): 2–16.
8. Pierre Ostiguy, "A Socio-Cultural Approach," in Pierre Ostiguy, C. Rovira Kaltwasser, P. Taggart, and P. O. Espejo, eds., *The Oxford Handbook of Populism* (Oxford University Press, 2017): 73–97; Benjamin Moffitt, *The Global Rise of Populism: Performance, Political Style, and Representation* (Stanford, 2017); Paul Taggart, *Populism* (Polity, 2000).
9. Margaret Thatcher, "Leader's Speech. Brighton 1976," http://www.britishpoliticalspeech.org/speech-archive.htm?speech=122.
10. Cas Mudde, "The Populist Zeitgeist," *Government and Opposition* 39, no. 4 (2004): 541–563; "thin ideology," Michael Freeden, *Ideology: A Very Short Introduction* (Oxford University Press, 2003), 98–100.
11. "I am for the people," quoted in Jennifer R. Mercieca, *Demagogue for President: The Rhetorical Genius of Donald Trump* (Texas A&M University Press, 2020), 76; "The only important thing," quoted in William Galston, *Anti-Pluralism: The Populist Threat to Liberal Democracy* (Yale University Press, 2018), 37; "The only antidote," in Donald J. Trump, "Let Me Ask America a Question," *Wall Street Journal*, April 14, 2016, https://www.wsj.com/articles/let-me-ask-america-a-question-1460675882. On political scientist Cas Mudde's rationale for excluding Trump as a populist, see "Neither Sanders nor Trump Is a Populist. Yes, You Read That Right, Neither Sanders nor Trump Is a Populist," http://www.sv.uio.no/c-rex/english/news-and-events/news/2016/the-power-of-populism-not-really%21.html. See also interview with Mudde, https://populismobserver.com/2016/05/30/interview-7-a-talk-with-cas-mudde-on-american-populism/.
12. Robert Michels, *Political Parties: A Sociological Study of the Oligarchical Tendencies of Modern Democracy* (Hearst's International Library, 1915), 2–7; "if you want to," quoted in Larry Tye, *Demagogue: The Life and Long Shadow of Senator Joe McCarthy* (HarperCollins, 2020), 40.

13. Agnes Akkerman, Cas Mudde, and Andrej Zaslove, "How Populist Are the People? Measuring Populist Attitudes in Voters," *Comparative Political Studies* 47, no. 9 (2014): 1324–1353.
14. E.g., B. Spruyt, G. Keppens, and F. Van Droogenbroeck, "Who Supports Populism and What Attracts People to It?," *Political Research Quarterly* 69, no. 2 (2016): 335–346, https://doi.org/10.1177/1065912916639138.
15. To measure populist attitudes, researchers have developed a range of scales with multiple dimensions and multiple questions. My own and other research has shown that *People-centrism*, *Anti-elitism*, and *Manichaean outlook* are weakly correlated with each other, meaning that bundling them together as a single attitude (*populism*) is very problematic; see Paul D. Kenny and Boris Bizumic, "Is There a Populist Personality? Populist Attitudes, Personality, and Voter Preference in Australian Public Opinion," *Journal of Elections, Public Opinion and Parties* 34, no. 4 (2023): 697–722, https://doi.org/10.1080/17457289.2023.2243587; on the importance of other policy preferences, see Steven M. Van Hauwaert and Stijn Van Kessel, "Beyond Protest and Discontent: A Cross-National Analysis of the Effect of Populist Attitudes and Issue Positions on Populist Party Support," *European Journal of Political Research* 57, no. 1 (2018); S. Jungkunz, R. A. Fahey, and A. Hino, "Populist Attitudes, Conspiracy Beliefs and the Justification of Political Violence at the US 2020 Elections," *Political Studies* (first published online July 30, 2024), https://doi.org/10.1177/00323217241259229; on non-Western European cases, see T. Hieda, M. Zenkyo, and M. Nishikawa, "Do Populists Support Populism? An Examination through an Online Survey Following the 2017 Tokyo Metropolitan Assembly Election," *Party Politics* 27, no. 2 (2021): 317–328, https://doi.org/10.1177/1354068819848112; B. Stanley, Populism, Nationalism, or National Populism? An Analysis of Slovak Voting Behaviour at the 2010 Parliamentary Election, *Communist and Post-Communist Studies* 44, no. 4 (2011): 257–270, https://doi.org/10.1016/j.postcomstud.2011.10.005; Bruno Castanho Silva, Mario Fuks, and Eduardo Ryô Tamaki, "So Thin It's Almost Invisible: Populist Attitudes and Voting Behavior in Brazil," *Electoral Studies* 75 (2022): 102434; On populists in power, see Sebastian Jungkunz, Robert A. Fahey, and Airo Hino, "How Populist Attitudes Scales Fail to Capture Support for Populists in Power," *PLOS One* 16, no. 12 (2021).

16. On the experimental approach, see Yaoyao Dai and Alexander Kustov, "The (in)Effectiveness of Populist Rhetoric: A Conjoint Experiment of Campaign Messaging," *Political Science Research and Methods* 12, no. 4 (2023): 1–8, https://doi.org/10.1017/psrm.2023.55. See also F. G. Neuner and C. Wratil, "The Populist Marketplace: Unpacking the Role of 'Thin' and 'Thick' Ideology," *Political Behavior* 44 (2022): 551–574, https://doi.org/10.1007/s11109-020-09629-y; "emaciated," Michael Freeden, "After the Brexit Referendum: Revisiting Populism as an Ideology," *Journal of Political Ideologies* 22, no. 1 (2017): 1–11.
17. On this dynamic, see the classic work by Daryl J. Bem, *Beliefs, Attitudes, and Human Affairs* (Belmont, CA: Brooks/Cole, 1970).
18. Lawrence Goodwyn, "Populist Dreams and Negro Rights: East Texas as a Case Study," *American Historial Review* 76, no. 5 (1971): 1435.
19. "populism revolves," Kurt Weyland, *Democracy's Resilience to Populism's Threat: Countering Global Alarmism* (Cambridge University Press, 2024), 20.
20. "a model ," Oliver Nachtwey, *Germany's Hidden Crisis: Social Decline in the Heart of Europe* (Verso, 2018), 191.
21. Gino Germani, *Authoritarianism, Fascism, and National Populism* (Routledge, 1978).
22. Nicos Mouzelis, "On the Concept of Populism: Populist and Clientelist Modes of Incorporation in Semiperipheral Polities," *Politics and Society* 14, no. 3 (1985): 329–348.
23. Kurt Weyland, "Clarifying a Contested Concept: Populism in the Study of Latin American Politics," *Comparative Politics* (2001): 14; Mouzelis, "On the Concept," 334.
24. "charismatic authority," Max Weber, *Economy and Society*, (University of California Press, 1978), 1119.
25. Ian Kershaw. "'Working Towards the Führer.' Reflections on the Nature of the Hitler Dictatorship," *Contemporary European History* 2, no. 2 (1993): 103–118.
26. Weyland, "Clarifying a Contested Concept," 14.
27. "the 99 percent," Jan-Werner Müller, *What Is Populism?* (University of Pennsylvania Press, 2016), 3.
28. "The only important thing," quoted in Jan-Werner Müller, "Real Citizens," *Boston Review*, October 26, 2016, https://www.bostonreview.net/articles/jan-werner-muller-populism/.

29. "illiberal democracy," Takis S. Pappas, *Populism and Liberal Democracy: A Comparative and Theoretical Analysis* (Oxford University Press), 2019; "anti-pluralism," William A. Galston, *Anti-Pluralism: The Populist Threat to Liberal Democracy* (New Haven: Yale University Press, 2017); Fareed Zakaria, "The Rise of Illiberal Democracy," *Foreign Affairs* 76 (1997): 22; Viktor Orbán, "Prime Minister Viktor Orbán's Speech at the 25th Bálványos Summer Free University and Student Camp," July 26, 2014, https://2015-2019.kormany.hu/en/the-prime-minister/the-prime-minister-s-speeches/prime-minister-viktor-orban-s-speech-at-the-25th-balvanyos-summer-free-university-and-student-camp.
30. Pascal D. König, "Support for a Populist Form of Democratic Politics or Political Discontent? How Conceptions of Democracy Relate to Support for the AfD," *Electoral Studies* 78 (2022): 102493.
31. Helena Rosenblatt, *The Lost History of Liberalism: From Ancient Rome to the Twenty-First Century* (Princeton University Press, 2018); "Everyone in turn," Benjamin Constant, *Principles of Politics Applicable to All Governments*, trans. Dennis O'Keeffe (Liberty Fund 2003), 35. "liberal democracy," Armin Schäfer and Michael Zürn, *The Democratic Regression: The Political Causes of Authoritarian Populism* (John Wiley, 2023). On the minimalist conception of democracy, see Adam Przeworski, "Minimalist Conception of Democracy: A Defense," in *Democracy's Value*, edited by Ian Shapiro and Casiano Hacker-Cordón (Cambridge University Press, 1999), 23–55.
32. Kurt Weyland and Raúl L. Madrid, eds., *When Democracy Trumps Populism: European and Latin American Lessons for the United States* (Cambridge University Press, 2019).
33. Being limited to populists in power, scholars working in the constitutional approach have generally adopted a case study approach, focusing on well-known cases where the categorization of an actor as a populist is taken as given.
34. See Paul Kenny, *Populism and Patronage: Why Populists Win Elections in India, Asia, and Beyond* (Oxford University Press, 2017), ch. 2.
35. Kenneth M. Roberts, "Latin America's Populist Revival," *SAIS Review of International Affairs* 27, no. 1 (2007): 5.

3

THE INSTITUTIONAL APPROACH TO POPULISM

Were the Populists populist?

No study of populism can avoid discussion of the first and only movement to explicitly adopt the populist moniker as its own. By the late 1880s, with the major exception that slavery had been formally abolished in America, the political status quo ante bellum had largely been restored. The nation's post–Civil War experiment with Reconstruction had come to an end, with Blacks effectively restored to their positions of political, as well as social and economic, subordination. Also returned to business as usual was the spoils system that had become the modus operandi of the main political parties in the decades before the war, although the scale of corruption was an order of magnitude greater. Again, like the antebellum period, this was an era of perennial economic boom and bust. The headlong expansion of the railroad network from 79,000 miles in 1877 to 166,000 miles in 1890 and the proliferation of independent operators had given way to bankruptcies and consolidation. Farming communities, especially in the West and South, became increasingly dependent on, and squeezed by, the middlemen—railroads, storage facilities, and banks—who stood between them and the major urban markets for their produce. The revival of national and global trade after the Civil War saw the wholesale price for American farm products decline by half between 1870 and 1896, with marginal southern cotton farmers and western staple producers living in fear of being pushed down to the status of former slaves. The financial panic of 1873 was so bad as to be known as "the Great Depression" until the even more severe crisis of 1929 hit. Americans—the majority of whom were rural—felt they faced a system that was stacked against them.

By the mid-1870s, farmers in the Midwest and the Upper South had begun to organize. The Farmers' Alliance was established in 1877 with local chapters sprouting up across much of rural America. The Alliance declared itself to be "against a government of politicians, by politicians and for politicians," and for "a government of the people, by the people and for the people." The party slogan was "special privileges to none." Initially attempting to lobby the incumbent Republican and Democratic parties to adopt policies such as mortgage relief and price supports, the Alliance soon became frustrated at the lack of progress being made with this indirect strategy. Leaders of the movement like William Peffer concluded that the parties were in the pockets of the railroads and banks. As he put it, "Republican legislatures of Kansas simply obeyed the orders of the railroad companies. . . . Nothing could be done without the consent of the railroad companies."[1]

The Populists were distinctive not because of their policies, but because of the way they went outside the party duopoly to challenge the status quo. By the late 1880s, it was clear to Peffer and other Alliance leaders that they would have to strike out on their own. Contesting state legislative elections in 1890, Alliance candidates made the most serious inroads in Kansas, sending Peffer to Washington, DC, as one of the state's two senators. Building on these state party organizations, a mass meeting called the National Union Conference assembled in Cincinnati on May 19, 1891, the outcome being the formation of a new national People's Party. With the then popular term "Pefferism" being too personalist and "Peopleists" having no ring to it, some bright spark coined the term

"Populists"—deriving from the Latin, *populus*, or people—to describe themselves. The name stuck.

The Populist platform was among the first to advocate a progressive income tax; national regulation or national ownership of finance, transport, and telecommunications networks; inflationary policies that would have benefited borrowers over creditors; direct elections to the United States Senate; and an end to the corrupt spoils system. Thomas Frank, bestselling author of *What's the Matter with Kansas*, insists that the true nature of populism is thus a kind of progressive, social democracy. Yet as historian Charles Postel notes, "No uniform doctrine prevailed within the Populist coalition." The movements' regionally diverse sections had discrete interests, with the result that the party eventually cohered on the minimal common shared policy preference of monetary deflation. In contrast, for Jan-Werner Müller, who insists that populism is inherently illiberal, the Populists (capital P) were not themselves populist. Which, if any, of these interpretations is correct?[2]

What the Populist experience suggests is that populism is not defined by a set of policies or a governing philosophy but by popular opposition to the institutional order. Moreover, this opposition to the status quo critically went beyond policy. It was, at the height of its success, anti-institutional in practice. The Populists came closest to upending the system when they rallied behind a charismatic outsider, who could credibly challenge the party duopoly. The sudden death of the popular Farmers' Alliance leader and People's Party founder, Leonidas Polk, in June of an election year, 1892, left the party short of a natural presidential candidate. In the short term, the Populists put forward General James Weaver, a perennial third-party candidate, as its leader in 1892. However, the party achieved its best performance with the nomination of the wildly charismatic William Jennings Bryan as its presidential candidate in 1896. Bryan was able to bring together a diverse coalition, united by little except its collective resentment of the status quo, and take it to the cusp of power. Bryan's failure, and the fact that the Populists had chosen to back a Democrat rather than put up their own candidate, led the party to fragment. The Populists fell to their most ignominious ebb in the turn to the white supremacist politics of Tom Watson after the turn of the century.

Populism, in short, could be both liberal and illiberal. What I call the *institutional approach* to understanding populism accounts not only for the anti-elite policies proposed by the Populists in the 1890s stressed by Frank, but also for the illiberal and nativist tendencies of populist movements typified by Watson that are of interest to Müller. The *institutional approach* provides an understanding of populism that fits the vast majority of those instances typically described as populist in other approaches, while also yielding a logically coherent concept. In the technical terms I introduced in Chapter 2, it is a conceptualization that performs well in terms of both *extension* and *intension*.

What is the institutional approach to populism?

As we saw in the last chapter, while the main approaches to understanding populism used today rightly give the people a prominent role, they disagree as to whom or what the people are allegedly opposed. Rather than thinking of the people's opposite as being the elite, political insiders, or minorities, as ideational, strategic, and constitutional approaches respectively tend to do, I propose that we instead view populism's opposite as being *institutions*. For populist supporters, the promises made by mainstream institutions—the pledges of fairness, of justice, of a system that works for all—feel like a lie. Populist voters reject the status quo. They reject the system.

What does a definition of populism look like according to the institutional approach? At the most general level, populism can be defined as *a politics of popular opposition to the institutional status quo*. Like other approaches, this conceptualization is centered on the people. It is a politics in which the views of the people—*populus* being the Latin root of *popular*—are of central importance. It is a politics of the people versus the system.

I deliberately use the general term "politics" here to convey the notion that populism can be used to refer to both ideas and actions; in other words, at the highest level of abstraction, we do not have to choose whether populism is an ideology (ideational approach), a type of movement (strategic approach), or a set of policies (constitutional approach). While populism may be evident in anti-institutional or anti-establishment rhetoric, it also implies a heterodox approach to policymaking, and an anti-institutional form or structure, in which (extraordinary) charismatic leadership predominates over (institutionalized) formal organization.

In this latter sense, populists themselves are *charismatic leaders who directly mobilize people resentful of the institutional order to win and retain power through the plebiscitary process.* A populist movement is one that has this personalistic form. My own interpretation of the politics of mass resentment of the institutional status quo prioritizes action and organization over ideology; but consistent with this definition, others could take a different view, placing more focus on anti-institutional discourse, attitudes, policy programs, or institutional reforms. Ultimately, this decision depends on the kinds of issues being investigated.

Although this is the first attempt that I know of which explicitly *defines* populism in institutional terms, it is far from the first to see the relationship with institutions as being central to what populism is about. In fact, the antipathy to institutions features prominently in many of the conceptions of populism that have been developed over the years. Sociologist Edward Shils observed in the 1950s that "populism proclaims that the will of the people as such is supreme over every other standard, over the standards of traditional institutions, over the autonomy of institutions and over the will of other strata. Populism identifies the will of the people with justice and morality." He continues: Populism has a "fundamental distrust of the dominant institutions and authorities of modern society." A decade later, political theorist Isaiah Berlin argued that populism "is not principally interested in political institutions" and that it "believes in society rather than in the state"; more recently, Jan-Werner Müller has observed that populists have a "noninstitutionalized notion of 'the people.'" Political scientist Julio Carrión identifies "mass discontent with existing political arrangements/institutions" as a key antecedent condition for the rise of populism. Barack Obama—again donning his sociologist cap—nailed the central role of institutions in the rise of populist anger in contemporary American politics: "Both on the left and the right, I think people feel separated from their government. They feel that their institutions aren't looking out for them."[3]

The idea that institutions are at the opposite pole to the people in populism is especially evident in the constitutional approach described in the previous chapter. As we noted then, that approach is heavily concerned with the implications of populism for the rule of law. Populists in power exploit their popular mandate to erode a range of institutions, from the free press to the independent judiciary, which would normally constrain their personal power. As Julio Carrión writes, populists aim to achieve permanency in power by "changing the rules of the game." Constitutional lawyer Eric Posner conceives of populism as "a political attitude that distrusts established institutions on the assumption that they thwart the popular will." As Wojciech Sadurski, another scholar of constitutional law, writes, "Formal institutions are viewed by populists as irritants, unnecessarily throwing obstacles on the path of implementing the leadership's will. . . . Populists do not like being straightjacketed by formal rules and institutions." Constitutional law specialist Samuel Issacharoff conceives of populism "as being grounded in political mobilization in disregard of the institutions of governance." It is a result of mass discontentment with "institutional failure." Populism, for Issacharoff, should be understood as "a form of democratic governance with weak institutions."[4]

Although studies like these affirm the importance of institutions to the concept of populism, surprisingly, the exact meaning of the term "institutions" is not always made clear. Usually, the concept is employed as the common-language categorical noun for entities such as the Federal Reserve or the European Court of Justice. However, this understanding runs in contrast to the usual meaning of institutions in the social sciences, which refers not to specific organizations, but to the *systems of rules* that such organizations create, refine, and enforce. Like most political scientists, I follow Nobel Prize–winning economist Douglas North's definition of institutions as "the rules of the game in a society, or, more formally . . . the humanly devised constraints that shape human interaction." This distinction might seem pedantic, but it helps us to keep separate the opposition to a particular organization like the European Commission, with its appointed and largely anonymous staff and leadership, and the broader body of European Union laws, rules, and regulations on issues like immigration and the environment.[5]

Like most political scientists, but in distinction to North, I reserve the term institutions for what are sometimes called *formal institutions*. Formal institutions can be defined as sets of rules that structure human behavior and expectations around a statutory goal by specifying actors and their roles, requiring, permitting, or prohibiting specified behavior, and defining the consequences of not complying with the rules. Formal institutions include the laws, directives, and regulations set forth by all levels of government. It includes also trade agreements and other supranational treaties. Formal institutions, moreover, can be private as well as public, including the enforceable codes and rules set out by industry associations and professional societies. Procedures around Diversity, Equity, and Inclusion (DEI) adopted by universities and many corporations are an example. Formal institutions exclude mere social norms, which political scientists typically label *informal institutions*. Including every type of social norm, rule, or guideline—such as proper table manners—risks equating institutions with the broader notion of culture. Preserving the conceptual distinction between institutions and culture is important because people are likely to feel very differently about formal and informal institutions. In fact, as we'll see, populism is often animated by the perceived gap between *formal institutions* and *informal ones*; for populists, folk wisdom and its associated norms may have a superior status to formal laws and regulations.[6]

Why stress something as abstract as institutions or "the rules of the game" and the opposition to them in understanding a concept like populism? As we'll see, populism is characterized by *resentment* of a system that is perceived to be *unfair*. Institutions are critical to how societies are organized, from setting interest rates on borrowing to determining how healthcare is provided. In a democracy, institutional systems or rules are expected to reflect what society believes to be *fair* at any given time. For liberals like philosopher John Rawls, there is an absolute standard of fairness, which demands a high level of equality of outcome. For more communitarian thinkers, the standard of fairness will change over time and from place to place, sometimes prioritizing individual rights, at others societal ones. Whatever the standard, fairness is the mental module we use to evaluate the acceptability of society's rules, and it is the sense of unfairness that appears to be almost universal among populist supporters.

When people perceive the rules to be unfair, they become embittered. Or as Lawrence Rosenthal, an expert on political extremism, writes, the "classic emotion associated with populist movements is resentment." Similarly, in her insightful study of the populist revolt against Wisconsin's progressive status quo in the 2010s, political scientist Katherine Cramer observes that working people in rural Wisconsin had come to feel that urbanites—privileged bureaucrats and dependent minorities—were unfairly benefiting at their expense; she aptly titled her book *The Politics of Resentment*. As a voter in a Trump stronghold in rural Kentucky put it to sociologist Arlie Russell Hochschild, "You feel like something out there is designed to keep you down. There's no specific person to get mad at. But I start thinking, whatever system is in charge here, I *hate* it and want to throw it out. . . . There are so many rules, it's hard to live with them all." Going back to the more general terms of sociologist Barrington Moore, as he concluded in his classic study of injustice, "social rules and their violation are crucial components in moral anger and a sense of injustice." In short, formal institutions are resented when they violate our informal expectations of what is just and reasonable.[7]

An advantage of focusing on the perceived fairness of institutions is that it is not cognitively demanding. To explain support for populism, we do not need to assume that people believe in multifaceted ideologies or understand complicated policies; they simply need to *feel* that the system is unfair. As revealed in a host of experimental studies, our sense of fairness is innate, arising primarily in the insular cortex part of the brain, otherwise known as the seat of emotions. In a devious psychology experiment known as the Ultimatum Game, two participants must divide a sum of money. The money, say $100, is allocated to only one of the participants. She must then decide on a fraction to offer to the other participant in the experiment, the subject. The subject is then free to accept or reject the offer. If he accepts, the money is divided as proposed. If the subject rejects the offer, then both participants walk away with nothing. Knowing these rules, we might expect the first player to make a minimal offer of say $10. Although the subject would be $10 better off if he accepted, such low-ball offers are systematically rejected. Even offers as high as $30 are often dismissed. Subjects expect fairness and will reject any outcome in which their playing partner walks away with a disproportionate share of the winnings. Nor is this sense of fairness felt only by the recipient players in these games. In another version of the game, called the Dictator Game, where subjects must accept any offer, dictators make less generous offers but still do not take the most selfish option of keeping all the money for themselves.[8]

These judgments of what is fair do not appear to be something we need to be taught. Experiments with child subjects suggest that we are born with a sense of justice. In fact, this intuition for fairness extends to many of our primate cousins and was thus a trait likely shared by a common ancestor. A famous study by ethologists Sarah Brosnan and Frans de Waal demonstrated that capuchin monkeys were content to accept a modest reward of cucumber for performing a simple task, but only as long as the same reward was received by the other monkeys in the experiment; if a monkey in an adjacent cage received a high-value reward (a grape) for the same task, then the cucumber was rejected—in some cases, unceremoniously thrown in the face of the experimenter! It seems increasingly likely that many other social animal species have rules of conduct for play (e.g., don't bite too hard or try to mate with your playing partner) and for the distribution of resources (e.g., sharing meat from the hunt). Our demand for fairness runs deep.[9]

Invoking deep-seated or evolved emotional pathways here is not to call on some irrational or illogical motivation that runs against self-interest—an all-too-common canard when it comes to explaining populism. Obama speaking in 2008 on the mounting opposition to his presidency illustrates the confusion here: "You go into these small towns . . . the jobs have been gone now for 25 years and nothing's replaced them. . . . And it's not surprising then they get bitter, and they cling to guns or religion or antipathy toward people who aren't like them or anti-immigrant sentiment or anti-trade sentiment as a way to explain their frustrations." Again, Obama the sociologist is both right and wrong. The disappearance of steady, well-paying work in small-town America is an important factor in the rise of populism. However, Obama erroneously implies that the bitterness and frustration, along with the search for community that follow, are muddled emotions, not clear thinking.[10]

In *Passions Within Reason*, economist Robert Frank proposed that emotions like anger and resentment are rational, operating in service of our long-run self-interest. Shame and anger might appear to be unproductive emotions. For sure, we've all said things to a loved one in the heat of the moment that we later regret. But from an evolutionary point of view, anger makes a great deal of sense. When people cheat, when systems are unfair, we need emotions like anger to get us to stand up and fight for what is right. Shame can be debilitating. It can cause people to engage in self-destructive behaviors like alcohol and drug abuse—shortcuts to avoid these unpleasant feelings. But the inherent desire to avoid feelings of shame can also drive people to change their circumstances in a more positive way—seeking out community and demanding institutional support. Without these "negative" emotions, we would "rationally" calculate that resistance is not worth the effort and the injustice would stand. The resentment of institutions that we perceive as unfair is thus far from irrational, even if we sometimes do a poor job of identifying precisely which policies, programs, and people are doing the harm or understanding why. Negative emotional reactions to a perceived decline in one's personal status—a loss of dignity—are quite logical from an evolutionary point of view. Moreover, even perceived drops in the status of the group to which one belongs can be understood as rational. Group status has real effects on an individual's physical and mental welfare. Populism's opposition to the institutional status quo may be a lot more rational than it seems.[11]

What institutions do populists oppose?

Claiming to stand for the unalloyed sovereignty of the people, populist leaders oppose institutions they argue are unfair in terms of outcome, process, or both. Support for these anti-institutional sentiments is not difficult to understand. Increasingly, as Obama noted, people simply feel as if institutions are not responsive to their needs. The system seems to have a way of defending itself, whatever the people say. When in 2015 Greek voters rejected the austerity measures imposed on the country by the Troika of international lenders—the European Commission, the European Central Bank, and the International Monetary Fund—as a condition for a financial bailout from its sovereign debt crisis, German Finance Minister Wolfgang Schäuble responded on behalf of the system: "Elections change nothing. There are rules." A similar story, which may be apocryphal, is told by Britain's Euroskeptic leader, Nigel Farage. After French and Dutch voters rejected a proposed new European Constitution in 2005 in separate referendums, Farage teased one of the document's drafters, German Member of the European Parliament, Jo Leinen, with an invitation to a celebratory drink. The latter responded, "You may have your little party; you may think this is a victory, but we have 50 different ways to win." Indeed, after the Irish earlier rejected the Nice Treaty by referendum in June 2001, they were asked to vote on it again in 2002. The process was repeated in 2008–2009, when the Irish took two votes to pass the Lisbon Treaty. Irish voters increasingly felt like they had to keep voting until they gave the *correct* answer. To more than a few critics, it seems that institutions like the European Union have little respect for the views of regular people. The system gets its way no matter what the people really want.[12]

Although individually named elites sometimes feature as the bogeymen of populist discourse, popular resentment is more often aimed at an anonymous system of rules and regulations that elites exploit to further their advantages over regular people. Populists

often claim to oppose a failing economic and political system, and vow to bring it down. As Argentina's libertarian populist president, Javier Milei, put it: "Let it all blow up, let the economy blow up, and take this entire garbage political caste down with it." Justifying his intention to replace Venezuela's constitution after winning the presidency in 1998, Hugo Chávez described his movement's goal as a "revolutionary process which seeks to destroy this system . . . ours does not seek to fix this system." Bernie Sanders called on voters to reject a political and economic system "that is fundamentally broken and grotesquely unfair." Sanders would lose to mainstream candidate Hillary Clinton in a primary process that even neutrals labeled "so rigged." The leader of Italy's Five Star Movement, Beppe Grillo, declared June 14, 2007, V-day (or "Vaffanculo Day"—"Fuck off day"), as he sought support to scrap the country's political system. To the extent that his popular movement had an agenda, it was a purely negative one, focused not on new policy but on abrogating a swath of existing laws and institutions. Nor is this anti-institutionalist quality of populism something new. Back in the 1940s, Wisconsin Senator Joseph McCarthy's rise to political prominence relied on the support not just of conventional anti-communists, but also those who "distrusted big institutions—government, labor, and business—as much as they hated Reds, radicals, and eggheads." Or as a commentator put it at the time, McCarthy built a "coalition of the aggrieved."[13]

If in many of today's Western democracies the institutions most resented are technocratic ones that sub in formal rules and procedures (e.g., central banks, international courts) for popular participation, in other parts of the world, institutional resentment takes on a different form. In places like India, populists have campaigned against the political corruption of the system rather than an unresponsive technocracy. Here, again, a plethora of rules and procedures are at work, but the problem is that insiders are able to game them for their own personal benefit. While the Indian National Congress (INC) government of Prime Minister Manmohan Singh (2004–14) presided over a period of impressive economic growth, it was also beset by a series of corruption scandals, from the acceptance of a politically connected bid for India's 2G mobile network license that cost the government some $25 billion in lost revenue to the massive cost over-runs for New Dehli's hosting of the Commonwealth Games in 2010 due to the awarding of dubious construction contracts. As I witnessed during fieldwork in New Delhi for my first book in 2009–10, middle class resentment of a corrupt status quo was growing. Before the Bharatiya Janata Party's (BJP) Narendra Modi made the breakthrough to become prime minister in 2016 on the back of promises to revivify a sagging economy, the upstart Aam Aadmi Party (AAP), led by the charismatic Arvind Kejriwal, displaced the long-standing INC government in Delhi in 2013, pledging to "sweep" away corruption—the party's emblem being a traditional broom. Even if nominally fair on paper, deeply corrupted institutions, from which the privileged few benefit while the rest lose out, are every bit as resented as those in which formally applied rules privilege some groups over others.

Understanding populism as being about opposition to institutions also helps to make better sense of the nationalist and nativist sentiments common to populist movements. International institutions are even more removed from the influence of regular people and so are particularly susceptible to allegations of unfairness by populist leaders. In the European Union, the separation of policymaking from public opinion was built into the very design of many European institutions, a democratic deficit that is effectively exploited by populist leaders like Britain's Farage and the Netherlands' Geert Wilders. The new nationalism owes much to this widespread sense of institutional unaccountability. In the United States, Trump, like Ross Perot before him, famously railed against the North American Free Trade Agreement (NAFTA) and other international institutions. Indeed, candidate Trump was obsessed with what he saw as China's unfair trade practices, graphically telling audiences: "We can't continue to allow China to rape our country, and that's what we're doing." Trump's framing was clearly much less a form of anti-elitism than it was a sense that China was unfairly breaking the rules. In his view, NAFTA and the World Trade Organization are institutions that are unfair to Americans.[14]

Historically, given America's prominent role in creating and running the most significant international institutions, nationalist populist opposition has tended to emerge in those places more marginalized by them. Venezuela's Hugo Chávez nationalized the oil industry at the expense of Western oil companies, making him an enemy of the United States. His suspicions of American involvement in a 2002 coup attempt against him further estranged him from the US international order and led him to later liken then-president George W. Bush to "the devil" and Hitler. Rodrigo Duterte sought to reorient the Philippines' economy away from the United States toward China. He also withdrew his country from of the International Criminal Court because of its threats (subsequently realized) to prosecute him over his government's violent war on illegal drugs.

In many instances today, it is institutions governing the treatment of immigrants and minorities that violate popular notions of fairness. Arlie Russell Hochschild, in her study of working-class, mostly white Tea Party supporters in Louisiana, captured something essential about this discontent: the sense of waiting patiently for one's turn, of playing by the rules, only to see others—immigrants and racial minorities—seemingly "cutting in front of the line." The result is mass resentment of the institutional order that allows this to happen—civil rights, welfare, and immigration systems that are perceived to benefit some (minority) groups at the expense of the "native" majority. And when political leaders—those entrusted with the responsibility of governing—plead that their hands are tied, that international law, supranational institutions, the European Union, or the courts that prevent them from acting, this only deepens the disillusionment. Because what these leaders are saying is that the system—the system that was supposed to be accountable to the people—is no longer theirs to control. It is broken. And if it is broken, then whose side, really, is the system on?[15]

Although the wealthy elite, liberal and conservative, are the primary beneficiaries of the immigration of low-skilled workers, whose labor keeps down the cost of everyday services, whose toil makes possible the conveniences of modern life—an Uber ride summoned with the tap of a finger, a hotel room cleaned without a thought as to who cleaned it—popular resentment is not primarily directed at the wealthy or the corporations who exploit these workers. Rather, resentment is directed at the immigrants who perform these services at subsistence wages. But as Hochschild notes, this institutional resentment is not simply about economics. It is about pride. The white working class has experienced downward mobility not just in the economic hierarchy but also in the pride hierarchy. While previously disadvantaged groups are encouraged to proudly identify with their race or gender, white straight ("cishet") men have seen their status downgraded. The corporate adoption of DEI policies, the sudden ubiquity of "woke" rhetoric in boardrooms, media, and universities—these developments have not only provoked anger among the right-wing elite but among the working class, the so-called normies, who see these shifts not as a long-overdue reckoning with social injustice but as yet another example of a system that no longer serves them. The institutional order, both public and private, is experienced as a direct threat to the status of these voters. I will have more to say specifically on the role of identity politics in populism later in this chapter.

The institutional approach may also make sense of the association between populism and conspiracy theories. Populist movements draw their strength not only from economic hardship and cultural anxiety but from something deeper—a conviction that the system itself is corrupt, that the institutions meant to serve the people have, in fact, betrayed them. And where that conviction takes hold, conspiracy theories are never far behind.

For those with a conspiratorial mindset, the answer is always the same. The hardships they endure, the political setbacks they suffer, are not the result of chance or mismanagement but of deliberate action—of unseen forces working against them, of a cabal of elites whose influence reaches into the highest echelons of power. It was this conviction that gave rise to one of the most infamous conspiracy theories of modern times: QAnon. In 2017, an anonymous figure, calling themselves "Q," emerged from the murky depths of the 4chan message boards, claiming to be a government insider with access to the truth—a truth that, if exposed, would reveal a vast, hidden ring of Satanic pedophiles conspiring to obstruct Donald Trump and even remove him from office. The details were lurid, and on their face, absurd. But the message resonated. Trump himself, the man QAnon's followers believed was leading the charge against the conspiracy, became known as the "conspiracy theorist in chief." And his supporters—many of whom already saw in him a warrior against the status quo—embraced the theory, because, to them, it confirmed what they already believed: that the system was against them.[16]

And it is not only in the United States. In Türkiye, in 2007, five years into the rule of the Justice and Development Party (AKP), Recep Tayyip Erdoğan's campaign for the newly empowered presidency was built not on triumph but on grievance—on *mazlum* (the feeling of being wronged) and *mağdur* (the feeling of being victimized). It was an argument not just against political opponents but against the system itself. Studies have shown that support for Erdoğan is better predicted by conspiratorial beliefs than by populist attitudes—because the issue, for many of his supporters, is not merely "the elite" as a class, but the existence of a vast and entrenched network of corruption working to keep the people down.[17]

Political parties are a core part of the institutional order. Again and again, however, populists have cast them not as instruments of democracy, not as the means by which the people's will is carried into government, but as obstacles—self-serving machines that exist not to serve the people but to preserve their own power. To the populist, the party is not a vehicle for representation. It is the problem itself. It is part of the institutional order that must be torn down. This is not just rhetoric. The distrust of parties runs deep in populist movements, and it is not just a matter of policy disagreements or ideological divides. It is something more fundamental. Populists do not see parties as legitimate arbiters of the democratic process but as factions—insular, self-perpetuating, and loyal not to the people but to their own survival. Scholars of populism have noted this antipathy to party for a long time. Shils writes that populism is characterized by the "distrust of professional politicians and party politicians, impatience with the traditional legal and political institutions which intervene between the people's desires and their execution by their elected representatives, belief in the moral superiority of the people, and a suspicion of privacy and withdrawal from the common culture." Canovan similarly argued that populists call on the people to bypass "professional politicians." Mudde, who stresses the primacy of people-centric and anti-elite ideology to populism, also observes that "populists argue that political parties corrupt the link between leaders and supporters." The British political theorist and social critic Bernard Crick has written that "the populist leader usually blames intermediary institutions for frustrating the will of the people. At various times, and, in various places, these intermediary and divisive institutions have appeared as the landlords, the bankers, the bureaucrats, the priests, the elite, the immigrants and, most popular of all for populists to denounce, *the politicians.*" To the populist, the party is, at best, a means to an end. Ultimately, like other institutions, the party is another enemy to be destroyed.[18]

While the foregoing indicates that most current scholarship acknowledges the tension between populists and political parties, the institutional approach has a particular explanation for why this relationship exists. Populism, at its core, does not merely reject the policies of the establishment. It rejects the establishment itself. It rejects the institutions that mediate power—parliaments, courts, and, of course, parties. In their recent book, *How to Save a Constitutional Democracy*, Tom Ginsburg and Aziz Huq similarly describe how populism entails cutting out the institutional middlemen. They write: "Because the populist leader alone channels and manifests the will of the people, there is no need for intermediary institutions of traditional representative democracy. Indeed by implication, institutions such as courts, legislatures, and ombudsmen that resist the populist program are instruments of a corrupt and illicit elite." Populism rejects these institutions because, as political theorist Nadia Urbinati puts it, it seeks to erase the space between the leader and the people. Populism does not want negotiation, or compromise, or slow-moving bureaucracy. It does not want institutions that stand between those who govern and those who are governed. "Blurring any mediation between leadership and the people," she writes, "so as to bypass indirect forms of politics"—this is not just a feature of populism, but its defining characteristic. This opposition to the intermediary role of the party gives populist movements their most distinctive feature: the charismatic leader. The singular figure who embodies the people's grievances, their hopes, their anger. And so populism's target is not just elites. It is not just minorities. Populism rejects the political party establishment as much as any other part of the institutional status quo. Five Star Movement leader Bepe Grillo captured this feeling best, targeting not just one party or politician, but La Casta—the Caste—his name for the whole political class.[19]

In lieu of the institutionalized political party, populism instead takes the form of a charismatically led movement. Populism's anti-institutional social movements may express the same resentments as those of populist ones, but without political leadership, these movements do not directly compete for power themselves. Oliver Nachtwey writes that Occupy

Wall Street and social movements like it represent a "strikingly anti-institutional form of politics." Despite the relatively high educational and economic status of its participants, Occupy quickly faded. In contrast, Spain's Indignados protest movement subsequently organized as a party, Podemos, under the leadership of Pablo Iglesias. Occupy remained a protest. Podemos became something more. For populism to endure, for it to be more than a fleeting expression of anger, it must have leadership. Not the slow, bureaucratic leadership of institutions but the kind that populism thrives on—the kind that is irregular, personal, charismatic. The kind that does not answer to rules but to the will of the people, as embodied in a single figure.[20]

Why is populism so puzzling?

Who would have predicted that a man with virtually no political experience, who had almost no plans for how he would govern the country, whose major accomplishment to date was to be the star of a popular television show, would become president? That is the reality that Guatemalans woke up to on October 26, 2015, as celebrity comedian Jimmy Morales was confirmed as the winner of the presidential election. Although Morales isn't as well known as another celebrity-cum-president a little to the north, his path to success tells us a lot about what populism is and how and why it works. Like Trump, Morales's celebrity status gave him a readymade connection to voters who were increasingly disaffected with the perennial corruption of the political system.

Relying on his fame alone, Morales built no party or campaign infrastructure. Instead, he appealed over the heads of the system's parties and political fixers directly to the people. His campaign slogan was blunt: "Not corrupt, nor a thief." A low bar, perhaps—but in Guatemala, it was enough. His predecessor, Otto Pérez Molina, had not just been accused of corruption. He had been forced from office, arrested, and imprisoned. And Guatemalans, weary of a system they saw as hopelessly, irredeemably corrupt, were no longer looking for a leader with experience. They were looking for someone who was not a paid-up member of the political class. It was the same anger with the status quo that fueled Trump's rise. The same belief that the system was rigged, that those in power had betrayed the people, that what was needed was not another politician but a reckoning. In Washington, Trump vowed to "drain the swamp." In Guatemala, Morales's voters wanted the same. When the system is rotten, when the people lose faith, they turn not to those who have been shaped by that system; they turn to those who stand outside it.

The simple interpretation here is that institutional distrust drives people to abandon the political establishment and rally behind populists like Morales and Trump. Yet by itself this explanation is incomplete. Mass distrust of political institutions makes people's voting for populist leaders not less of a puzzle, but *more*. It is true that those who resent the status quo, who no longer trust the institutions that govern them, are less likely to vote for mainstream parties. But just as important—if almost entirely neglected in existing research—is that these disaffected voters are also less likely to vote *at all*. When faith in the system collapses, when people believe that government is no longer theirs to influence, their first instinct is not rebellion, but withdrawal. Well before the recent surge in populist support in Western Europe and North America, voter turnout rates were in historic decline. The disillusioned, the working class, the dispossessed—those who once formed the backbone of social democratic and labor parties—had been slipping away from the political process for decades. And so the question is not simply why they turned to the likes of Trump. It is why, after years—sometimes generations—of absence, they decided to vote at all.

Simply having *policies* that disaffected voters like is not enough to get them out of bed on election day. For decades, political scientists assumed that voters made their choices based on a rational calculation of self-interest—that they weighed the policies of competing parties, measured how those policies would affect their lives, and then cast their ballots accordingly. But that assumption, the foundation of early voting behavior models, has not held up. Because if voters were truly rational calculators, if they were measuring costs against benefits, they would do something else entirely. They would stay home. Voting takes time and effort. And for any one individual, the marginal impact of a single vote on the outcome of an election is vanishingly small. In a strict, rational sense, it does not make sense to vote at all. Why should I make the effort to get up early and spend hours queuing to vote when my vote has a vanishingly small impact on the result? In their book, *Why Bother?*, political scientists S. Erdem Aytaç and Susan Stokes propose that the answer is civic duty. People vote, they suggest, because they feel an obligation to participate in the democratic process. This could make sense for some voters, but for those who are resentful of the institutional status quo, it seems unlikely. In short, we're still left with the problem of explaining why resentful and apathetic citizens vote at all.[21]

The discontented and disorganized masses most likely to vote for anti-institutionalist populist outsiders face an acute collective-action problem. A collective action problem arises when people stand to benefit from an outcome but have little reason to personally contribute to making it happen. It is one of the great paradoxes of human behavior: Everyone wants the reward, but few are willing to do the work, since they can free-ride on the efforts of others. Why should an individual sacrifice time, effort, or resources when they can simply wait for others to act—when they can reap the benefits without ever lifting a finger? This is why societal change so often fails to come, even when the need for it is clear. It is why, despite the overwhelming consensus on the dangers of climate change, emissions remain high. Because while we may all agree that reducing greenhouse gases would be beneficial, the incentives to act—on an individual level—are weak. Why should *I* change my lifestyle, pay more for cleaner energy, or cut back on consumption when others refuse to do the same? And if they do nothing, why should I? The logic feeds on itself. The result is paralysis.

It is important to stress here that the mere framing of the political debate is insufficient to overcome this problem of apathy. Simply telling people they share a common interest—in the environment, or an economic policy, etc.—won't make it so. The problem is deeper than that. It is not just about belief; it is about incentives. Economist Mancur Olson understood this well. He argued that for collective action to succeed, individuals who contribute must be given *selective incentives*—real, tangible benefits—which non-participants do not get. For generations, this is how political machines thrived. At the turn of the twentieth century, people did not vote for New York's Tammany Hall machine out of ideological loyalty. They voted because it gave them something in return. A job. A favor. Something that non-Tammany voters didn't get.[22]

For parties that do not provide these gifts to their supporters, the motivation is different. A major reason that people turn out to vote for programmatic parties like the British Labour Party or the Conservative Party is because of the interpersonal rewards (and sanctions) provided by the broader social networks in which these parties are embedded. These networks—labor unions, churches, social clubs, neighborhoods, and so on—provide affective rewards for voting and punishments for non-voting that are a critical part of how mainstream democracy operated in the second half of the twentieth century. Vote, and you can hold your head high. Stay home, and you are shunned. French sociologist, Didier Eribon, observes that "the act of voting, while fundamentally individual in appearance, can be experienced as part of a collective mobilization, as a political action carried out in common with others." The act of voting is less about civic duty in an abstract sense than about a collective solidarity with one's peers, colleagues, and neighbors. You vote so you can be *seen* to be helping your side.[23]

But without well-organized parties or institutions to provide these kinds of selective rewards for participation, how do populist movements manage to mobilize their supporters? The answer is charisma. Contrary to the view of many scholars that charismatic leadership is incidental to populism, I'll argue in the rest of this chapter that it is necessary to coordinate resentments of the institutional status quo. Failing the emergence of a charismatic leader, potentially populist movements tend to be ephemeral (e.g., Occupy Wall Street) or to institutionalize into regular parties (e.g., Green Parties). Charismatic leadership has been notoriously difficult to operationalize as a social scientific concept. In the rest of this chapter, I propose a new schema of what charismatic leadership does at the level of the follower, which helps explain its centrality to populist politics.

Why is charismatic leadership so important to populism?

Charisma is one of those qualities—like beauty, like genius—that we recognize instantly but struggle to define. John F. Kennedy had it. Richard Nixon did not. Donald Trump has it. Kamala Harris did not. But what is it, really? The concept is ancient, its roots stretching back to St. Paul of Tarsus, the man who, more than any other, shaped the early Christian church. Paul used the Greek word *charisma* to mean a divine gift—what would later be understood as *grace*—bestowed by God upon the faithful. These gifts, these talents, were signs of God's favor, evidence that an individual had been touched by the divine. Yet Paul's message was clear: Such gifts were not reserved for the few, for those who could work miracles or speak in tongues. All believers had them. Paul understood something else about charisma—something that would resonate centuries later in politics. Paul insisted that he himself was as gifted in glossolalia as any man. But he urged early Christians to practice it sparingly, to avoid alarming outsiders.

Charisma, it seemed, was not just a gift. It was something that could be controlled, wielded. It could be turned on and off.[24]

The meaning of charisma shifted profoundly with the work of Max Weber. For Weber, charisma was no longer merely a divine gift but "a certain quality of an individual personality by which he is set apart and treated as endowed with supernatural, superhuman, or . . . exceptional powers or qualities." He tells us that charisma "rejects all external order," "transforms all values," and compels the "surrender of the faithful to the extraordinary and unheard of, to what is alien to all regulation and tradition, and therefore is viewed as divine." Weber was right in recognizing that, throughout history, leaders have often been seen as possessing mystical, even godlike powers. In the ancient world, the association was explicit. Those who led rebellions, those who inspired movements, those who upended the existing order—these figures were not merely men. Spartacus, the gladiator who led Rome's greatest slave revolt, was believed to have had the favor of Dionysus. His near contemporary, Jesus of Nazareth, was assumed by contemporaries to have communed directly with God. His deification would come later. Even in modern times, charismatic leadership is associated with some mystical if not religious quality. After reading *Mein Kampf*, Joseph Goebbels confided in his diary, asking of Hitler: "Who is this man? Half-plebian, half-god! Is this really Christ or just John the Baptist?" Hugo Chávez, in the days before he assumed Venezuela's presidency, sat for an interview with Gabriel García Márquez. The novelist, a man attuned to the myths that shape history, wrote afterward that Chávez "has a great sense of timing and a memory that has a touch of the supernatural." After Chávez's death, his followers took this idea further still, praying to him: "Our Chávez who art in heaven, in the earth, in the sea and in us, the delegates." At the height of his power, Brazil's Jair Bolsonaro was not merely a president. He was *o mito*—the myth, the legend.[25]

It is not entirely clear why Weber chose the word *charisma* to describe this extraordinary, quasi-divine quality. The resemblance to Paul's original notion—grace as a gift bestowed by God—is faint. But one consequence of Weber's choice is the persistent belief that charisma is an inherent trait, a quality that some individuals simply *possess*. In this sense, charisma at its core captures the quality of "presence"—of being fully immersed in the moment and not distracted by other thoughts—which makes its users especially effective interpersonal communicators. Over time, charisma has come to be understood in more casual terms—synonymous with charm, with personal magnetism. By 2023, the *Oxford English Dictionary* had even declared "rizz" its word of the year, a term supposedly derived from the middle syllable of *charisma*, referring to the male ability to pick up women.

Management gurus insist that charisma can be cultivated, broken down into a series of techniques—learnable, repeatable, available to anyone willing to buy a book or subscribe to a podcast. One problem with understanding charisma in this way is that it is unclear precisely which traits or behaviors it captures. In management studies, charisma has been mapped onto an assortment of positive traits: vision, pride, selflessness, optimism, enthusiasm, confidence, respect, power, morality, deeply held values, a sense of mission. But if charisma is nothing more than a bundle of admirable qualities, how is it that men like Adolf Hitler and Benito Mussolini so often top the lists of history's most charismatic leaders?

The same outward behaviors we associate with charisma are also common among those high in what psychologists call the *dark triad*—narcissism, Machiavellianism, and (subclinical) psychopathy. These traits, when named explicitly, are universally condemned. Yet in practice, they often produce behaviors that people find highly compelling. Narcissism, for example, is not just selfishness—it is extreme self-confidence, a quality nearly always associated with charismatic leaders. Narcissists speak more loudly and more often, drawing attention, commanding a room, making others instinctively follow their lead. Psychopathy, with its lack of empathy, and Machiavellianism, with its talent for manipulation, are typically seen as destructive. But in times of crisis, particularly in war, these very qualities can be mistaken for the decisiveness and ruthlessness of effective leadership.

Consider the classic case of the dark power of charisma. As World War II entered its final stretch, the US government sought to penetrate the mind of the man whose obsessions had set Europe ablaze. Around the turn of 1944, it commissioned two highly classified psychological reports—their purpose: to anticipate how Hitler might behave as Germany's defeat loomed. The reports, written from a distance, relied on a patchwork of secondhand accounts, rumors, and speculation. Looking back, they reveal less about Hitler's psychological collapse than they do about the intellectual climate of the time—specifically, the influence of psychoanalysis on both social science and public policy. Sigmund Freud's theories loomed over both assessments. For Freud, the unconscious was a battleground, a place where the rational ego struggled against the dark forces of the id—forces driven by repressed traumas, thwarted ambitions, unfulfilled desires. And in Freud's view, those desires, more often than not, were sexual. Predictably, the first report would diagnose Hitler as deeply neurotic, a man whose sadomasochism and repressed homosexuality had shaped his pathology; the second report went further, declaring him a schizophrenic and a coprophile — a man whose deviance had metastasized into something far beyond neurosis.

The attempt to explain Nazi Germany's continentwide war of aggression and the butchery of the Holocaust with reference to its leader's sexual proclivities might now seem naïve, if not offensive, but psychoanalysis continues to have a profound influence on the study of political leadership. In one of the best-selling books on the Trump presidency, Mary Trump, a clinical psychologist and Donald Trump's niece, argues that the populist and even authoritarian impulses of America's forty-fifth and forty-seventh president are due to the psychological scars of repeated childhood traumas. In 2019, a group of professional psychologists and psychiatrists went as far as issuing a warning to Congress over the "dangerous" state of Trump's mental health and the "threat to the safety" of the nation posed by his "brittle sense of self-worth." Regardless of the validity of these at-a-distance psychological profiles, the point remains: Traits that outside observers identify as pathological—narcissism, grandiosity, an insatiable need for admiration—are often seen by followers in a very different light. What critics interpret as delusion, they perceive as confidence. What analysts call dominance, they recognize as strength. What appears to be recklessness to outsiders can, in the eyes of the devoted, look like courage. This is the paradox of charismatic leadership. The very qualities that alarm opponents are the same ones that inspire the faithful.[26]

Human beings may have evolved beyond many of the traits that once governed our ancestral past. But deference to dominance—to the *alpha*—remains. We do not reserve leadership status only for those with moral virtue or intellectual brilliance. We grant it just as readily to those who impose their will through force, through confidence, through sheer presence. All of which suggests something fundamental: Charisma is not a personality trait. It is not an innate quality, possessed or absent. It is, at its core, an interaction between leader and follower, shaped as much by those who grant it as by those who wield it.[27]

Indeed, when reading Weber more closely, it becomes clear that charisma describes a relationship. An individual is charismatic to the extent that his followers treat him as endowed with desirable traits. Weber contended: "It is recognition on the part of those subject to authority which is decisive for the validity of charisma." Charismatic leadership, by definition, requires the existence of a people to lead, even if any such popular movement is relatively fluid and temporary. Charismatic leadership, and hence populism, is not a performance put on by some individual but a collective process in which both leader and supporters play their role. The leader is nothing without his followers. His power, his influence, his very existence is shaped by their belief, their devotion, their willingness to follow. For this power to fully take root, there must be no mediation between them. No buffer, no intermediary—only the direct, unfiltered connection between leader and follower. Charismatic leadership is distinctive in terms of "the absence of significant mediation of the relationship [between leader and follower], either by formal structures or informal networks."[28]

Arguably, it is the followers, not the leader, who play the primary role. To quote Weber again, "What is alone important is how the individual is actually regarded by those subject to charismatic authority, by his 'followers' or 'disciples.'" According to two later Weberian scholars, charisma is "an attribute of the belief of the followers and not of the quality of the leader." It is the "emergent following which sets the charismatic figure apart from ordinary mortals." Reverence for the leader is one of the key traits of followers. Max Weber argued that people are drawn to charismatic leaders because of their extraordinary needs—needs that the leader, by virtue of his charisma, promises to fulfill. Yet, Weber's insight raises a crucial question: What are these needs, and why do people place such unwavering trust in someone who, in the eyes of many, should not be trusted at all?[29]

One answer to the question of why people follow charismatic leaders lies in a psychological predisposition to submit to authority. This was first articulated by William Reich, one of Freud's followers, who, in *The Mass Psychology of Fascism* (1933), argued that psychoanalysis could explain why the masses were drawn to figures like Hitler. For Reich, the modern repression of children's natural sexual urges created an underlying psychological condition, one that led people to seek out authoritarian figures who could dominate them. Freud himself, ever confident in the applicability of his theories, offered his own take on the phenomenon. On the eve of World War II, he wrote, "Why the great man should rise to significance at all we have no doubt whatsoever. We know that the great majority of people have a strong need for authority which they can admire, to which they can submit, and which dominates and sometimes even ill-treats them." Freud's assertion draws on the deep, primal need for authority embedded in the human psyche—a need shaped by childhood experiences. He argued that this need stems from the unconscious longing for the father figure, a psychological relic from early development that persists into adulthood.[30]

The problem with Freud's explanation lies not only in his preoccupation with incestuous desires but in its failure to account for the timing of such behavior. Why, one might ask, does this inherent craving to submit to authority suddenly emerge in certain places, at certain times, but not others? The answer, as offered by Freud's follower, the German American psychologist Erich Fromm, lies not in the shadows of the unconscious but in the harsh realities of economic collapse. Fromm, observing the sharp economic decline of the interwar period, saw its effects firsthand. As the middle class—those with the most to lose—grappled with the destabilizing forces of depression and uncertainty, they were consumed by anxiety. Their old certainties had crumbled, and with it, their trust in traditional institutions. In this moment of crisis, they looked for something, or someone, to restore the stability that had been so violently stripped away. Fromm's analysis, most famously articulated in *Escape from Freedom* (1941), proposed that it was this profound insecurity, this fear of living in a world without clear order, that fueled their yearning to surrender to an authoritarian figure.

Fromm's approach, grounded in his own experiences, was more theoretical than empirical. It was only after the war that a more systematic and empirical study of authoritarianism took root. In *The Authoritarian Personality* (1950), Theodor Adorno and his colleagues laid the foundation for a more rigorous psychoanalytical investigation. Using a series of personality questionnaires, they studied thousands of respondents in the United States, identifying what they called the "F-scale"—or fascism scale—an indicator of susceptibility to authoritarian tendencies. The results were striking. Those who scored high on the F-scale, they found, were predisposed to follow a strong leader. These individuals were not just seeking authority; they were inherently anxious people who craved order, structure, and security, especially when they felt threatened by forces they couldn't control. It was in times of crisis that their longing for stability became most pronounced—and that a charismatic leader, promising control, could most effectively fill the void.[31]

The idea of a collective threat is central to the dynamics of charismatic leadership, yet whether it can be neatly captured by the concept of an authoritarian personality is far from clear. Measuring "authoritarianism" at the level of individual personality has long posed significant challenges. The initial scales developed by Adorno and his colleagues, though influential, proved deeply flawed—both in statistical rigor and in their inherent biases. Recognizing these issues, later scales such as right-wing authoritarianism (RWA) and social dominance orientation (SDO) (each stripped of attitudes toward sex) aimed to pick out the more salient aspects of the supposed authoritarian personality type. However, these too carried their own set of complications. These newer scales sometimes had embedded assumptions about attitudes toward other groups—attitudes like nativism or racism—which authoritarianism itself is often employed to explain. The problem is that one cannot use authoritarianism to explain prejudice against out-groups if the very construct includes such biases. It's true by definition.

In response, more recent approaches have sought to strip authoritarianism of overt political views, aiming instead for a more neutral measure that captures underlying psychological tendencies. These newer frameworks often define authoritarianism as a negative disposition toward difference or an intrinsic fear of change. By moving away from political labels, they empirically use attitudes toward childrearing as a more accessible and less ideologically charged way to measure authoritarian tendencies. This scale involves asking respondents which of two traits is more important in children: (1) independence or respect for their elders; (2) curiosity or good manners; (3) self-reliance or obedience; (4) being considerate or being well-behaved. Those who favor obedience, conformity, and respect for authority are regarded as having a "fixed" approach to childrearing—an indicator of a more authoritarian disposition. This method offers a picture of authoritarianism that is unclouded by political assumptions while still shedding light on the personality traits that may predispose individuals to follow charismatic leaders. Yet the evidence linking the authoritarian personality to support for populist leaders is ambiguous.[32]

What people are after is not the masochistic submission or desire for domination that Freud and his disciples once theorized. What they are searching for is a leader, a figure who stands above the crowd—not for his own glory, but for theirs. People want a strongman: not one who will dominate them, but who will dominate others on their behalf. Here, recent research in evolutionary psychology offers a telling insight into the probable function of charisma. As mentioned, dominance behavior remains a classic route to leadership. While expertise undeniably matters, studies show that we are more likely to perceive someone as competent if they possess physical traits like height, strength, and maleness—traits that would have been useful in identifying warrior leaders among our early ancestors.[33]

Take the 2016 presidential debates. When Trump paced menacingly around Hillary Clinton, some saw misogyny and aggression; his supporters, however, saw confidence and strength. Fast forward to July 2024, after the assassination attempt on Trump. A bullet grazed his right ear and sent him to the ground, but he immediately rose, pumped his fist, and shouted, "Fight! Fight! Fight!" Mark Zuckerberg, a recent Trump convert, summed up the moment: "That was one of the most badass things I've ever seen in my life!" In that moment, Trump's ability to project strength, even in the face of physical threat, resonated with his followers—a manifestation of a deeper, more primal form of leadership.[34]

Another aspect of leadership, one more cultivable than height or jawline, is speaking skill. Hitler was an absolute master at manipulating and controlling the masses through speech. Not that this ability was purely innate. In an incredible series of photos from 1925, Hitler can be seen with his photographer, Heinrich Hoffman, rehearsing the poses he would use during a speech (see Figure 3.1). Much as Hitler sought to appear spontaneous, he would recite, record, replay, and repeat his speeches so that they achieved the best effect. Hitler was not the first to see the potential in cultivating one's charismatic appeal. The feted Athenian orator, Demosthenes, would practice speaking with rocks in his mouth as the waves crashed against the shore in the background, in an effort to perfect his voice and delivery.

Not all effective speech-making, however, is rooted in grand oratory. Trump's style—often criticized for being disjointed and rambling—provides a contemporary example of how charisma can manifest in unexpected forms. His speeches are typically a jumble of thoughts, a style he calls "the weave." As he explained to podcaster Joe Rogan, "I'll talk about like nine different things and they all come back brilliantly together." To critics, this might appear incoherent, especially when examined as a written transcript or broken into discrete parts. But to focus on the disjointedness is to miss the emotional, even unconscious, connection that Trump's speeches create with his audience. His conversational approach—marked by incomplete sentences and abrupt transitions—invites his followers into the dialogue. In this way, his audience feels as if they are engaging with him directly, filling in the blanks and

Figure 3.1 Hitler Hones His Charisma (from Getty Images: 3289891)

participating in a personal exchange. This style taps into a deeper, more primal need for connection, a key aspect of charismatic leadership.[35]

An alternative route to leadership, distinct from the dominance path, is through success or prestige status. Successful individuals are often attributed a kind of genius, a quality that at one time might have been directly associated with divine favor. In ancient Greece, heroes were believed to be under the protection of the gods, their triumphs seen as signs of celestial blessing. Yet even in modern times, success has a way of breeding followership. Entrepreneurs like Steve Jobs, Bill Gates, and Elon Musk—despite their well-documented social awkwardness—are frequently considered charismatic figures, their achievements alone lending them an aura of power and influence.[36]

More commonly, however, what endows individuals with charisma is success in serving the welfare or defense of the social group. Military leaders, in particular, have long enjoyed a fast track to charismatic status. Figures like George Washington, Napoleon Bonaparte, Toussaint Louverture, and Andrew Jackson all rose to prominence for their brilliance on the battlefield. Sometimes, a military leader's success is driven by tactical innovations, as Napoleon demonstrated when he seized Toulon by recognizing the strategic importance of controlling the bluffs surrounding the city. Other times, the outcomes are more a result of luck—yet even then, luck can endow a leader with the same aura of charisma. As Napoleon himself allegedly remarked, "I'd rather have lucky generals than good ones." In the end, what matters is winning. People follow winners, and as Trump famously promised, "We're gonna win so much, you may even get tired of winning." Whether through tactical brilliance or sheer fortune, successful leaders inspire loyalty. Charisma, in this sense, is not always the product of personal charm but rather the result of an ability to achieve and to lead others to victory.[37]

The politically disaffected need not all be persuaded by these leadership displays at the same rate. Critically there is a social dynamic that enhances this tendency to support those who already lead. Once a critical mass of individuals begins to support a particular leader, the likelihood of that leader's success in future elections increases significantly. The larger the movement, the greater the social and network benefits of belonging to it—and conversely, the greater the cost of remaining on the sidelines. There is a powerful bandwagon effect at play, one rooted in our inherent drive to be part of some successful group endeavor. Part of this dynamic can be traced to an innate desire to participate in collective rituals. Whether these rituals involve synchronized movement—such as marching—or coordinated vocal expressions, like chanting, they are pleasurable and deeply reinforcing. Through these collective acts, group identities are forged and solidified, something religious cults have long understood and exploited. These rituals don't necessarily require a leader at their center, but it is clear that charismatic leaders can manipulate these instincts to their advantage—watch the millions respond to Hitler's call and response at national rallies. The leader becomes not just a symbol of power but the very focal point of an emotional and social force that sweeps through the masses.

Humans are, at their core, mimics. We tend to follow the crowd, especially when others show unwavering belief in a leader. As Allen Grabo and his colleagues explain, "Charisma has evolved as a credible signal of a person's ability to solve a coordination challenge requiring urgent collective action from group members." In other words, if I observe many others placing their trust in a leader, I interpret that as a signal that they possess some crucial knowledge or insight that I lack. This collective judgment becomes a key factor in my own decision to follow. This social dynamic helps explain how charismatic leaders can overcome the typical obstacles to collective action. They often begin with a small, committed base of followers—a "cult," if you will. But as their influence grows, these initial adherents serve as the catalyst for a broader social cascade, wherever more people are drawn in, either because of their own convictions or the compelling influence of the growing movement. Charisma, then, is not just an individual trait; it's a social process, a signal that spreads through a community, ultimately shifting the collective understanding of who is worth following.[38]

At the same time, it's important to note that leadership status, and charisma, can be fleeting. Consider the fate of Max Weber's own beau ideal of the charismatic leader, General Erich von Ludendorff. During World War I, Ludendorff had brought Germany a thumping victory against Russia on its eastern front and nearly did the same in the west. After Germany's eventual defeat and the abdication of the monarchy, Weber wanted to see Ludendorff as the charismatic master of all Germany. For a time, Ludendorff seems to have shared this vision. He participated in the botched Nazi 1923 putsch, in which he (not Hitler) was to become the figurehead of the revolutionary government. But Hitler soured on Ludendorff as a figurehead. As Hitler recognized, failure was detrimental to one's ambitions for charismatic leadership. When Ludendorff obtained a negligible share of the presidential vote in 1925, Hitler privately gloated to a confidant that the general was now finished in politics. Charismatic leadership, after all, is rooted in the belief that the leader can perform miracles, that they can guide their followers through crises. But when that belief is shattered—when the leader fails to deliver, when they no longer seem capable of miraculous feats—their power wanes. Charisma, more than other sources of authority, is fragile. It is not merely the traits of the individual that sustain it but the ongoing conviction of the followers who believe in that leader's unique ability to lead them.

Why is populism associated with identity politics?

Populism is founded on resentment of the institutional status quo. At its core, populism speaks to the divide between the winners and losers created by the existing system. Invariably, this results in resentment from those left behind—those who see themselves as having been marginalized, sidelined, or disregarded. Müller observes that "populism is always a form of identity politics." Which groups become the subject of collective action is a matter of context. The usual suspects are those related to ethnicity—a set of identities based on a shared belief in common descent. It is important, however, to resist simplifying populism as solely a nativist, nationalist, or ethnocentric phenomenon. While ethnicity and race can become focal points for populist movements, the power of populism lies in its ability to form new group identities. These identities are often forged by charismatic leaders who are able to shape and channel collective discontent. As Grabo and his coauthors write: "A charismatic leader is one who is able to attract the attention of other *group members* and serve as a focal point for aligning and synchronizing prosocial orientations in followers, suppressing sensitivity to cooperative risks, and enhancing the salience of perceived cooperative rewards." Charismatic leaders synchronize group sentiments, enhancing cooperation while suppressing fears of mutual distrust or risk. In this way, charismatic leadership becomes a powerful force, turning disparate individuals or factions—united only by a sense of alienation or shared grievance—into a unified group with a common cause.[39]

This is not to say that charismatic leaders can make groups out of whole cloth, that someone like Trump could create a sense of white working-class grievance out of thin air. Everyone is simultaneously a member of multiple groups: employees in a firm, speakers of a dialect, devotees of a religion, and so on. Not all of these groups have political relevance. To the degree that charismatic leadership has a basis in our evolutionary past, it would make most sense if the salient groups are the ones that affect our core needs: safety, welfare, and, importantly, status.

The need for status makes us sensitive not only to our personal standing within our social group but also to the standing of our group relative to others. This is not to assert that evolution has fashioned selection on a purely group level—a notion long discredited—but rather to acknowledge that an individual's prospects for amassing material wealth and social honor are intricately tied to the collective resources of his community. In short, what is critical to the group is some sense of shared fate, with a basis in material reality, even if it is not automatic. Groups become especially salient when their status is under threat. As we'll see, a perceived loss in group status appears to be a strong correlate of populist support. What charismatic leaders accomplish, then, is to rally these emergent factions—resentful of the prevailing order yet grappling with the perennial challenge of unified action—into a force capable of winning and keeping power.[40]

In conclusion, I maintain that the force of charismatic leadership emerges only when followers experience three essential sentiments. First, they must feel a deep belonging to a collective—a shared identity anchored in common circumstance. Second, they are stirred by a palpable crisis that threatens the status or safety of their group. Third, they embrace a belief in a savior, a figure capable of restoring the group's rightful place. Consequently, populist supporters tend to rally around a leader who promises deliverance from a status under siege. Charisma thus serves to unite a disorganized multitude against an institutional status quo deemed unjust.

Yet, it is insufficient merely to acknowledge the need for such leadership; ideally, we should be able to foresee its emergence in time and place. Populist success depends on both demand and supply. Chapters 4 and 5 will examine how these factors play out. Understanding populism as mass anti-institutionalism makes sense of several of populism's key features. On the demand side, populism is spurred by a profound resistance to an entrenched status quo, one that is widely perceived as both unfair and unyielding. On the supply side, populism provides a way of cost-effectively mobilizing an otherwise diffuse and disorganized body of supporters. In its very opposition to the established political party, populism finds its lifeblood in charismatic leadership, a force that mobilizes and unites. This intricate interplay explains not only populism's deep ties to group-based identity politics but also its relentless antagonism toward the institutional status quo.

Notes

1. "against a government," quoted in Vivien Hart, *Distrust and Democracy: Political Distrust in Britain and America* (Cambridge University Press, 1978), 86; "Republican legislatures," quoted in Peter H. Argensinger, *Populism and Politics: William Alfred Peffer and the People's Party* (University of Kentucky Press, 2014), 7; "special privileges," quoted in James M. Beeby, *Revolt of the Tar Heels: The North Carolina Populist Movement, 1890–1901* (University Press of Mississippi, 2008), 89.
2. "soulless despot," William M. Stewart, quoted in Benjamin F. Alexander, *Coxey's Army: Popular Protest in the Gilded Age* (Johns Hopkins University Press, 2015), 52; "no uniform," Charles Postel, *The Populist Vision* (Oxford University Press, 2009), 14.
3. "populism proclaims," Edward Shils, *The Torment of Secrecy: The Background and Consequences of American Security Policies* (W. Heinemann, 1956), 133, 31; "noninstitutionalized notion," Müller, *What Is Populism?*, 31–32; "is not principally interested," Isaiah Berlin, "To Define Populism," *Government & Opposition* 3, no. 2 (1968): 174; "mass discontent," Julio Carrión, *A Dynamic Theory of Populists in Power: The Andes in Comparative Perspective* (Oxford University Press), 53; "Both on the left," Devin Dwyer, ABC News, October 18, 2011, https://abcnews.go.com/blogs/politics/2011/10/obama-occupy-wall-street-not-that-different-from-tea-party-protests.
4. "changing the rules," Carrión, *A Dynamic Theory of Populists in Power*, 19; Eric A. Posner, *The Demagogue's Playbook: The Battle for American Democracy from the Founders to Trump* (All Points Books, 2020), 8; "Formal institutions," Wojciech Sadurski, *A Pandemic of Populists* (Cambridge University Press, 2022), 5; "as being grounded," "institutional failure," "a form," Samuel Issacharoff, *Democracy Unmoored: Populism and the Corruption of Popular Sovereignty* (Oxford University Press, 2023), 8, 10, 85.
5. Douglass C. North, *Institutions, Institutional Change and Economic Performance* (Cambridge University Press, 1990), 3.

6. On this understanding of institutions, see Steven Levitsky and María Victoria Murillo, "Variation in Institutional Strength," *Annual Review of Political Science* 12, no. 1 (2009): 115–133.
7. Lawrence Rosenthal, *Empire of Resentment: Populism's Toxic Embrace of Nationalism* (New Press, 2020), 8; Katherine J. Cramer, *The Politics of Resentment: Rural Consciousness in Wisconsin and the Rise of Scott Walker* (University of Chicago Press, 2016). "You feel," quoted in Arlie Russell Hochschild, *Stolen Pride: Loss, Shame, and the Rise of the Right* (New Press, 2024), 91; "Social Rules," Barrington Moore, *Injustice: The Social Bases of Obedience and Revolt* (M. E. Sharpe, 1978), 5.
8. K. McAuliffe, P. R. Blake, N. Steinbeis, and F. Warneken (2017). "The Developmental Foundations of Human Fairness," *Nature Human Behavior* 1:0042, https://doi.org/10.1038/s41562-016-0042; G. Tabibnia and M. D. Lieberman, "Fairness and Cooperation Are Rewarding: Evidence from Social Cognitive Neuroscience," *Annals of the New York Academy of Sciences* 1118 (2007): 90–101; J. A. List, "On the Interpretation of Giving in Dictator Games," *Journal of Political Economy* 115, no. 3 (2007): 482–493.
9. Sarah F. Brosnan and Frans B. M. de Waal, "Evolution of Responses to (un) Fairness," *Science* 346, no. 6207 (2014): 1251776; Marc Bekoff and Jessica Pierce, *Wild Justice: The Moral Lives of Animals* (University of Chicago Press, 2009).
10. "You go into these," David Gura, "Guns and God: A Bitter Brew," NPR, April 14, 2008, https://www.npr.org/sections/talk/2008/04/guns_and_god_a_bitter_brew.html.
11. Robert Frank, *Passions Within Reason: The Strategic Role of Emotions.* (W. W. Norton 1988); Cameron Anderson, John Angus D. Hildreth, and Laura Howland, "Is the Desire for Status a Fundamental Human Motive? A Review of the Empirical Literature," *Psychological Bulletin* 141, no. 3 (2015): 574. For a popular introduction to the research on status, see Will Storr, *The Status Game: On Human Life and How to Play It* (William Collins, 2021).
12. Gavin Hewitt, "Greece: The Dangerous Game," BBC, February 1, 2015, https://www.bbc.com/news/world-europe-31082656; "You may have," quoted in Michael Crick, *One Party After Another: The Disruptive Live of Nigel Farage* (Simon & Schuster, 2023), 176.

13. "Let it all blow up," Vera Bergengruen, "Javier Milei's Radical Plan to Transform Argentina," *Time*, May 23, 2024, https://time.com/6980600/javier-milei-argentina-interview/; "revolutionary process," quoted in Allan Brewer-Carias, *Dismantling Democracy in Venezuela: The Chávez Authoritarian Experiment* (Cambridge University Press, 2010), 49; "Sanders Calls for 21st Century Bill of Rights," https://berniesanders.com/sanders-calls-21st-century-bill-rights/; John Foot, "Beppe Grillo: A Comedian to Be Taken Seriously," *The Guardian*, October 31, 2012, https://www.theguardian.com/commentisfree/2012/oct/30/beppe-grillo-comedian-italy-five-star; "distrusted big institutions," "coalition of the aggrieved," Larry Tye, *Demagogue: The Life and Long Shadow of Senator Joe McCarthy* (HarperCollins, 2020), 370, 371.
14. "We can't continue," Danielle Kurtzleban, "Trump Can't Bring Back All Those Jobs from China. Here's What He Can Do," *NPR*, April 7, 2017, https://www.npr.org/2017/04/07/522879370/trump-can-t-bring-all-those-jobs-back-from-china-here-s-what-he-can-do.
15. "cutting in front," Arlie Russell Hochschild, *Strangers in Their Own Land: Anger and Mourning on the American Right* (The New Press, 2018).
16. Chris Cillizza, "Conspiracy Theorist in Chief?" *Washington Post*, March 5, 2017, https://www.washingtonpost.com/politics/conspiracy-theorist-in-chief/2017/03/05/b278e6a6-01da-11e7-a391-651727e77fc0_story.html; Dan Cassino, "Fairleigh Dickinson University's PublicMind Poll Finds Trump Supporters More Conspiracy-Minded Than Other Republicans," The FDU Poll (press release), Fairleigh Dickinson University, May 4, 2016, https://portal.fdu.edu/fdupoll-archive/160504/.
17. M. Hakan Yavuz, *Erdoğan: The Making of an Autocrat* (Edinburgh University Press, 2021), 153; E. Balta, C. R. Kaltwasser, and A. H. Yagci, "Populist Attitudes and Conspiratorial Thinking," *Party Politics* 28, no. 4 (2022): 625–637.
18. "the standards," "Distrust of," "fundamental distrust," Shils, *The Torment of Secrecy*, 133, 131; "the populist leader," Bernard Crick, "Populism, Politics and Democracy," *Democratisation* 12, no. 5 (2005), 626; "professional politicians," Margaret Canovan, "Trust the People! Populism and the Two Faces of Democracy," *Political Studies* 47, no. 1 (1999), 6; "populists argue," Cas Mudde,

"The Populist Zeitgeist," *Government and Opposition* 39, no. 4 (2004), 546

19. "Because the populist," Tom Ginsburg and Aziz Z. Huq, *How to Save a Constitutional Democracy*. (University of Chicago Press, 2020), 81; "Blurring any," Nadia Urbinati, "Democracy and Populism," *Constellations* 5, no. 1 (1998): 119.
20. "strikingly," Oliver Nachtwey, *Germany's Hidden Crisis: Social Decline in the Heart of Europe* (Verso, 2018), 189.
21. On the collective action problem inherent in early populist movements, see Philip Oxhorn, "The Social Foundations of Latin America's Recurrent Populism: Problems of Popular Sector Class Formation and Collective Action," *Journal of Historical Sociology* 11, no. 2 (1998): 212–246; S. Erdem Aytaç and Susan C. Stokes, *Why Bother? Rethinking Participation in Elections and Protests* (Cambridge University Press, 2019).
22. Mancur Olson, *The Logic of Collective Action: Public Goods and the Theory of Groups* (Harvard University Press, 1965).
23. "the act of voting," Didier Eribon, *Returning to Reims* (Penguin, 2019), 129.
24. John Potts, *A History of Charisma* (Palgrave Macmillan 2009)
25. "a certain," "rejects all external order," "transforms all values," "surrender," Max Weber, *Economy and Society: An Outline of Interpretive Sociology*, trans. Guenther Roth and Claus Wittich (University of California Press, 1978), 241, 1115–1117; "brilliant," "who is this man," "people's tribune," in Peter Longerich, *Goebbels* (Vintage Arrow, 2016), 56, 63; "has a great sense," quoted in Roy Carroll, *Comandante: The Life and Legacy of Hugo Chávez* (Canongate Books, 2013), 4; "o myto," in Vincent Bevins, *If We Burn: The Mass Protest Decade and the Missing Revolution* (Wildfire, 2023), 229.
26. Mary L. Trump, *Too Much and Never Enough: How My Family Created the World's Most Dangerous Man* (Simon & Schuster, 2020); Tom Porter, "350 Health Professionals Sign Letter to Congress Claiming Trump's Mental Health Is Deteriorating Dangerously Amid Impeachment Proceedings," *Business Insider*, December 6, 2019, https://www.businessinsider.com/psychiatrists-submit-warning-trumps-mental-health-deteriorating-2019-12.
27. Dan P. McAdams, "The Appeal of the Primal Leader: Human Evolution and Donald J. Trump," *Evolutionary Studies in*

Imaginative Culture 1, no. 2 (2017): 1–13, https://doi.org/10.26613/esic.1.2.45.

28. "It is recognition," Weber, *Economy and Society*, 242; "the absence of significant," Douglas Madsen and Peter G. Snow, *The Charismatic Bond: Political Behavior in Time of Crisis* (Harvard University Press, 1991), 5.
29. "what alone," Weber, *Economy and Society*, 1112–1113; "an attribute of the belief," Joseph Bensman and Michael Givant, "Charisma and Modernity: The Use and Abuse of a Concept," *Social Research* 42, no. 4 (1975): 578; "emergent following," Madsen and Snow, *The Charismatic Bond*, 2; see also Jay A. Conger, Rabindra N. Kanungo, and Sanjay T. Menon, "Charismatic Leadership and Follower Effects," *Journal of Organizational Behavior* 21, no. 7 (2000): 747–767, http://www.jstor.org/stable/3100311
30. "Why the great man," Sigmund Freud, *Moses and Monotheism*, trans. Katherine Jones (Hogarth Press, 1939), 173.
31. For a recent psychoanalytic take, see Mattias Desmet, *The Psychology of Totalitarianism* (Chelsea Green, 2022).
32. Marc J. Hetherington and Jonathan Weiler, *Prius or Pickup? How the Answers to Four Simple Questions Explain America's Great Divide* (Houghton Mifflin Harcourt, 2018).
33. Mark Van Vugt and Anjana Ahuja, *Naturally Selected: The Evolutionary Science of Leadership* (HarperBusiness, 2011).
34. Melvyn R. W. Hamstra, "'Big' Men: Male Leaders' Height Positively Relates to Followers' Perception of Charisma," *Personality and Individual Differences* 56 (2014): 190–192; D. E. Re, D. W. Hunter, V. Coetzee, B. P. Tiddeman, D. Xiao, L. M. DeBruine, B. C. Jones, and D. I. Perrett, "Looking Like a Leader—Facial Shape Predicts Perceived Height and Leadership Ability," *PLOS One* 8, no. 12 (2013): e80957.
35. "I'll talk about," "Joe Rogan Experience #2219—Donald Trump," October 25, 2024, https://www.youtube.com/watch?v=hBMoPUAeLnY.
36. For more on the idea that we take our cues for whom to follow from others, see Robert B. Cialdini, *Influence, New and Expanded: The Psychology of Persuasion* (HarperCollins, 2011).
37. On the military roots of charisma, see David A. Bell, *Men on Horseback: The Power of Charisma in the Age of Revolution*. (Picador, 2021); "We're gonna win," "Transcript of Donald Trump's Dec.

30 speech in Hilton Head, S.C.," *The Kansas City Star*, January 20, 2016, https://www.kansascity.com/news/local/news-columns-blogs/the-buzz/article55604115.html.

38. "charisma has evolved," Allen Grabo, Brian R. Spisak, and Mark van Vugt. "Charisma as Signal: An Evolutionary Perspective on Charismatic Leadership," *Leadership Quarterly* 28, no. 4 (2017): 473–485.
39. "populism is always," Jan-Werner Müller, *What Is Populism?* (University of Pennsylvania Press, 2016), 3; "A charismatic leader," Allen Grabo and Mark van Vugt, "Charismatic Leadership and the Evolution of Cooperation," *Evolution and Human Behavior* 37, no. 5 (2016): 399–406.
40. M. Marchlewska, A. Cichocka, O. Panayiotou, K. Castellanos, and J. Batayneh. "Populism as Identity Politics: Perceived In-Group Disadvantage, Collective Narcissism, and Support for Populism," *Social Psychological and Personality Science* 9, no. 2 (2018): 151–162, https://doi.org/10.1177/1948550617732393.

4

THE DEMAND SIDE

Why do people want populism?

From the moment Donald Trump first entered the political spotlight in the late 1980s, he was seen as a potential presidential candidate. Trump was already a household name, not just for his towering skyscrapers but also for his brash commentary on race, crime, and the nation's economic decline. But Trump was different from the usual parade of political figures. For Trump, America was not just a nation to be governed. It was a business to be managed, and the world was a marketplace where others, from enemies to allies, were taking advantage of the country's generosity and power. This was the lens through which he saw the world — through the narrow, calculating perspective of a real estate magnate, where everything was a transaction, and every gain by another was a loss to him.

And so, when in January 2012 a group of his supporters in Texas registered the "Make America Great Again Party" in anticipation of a third-party run, they tapped into a sentiment that Trump had long cultivated—a sentiment that, four years later, would fuel his journey to the White House. Trump would later claim credit for coining the phrase himself. In truth, it had been around long before, but by late 2012, he had registered it as his own trademark, an encapsulation of his political brand. To Trump, it was less about ideology and more about tapping into the anxieties of a nation that felt it was losing its place in the world. More than any political theorist, Trump had an instinct for what Americans wanted to hear.

By the time 2016 came around, Americans were afraid and anxious about pretty much everything from job losses and illegal immigration to rising crime and the threat of terrorism. What people wanted was not blind optimism—"hope" being indelibly associated with Obama thanks to Shepard Fairey's iconic 2008 poster—but nostalgia. People wanted to feel safe, and who better to protect them from a scary world than a boss like Trump. Make America Great Again baseball caps became the uniform of Trump's army of aggrieved and fearful supporters. The establishment sneered; the *Washington Examiner*'s columnist, Philip Wegmann, wrote, a month out from the election, "The millions of hats will make excellent keepsakes for those who thought his populist bravado could overcome Clinton's unimaginative and conventional but well-oiled political machine." It wasn't long before Wegmann and other pundits were eating crow.[1]

Even though most political analysts—myself included—had failed to predict Donald Trump's 2016 presidential election win, after the fact, commentators quickly seemed to converge on an explanation: Trump's unexpected triumph occurred because he won over "white working-class" voters, breaching the so-called Blue Wall of solid Democratic support that extended through the Rust Belt region from the Midwest to the Mid-Atlantic. Voters in the parts of America "left behind" by financialization and globalization were economically insecure and frustrated with Washington's liberal elite. They readily fell back on their old prejudices toward immigrants and minorities, who they felt were benefiting at their expense. Despite the Republican Party's historic record of fiscal and regulatory policies that disproportionately benefit the rich, poorer Americans (at least if they were white) were the ones tempted by Trump's wishful promises to move out of the Democratic fold. Almost a third of the counties that had voted for Obama in 2008 and 2012 switched to Trump in 2016. In the years that followed, more detailed research confirmed that this remarkable volte-face was driven by the white working class. While around 13 percent of white voters switched their support from Obama in 2012 to Trump in 2016, the figure was more than double that (27 percent) for those in the working class.[2]

Despite this apparent consensus on the source of Trump's victory, interpreting the change in the political loyalties of the white working class has proven extremely contentious. Was the white working-class vote for Trump driven by resentment of an economic system that excluded them? Or was it instead triggered by cultural and racial resentments against a system that supposedly served the interests of minorities? Pitting these economic and cultural interpretations against one another has become a common trope not just in studies of Trump's rise to power but of populism in general. These explanations, and others like them, are concerned with the *motivations* of populist voters. Or put somewhat differently, they locate the causes of populism on the "demand side."

As we'll see, something of a coherent picture is emerging from these demand side approaches: Economics and culture matter, but these factors do not work in isolation. First, at least in highly developed economies like the United States, *places* (like counties) that have experienced economic decline or disruption are more likely than those with prosperous, well-integrated economies to give populists their support. This suggests that there is a real material basis for the feeling that government institutions are failing to do their job. Ultimately, however, individuals vote, not places. Second, and rather confoundingly, individual data gleaned from representative sample surveys show that cultural preferences—concerning diversity, sex, and immigration—appear to be better predictors of populist support than things like income or evaluations of one's own economic prospects. In this sense, populism seems to be a form of identity politics. How do we explain these seemingly conflictual results?

At the heart of populist support lies a powerful, unyielding resentment of an institutional status quo that people believe has failed them. This is not merely about dissatisfaction with policy or ideology. It is a deeply felt belief that the system itself is unjust, that it is rigged, that it benefits the few at the expense of the many. And this resentment is tightly bound to a profound distrust of institutions. Such institutional skepticism is related, if imperfectly, to real failures whether in the economic or sociocultural realms: financial crises, inequality, and surges in immigration. Critically, however, if poor economic prospects are blamed on institutions, rather than personal circumstances, grievances are likely to be expressed geographically and collectively, rather than individually. When institutions fail, they fail *groups*. People are, moreover, especially sensitive to changes in their group's relative status. And it is here, in this deeply ingrained sense of collective injustice, that populists find fertile ground. As the previous chapter highlighted, populist leaders—masters of rhetoric and opportunists of resentment—are uniquely positioned to channel these group-based grievances, transforming them into a rallying cry for a movement that promises to upend the very system that caused the pain.

Is it the economy, stupid?

In 1992, US President George H. W. Bush was up for re-election. Contrary to the idea that American voters automatically rally around the flag in times of international conflict, Bush Sr. was unable to hold on to the presidency even though he had presided over both America's victory in the more than four-decade Cold War against the Soviet Union and its rapid, and relatively low-cost, military defeat of Saddam Hussein's Iraq in the First Gulf War (1990–1991). Bush's main opponent (and eventual defeater) was Bill Clinton, then governor of Arkansas and star of the moderate wing of the Democratic Party. Also in the mix, however, was a third-party candidate, Ross Perot, best known as a highly successful and wealthy tech entrepreneur. With no political experience and no party machinery to speak of, Perot was a classic populist who railed against the two-party establishment.

Even if "Poppy" Bush hadn't done a great deal wrong in policy terms, he had little rapport with the average American—an awkwardness memorably depicted in the 1996 episode of *The Simpsons* in which Bush and Homer Simpson came to blows. In the dawning age of twenty-four-hour cable news coverage, Bush's lack of charisma mattered. He was also unfortunate in that his re-election campaign got under way in late 1991, with the nation still suffering from a cyclical recession that began the previous year. The downturn was comparatively mild, but it forced Bush to break his core campaign pledge of "no new taxes." Clinton's serpentine campaign strategist, James Carville, went after Bush's Achilles's heel, coining the term that defined the election: "It's the economy, stupid." However, with Bush struggling and Clinton promising a similar centrist economic policy mix, the outsider Perot began to surge in the polls. Just five months out from the election, Perot was the clear front runner, with 37 percent support compared to 24 for each Bush and Clinton. In the end, tactical blunders and greater public scrutiny killed off the Perot campaign, but he still obtained nearly 19 percent of the popular vote—the highest third-party vote share since former president Theodore Roosevelt's runner-up showing eight decades earlier. Economic insecurity was not enough for a populist like Perot to capture the presidency on this occasion, but it gave the Democratic–Republican duopoly an extraordinary shock.[3]

Perot's historic performance fits well with one of the most common explanations for populist success: Anti-establishment appeals will be most relevant to voters in times of economic hardship. Even if voters are ill-informed about political parties' prospective economic policies, they tend to have a fair sense of past economic performance. Voters may not have known a great deal about the economic policies of Bush, Clinton, or

Perot, but they certainly weren't happy with the end to the economic good times of the 1980s. Real disposable income grew only 1 percent during Bush's first term, compared to 8.5 and 6.6 percent during Reagan's two terms, and even 7.3 percent during the crisis-racked presidency of Jimmy Carter. Although scholarship is divided on this question, as I'll describe below, the best evidence tends to support the idea that populists do well in times of economic crisis or decline.[4]

What is it about a stagnant or crisis-ridden economy that drives people toward populism per se? One argument is that support for populism during times of economic stress is driven by resentment of the well-off and the elitist policymakers of *all* mainstream parties who cater to them. For decades now, since the late 1970s, political parties in the industrialized West have converged around a single, unmistakable pro-market orthodoxy. To the average voter, this convergence has the look of a cartel—a carefully constructed illusion of alternatives, where every option ultimately serves the same narrow elite interests. At one time, working-class voters knew where their allegiances lay. But that certainty is now gone. The Democratic Party of Franklin D. Roosevelt, once the champion of the working class, has become the party of highly educated, high-earning professionals, particularly those in the creative industries. These professionals, often progressive in their views on social justice, may not perceive themselves as part of the country's super elite. Yet they are undeniably well off in relative terms, navigating a world where their economic power gives them access to privileges the majority will never know. By partnering with others in their own social and economic strata, they ensure their children's access to the private tutoring, internships, and cultural capital that can open doors to elite universities. This cycle of elite reproduction, in turn, perpetuates a system of economic inequality that has become ever more entrenched. Given this, it may be little wonder that those at the bottom resent the well-off of all political persuasions who seem to be able to ride out economic hard times better than they can.

Problematically, however, anti-elite sentiment doesn't necessarily drive voters to populism per se. It is common to the supporters of socialist or left-leaning parties in general. Moreover, despite their dissatisfaction with the economy, many populist voters self-identify as being on the right (favoring a limited welfare state), while many populist leaders have been open advocates of neoliberal economic policy. The question remains, why do tough economic conditions lead to populism per se?

Another possibility is that extremely hard economic times, especially over a sustained period, lead voters to abandon the mainstream altogether. When both the center-left and center-right have tried and failed to fix things, the vague, if not heterodox, policies of populist candidates like Perot and Trump are given a hearing that they wouldn't get under normal circumstances. This is very likely part of the story. Distrust in mainstream political parties is associated with populist support. Yet to leave it there neglects the degree to which populist voters believe the economic system itself is rigged against them. That is, populist voters aren't merely looking for alternative economic policies, but are expressing their rejection of the institutional status quo.[5]

Some of the clearest evidence comes from the surprising election win of Donald Trump in 2016. The economic resentments that led to that point were a long time in gestation. When the inflated market for mortgage-backed financial derivatives imploded in 2007, the venerable—but risk-taking—Wall Street investment bank, Lehman Brothers, went bankrupt, setting off a global cascade of bank failures and the deepest worldwide recession since the 1930s. By the time Obama took office in January 2008, the economy was in freefall, with unemployment doubling to hit nearly 10 percent by late 2009. Although the Obama administration bore no direct responsibility for the onset of the crisis, the economy's anemic recovery meant that he quickly became associated with it. Very quickly, opposition to Obama took on a populist hue.

In the February 2009 "rant" heard around the world, CNBC reporter, Rick Santelli went off on the Obama administration's use of bailouts and fiscal stimulus in response to the crisis. Echoing the resentful language of Richard Nixon, Santelli called on the "silent majority" of upstanding, mortgage-paying, middle-class Americans to take a stand against a government that was bailing out "losers" at their expense. Harking back to America's libertarian past, he called out to President Obama, "We're thinking of having a Chicago Tea Party in July." Within days, "Tea Party" rallies and groups sprang up across the country. Much of this early activity appeared to be spontaneous and directed mostly at pressuring the government for a change in policy. However, as big donor money flowed into the movement, the Tea Party began unseating establishment Republican incumbents, eventually forming a sizable caucus within Congress.

While banks were bailed out by gigantic federal loans, the middle class saw little relief of its mounting mortgage, student, and consumer debt. In late 2011, some 2,000 protestors descended on New York's financial district, occupying Zuccotti Park in opposition to the gross inequalities produced by a brand of finance capitalism in which both major political parties were complicit. A self-consciously leaderless social movement, Occupy Wall Street faded quickly, although social democratic Senator Bernie Sanders would mobilize some of the group's energy in his 2015–16 campaign for the presidency. Yet even as many of the technologically savvy, middle-class millennials and Gen Xers who made up the core of Occupy benefited from the eventual rebound in the economy, less educated, poorer voters saw no such recovery. Low-skilled jobs, especially in manufacturing and heavy industry, simply never returned. The result was a massive "left behind" constituency ready to be mobilized.

Evidence on the role of personal economic circumstances and Trump voting is mixed. In the 2015–16 Republican Party primary, Trump stood out for his advocacy of protectionist measures on trade and immigration. Support for these policies was strongly associated with Trump support in the primaries. Moving to the general election, however, where the views of mainstream Republicans as well as hardcore Trump supporters are aggregated, non-economic attitudes take on greater significance. Survey research shows that individual concerns about personal finances or the state of the economy were secondary to hot-button cultural issues such as immigration in motivating Trump voters. Trump's support did not come from the poorest voters we might normally classify as working class. Indeed, the typical Trump voter had an income of $72,000, well above the national average. Hillary Clinton beat Trump among voters in the lowest income quintile, both Black and white.[6]

However, if we think of class in terms of education rather than just income, there was a strong class basis to Trump's support. Evidence shows that those with lower educational levels have been relative economic losers in the wake of globalization and automation. In 2016, Trump won 50 percent of non–college graduates compared to 43 percent for Clinton. This remained true in 2024, when he increased his support to 56 percent among voters without college degrees. No wonder Trump said "I love the poorly educated"; they clearly love him. These voters have been trending toward the Republican Party since before Trump, but he has clearly tapped into a rich vein of support among those with grievances against the institutional status quo. It is also the case that low education is associated with greater prejudice toward other groups, but the direction of causality is difficult to disentangle.

Although this individual-level evidence is mixed, there is especially compelling research which shows that economically depressed regions were those most likely to lean toward Trump in 2016 and in 2020 (we don't yet have the data for 2024). Using a locality's exposure to trade competition from China or the susceptibility of its economy to automation, researchers have shown that local labor market changes have effects on political outcomes at the aggregate level. Places that had been most exposed to trade shocks and automation were more likely to vote for Trump. Going back a little further, although survey research has shown that individual economic anxiety was unrelated to early support for the Tea Party, it's also the case that Tea Party activity was higher in those places most exposed to the fallout of the financial crisis. Left-behind *places* seem to vote populist, if not left-behind individuals.[7]

This more aggregated economic approach finds support in the survey data if we consider voters' concerns about the economy as a whole rather than their personal economic circumstances. So-called *sociotropic* voting is not as irrational as it might seem. We all live in communities that affect our personal lives in various ways, and we benefit indirectly when those communities are economically healthy. The opposite is true when those areas are in decline. For a small business owner, say, of a furniture store or a café, it is of fundamental importance that the local economy is doing well. Even professionals like lawyers and dentists, despite their high, recession-proof personal incomes, prefer to live in localities that are thriving, not ones in decline, because of the knock-on effects of the latter on social cohesion, crime, and so on. As jobs leave, depression, disease, and drugs come in. Alarmingly, Trump's support was higher in those places most affected by what economists Anne Case and Angus Deaton called "deaths of despair"—suicides, overdoses, and liver disease. Economically left behind places in the United States have become wells of collective unhappiness and grievance—feelings that have driven people to abandon the status quo.[8]

The evidence from post-crisis Europe points in the same direction. Although economic motivations are somewhat mixed at the individual level, struggling localities seem to provide the bedrock of populist support. As the impact of the Great Recession rippled out across the global financial system, European banks were forced to tighten their lines of credit. The treasuries of heavily indebted nations like Greece, Ireland, and Italy soon found themselves under immense pressure, as bond traders fled the market. Compelled into extreme austerity measures by the European Commission (EC), the European Central Bank (ECB), and the International Monetary Fund (IMF)—the Troika—Greece came close to repudiating its debts and withdrawing from the Eurozone. Unemployment shot up from 7.5 percent in 2005 to 23.1 percent by May 2012; youth unemployment hit a staggering 54.9 percent. For proponents of the economic theory of populism, it is no surprise that Greece was the first European state for several decades to come under a populist government.[9]

Syriza was formed as a political coalition of socialist and radical parties in 2004, and in 2007, it elected Alexis Tsipras, a popular member of the Athens municipal council as its leader. Syriza had won just under 5 percent in the last pre-crisis legislative elections of October 2009. However, as the effects of the debt crisis began to bite, opinion polls showed a boost in support for Syriza, and in elections in May 2012, it became the second largest party in parliament with 16 percent of the vote. With no party able to form a government, however, fresh elections were held in June. Syriza's vote share rose to 27 percent, although it remained behind the center-right New Democracy (ND) party. The economic and political instability persisted, and in legislative elections in January 2015, Syriza received 36 percent of the vote, allowing Tsipras to form a coalition government. Tsipras campaigned on promises to put an end to austerity, but the Troika faced his government down, leaving his supporters disappointed and disaffected.

Individual survey data from Europe provides some support for the economic model of populism, but again the results are not consistent. Using pre- and post-crisis survey data, one study of twenty-four EU countries from 1980 to 2020 finds that individual perceptions of global economic uncertainty are associated with a greater preference for populist parties. There is also evidence that employment status, income difficulties, and exposure to globalization are associated with populist support, along with evidence that voters who feel that inequality is unfairly high are more likely to support populist parties. Overall, evidence from pan-European surveys, which test the effect of national economic conditions on political outcomes, indicates a modest relationship between various measures of economic insecurity and political distrust or populist voting. Another study based on large-scale survey data shows that economic distress is related to a drop in confidence in the political establishment, arguably a precondition for the success of populist outsiders. Other research suggests that the effects of economic decline may differ for populist parties on the left and the right, although the results are not consistent.[10]

In contrast to all of this, however, the most comprehensive study of public opinion in Western Europe finds that of attitudes toward several issues, including immigration and the European Union, economic dissatisfaction had the least effect on support for right-wing populist parties over the last two decades. Sometimes economic distress leads to populist success; at other times it does not. Among European countries, it had a measurable effect only in Sweden and the Netherlands, countries that had done relatively well economically over the period. In Eastern Europe also, populist parties seem as likely to emerge in good economic times. Even among those economies that crashed hardest after 2008, the effect was inconsistent. Although Italy saw a return to populist government with the success of Beppe Grillo's Five Star Movement (M5S) and Matteo Salvini's Lega Nord in 2018, and subsequently with Giorgia Meloni's Brothers of Italy in 2022, in the equally hard-hit economies of Ireland and Portugal, the populist dog failed to bark. At the national and individual levels, at least, the picture is suggestive, but inconsistent.[11]

As in the United States, economic distress in Europe has a much more predictable effect on populist voting at the level of place. A recent study finds that across 240 sub-national regions in twenty-six European countries, a 1 percentage point increase in the unemployment rate translates to a 1 percentage point higher populist vote share. Similarly, the United

Kingdom Independence Party (UKIP) —a major force behind Brexit—consistently overperformed in Britain's former industrial heartland. Support for Leave in the Brexit referendum was itself strongest in those "left behind" regions of England and Wales. In France, the stronghold of the Front National, the party of Jean-Marie and Marine Le Pen, also lies in France's deindustrializing areas. We see the same thing in Germany, where the AfD (Alternative for Germany) does best in declining and depopulated areas of Eastern Germany. Other evidence from across the continent points in the same direction.[12]

What we see, in short, is that economics has a powerful effect at the level of place although this doesn't seem to show up at the individual level. As a result, a good deal of research argues that culture and identity are the real causes of populist support. On aggregate, there is some evidence of an association between nativist, ethnocentric views and populism. Yet, these feelings are heightened during periods of economic distress, raising questions of what is causing what. After we examine the cultural argument for populism, I'll examine how the institutional approach can help to make sense of these somewhat conflicting findings.

Is populism a cultural backlash?

If at one time, political and economic commentators could confidently assert that vote choice was primarily a matter of "pocketbook" concerns, these arguments are today treated as quaint, if not reactionary. Those turning to populist candidates, critics of the economic approach argue, are motivated by threats to the status of their identity and to that of their group. Not long after Trump's shock win, headlines like the following made the rounds in the nation's leading newspapers and magazines: "Economic anxiety didn't make people vote Trump, racism did," and "It was the racism, stupid: White working class 'economic anxiety' is a zombie idea that needs to die." While establishment parties focus on economic policy issues like taxes and welfare, populists appeal to voters' sense of ethnic, national, or religious identity.[13]

Yet there is a link here between the economic and cultural realms. The regions that have benefited from the global economy, say, Silicon Valley and the City of London, have also become culturally distinct. They have become increasingly liberal on family matters, religion, immigration, race, and gender. In contrast, those parts of the West that have not benefited from globalization retain more traditional social values. As journalist David Goodhart has put it, politics has become culturally divided between the "Anywheres"—the green-alternative-libertarian globalists—and the "Somewheres"—the traditional-authoritarian-nationalists. Populist supporters are the "deplorables" of Hillary Clinton's nightmares: racists, xenophobes, chauvinists, and transphobes. Their opponents are the "wokies" who'll stop at nothing in their pursuit of social justice. In contrast to the establishment parties that came of age in the first half of the twentieth century, which stress their differences along the classic left-right economic axis, populist parties have disrupted the political space, focusing on these cultural cleavages instead. Immigration, secularism, gay marriage, affirmative action, and abortion are more relevant to the rise of populism than the unemployment or inflation rate.[14]

It is not hard to see why a cultural narrative of populism has become so prominent in the Trump era. In the announcement of his candidacy way back in mid-2015, Trump labeled Mexicans drug dealers and rapists. He promised to build a wall to keep them out. In office he bemoaned having to deal with people from "shithole countries"—in Latin America, the Caribbean, and Africa—coming to America. One of his first executive orders was to ban travel to the United States for the citizens of seven Muslim-majority countries. He refused to condemn white nationalists, even after the murder of a counter-protestor during a rally in Charlottesville in August 2017, opining that there were "very fine people on both sides." During his 2020 re-election campaign, he winked at his most notorious white supremacist supporters, telling the Proud Boys to "stand back and stand by," while deriding Black Lives Matter protestors as looters and rioters. In 2024, Trump went even further, promising to deport millions of undocumented immigrants in his second term. In the first few months since his return to office, he has begun to make inroads on these commitments. Trump, in short, seems to stand for the same things as white nativist movements have throughout American history.

Nor is Trump unique. At the turn of the twenty-first century, reactionary, nostalgic nationalism went global. Just as the European project seemed to be progressing irrevocably toward a full political union—a United States of Europe—new and old nationalist parties began to make deep inroads into the political mainstream. Nine days before the 2002 Dutch parliamentary election, Pim Fortuyn was assassinated, but his avowedly nativist eponymous party became the second largest in parliament. Although the Pim Fortuyn List soon broke up without its charismatic leader, Geert Wilders picked up the nationalist mantle, and after two decades of more or less steady growth, in 2023 his Party for Freedom and Democracy (PVV) became the largest in the Dutch parliament. The Front National, and its nationalist successor, the National Rally (RN) have become the main opposition party in France. Marine Le Pen has twice been runner-up in the presidential runoffs (2017 and 2022), replicating the breakthrough success of her father, Jean Marie, in 2002. Even though the British Labour Party's Jeremy Corbyn and Alexis Tsipras's Syriza party in Greece are usually located on the left, they were also both protectionist and nationalist, with ambiguous, if not hostile feelings toward the European Union and other international institutions including the IMF. Allegations of antisemitism have dogged Corbyn for decades. It is not hard to see why many scholars have virtually equated populism with nationalism.[15]

As with economic explanations, the evidence for cultural accounts comes at different scales. Survey research suggests that identity was the key factor driving Trump's success. The major study of his 2016 election, titled *Identity Crisis*, found that identity concerns rather than material interests were the main motivations of Trump's supporters. Specifically, negative feelings toward immigrants, Blacks, and in some studies women were positively associated with support for Trump. To the extent that perceptions of the economy mattered, they argue, it was through the lens of racial attitudes. Other studies similarly "control" for economic factors and find that once views toward immigrants and minorities are measured, economic issues had no effect on support for Trump. In fact, hardcore Trump supporters score low on measures of resentment toward the rich and educated. Pivoting to Trump's reelection campaign in 2020, identity issues again outweighed economic ones. Tax policy made no impact on Trump's popularity among Republicans, but the border wall did. Trump's populism was seemingly less about opposition to economic elites than to racial or national *others*.[16]

Yet not all evidence points in the same direction. In 2024 Trump won the support of a third of non-white voters. This compares with the 15 percent of non-white voters won by Mitt Romney in 2012. Clearly something other than their ethnic identity was driving the behavior of these voters. Moreover, when scholars have used experimental setups to test the effect of threats to the racial status of whites, many of the correlations between racial anxiety and political preferences disappear. This means that when we see a link between identity and support for populism in surveys, we might be missing some factor that connects them. The implication is that racial or ethnic identity per se could be a problematic explanation for the sustained popularity of Trump and other populists.[17]

Some of the inconsistency in the evidence may also be due a conflation of anti-immigrant sentiment with ethnocentrism (or racism). As the 2024 election approached, Trump exclaimed that an "invasion" of immigrants was "poisoning the blood of our country." While this statement may well be racist and fascist, as others have argued, it also reflects a straightforward opposition to immigration that is distinct from these other belief systems. Trump's nationalism seems to have had an appeal to those who self-identify as American patriots, regardless of their own ethnicity. Immigrants, irrespective of their color, are not Americans. Between Trump's loss in 2020 and his victory in 2024, the proportion of Americans supporting a *decrease* in immigration rose from 28 to 55 percent. Importantly, this rise in anti-immigrant sentiment was not restricted to whites. In mid-2024, three quarters of Hispanics said that the increase in number of migrants crossing the border was a "crisis" or a "major problem," the same proportion as non-Hispanics. And by a 2-to-1 majority, they felt the government was failing to manage the problem. Over the last three presidential elections, Trump's vote share has consistently gone up in many of America's most ethnically diverse counties, especially those along the border. Trump's promises of a mass deportation program fit the national mood. Yet it is far from clear that the underlying motivation here is racism or ethnocentrism rather than resentment of government failures that were imposing costs on others. Trump supporters were motivated by a loss of trust in a system that they felt favored immigrants and minorities, who "cut in line" for benefits, while the lower middle class gets stuck with higher taxes.[18]

In Europe, concerns over immigration have been a driving force behind the success of populist movements. The wars in Afghanistan and Iraq led to a surge of refugees in the early 2000s. As immigration to Western Europe from North Africa, the Middle East, and Central Asia increased after 2001, the proportion of Muslims residing there skyrocketed. Similarly, after 2004, millions of Eastern Europeans who had just joined the European Union gained access to Western European labor markets, resulting in a surge in East-West migration. The establishment, the old guard of politics, responded with a sort of helplessness, arguing that they were bound by international law, by the European Union, by the European Court of Human Rights. Populists promised what the establishment could not: a closure of the borders, a stemming of the flood, even if this meant reneging on international treaties.

The process was Europe-wide, but the British case is instructive. It has been shown that asylum seeker immigration during the 2000s caused a substantial uptick in support for the far-right populist British National Party (BNP). The BNP was poised to expand its appeal under its charismatic leader, Nick Griffin, but it was soon outflanked by UKIP. Originally more concerned with the wonkish issue of European encroachment on British sovereignty, UKIP had none of the old neo-Nazi baggage of the BNP. By the mid-2010s, when Nigel Farage realized that there were votes to be won in opposing immigration, UKIP's popularity surged. In the lead-up to the Brexit Referendum of 2016, UKIP pushed the boundaries of political decency, rolling out the now-infamous poster—an endless line of refugees, seemingly on their way to Britain. Immigration became by far the most important issue to a majority of voters. Brexit was not an idea born of sovereignty alone. It was born of this mass opposition—this fear, this anger over immigration. Having exited the EU, however, the British government, even led by another populist, Boris Johnson, struggled to make good on its promises. Immigration did not stop. In fact, it surged. While immigration numbers fell from their pre-COVID-19 peak of around 200,000 during the pandemic, in 2022 they surged to a record 745,000. At the 2024 general elections, the ruling Conservative Party was unceremoniously dumped out of office, while Farage's latest anti-immigrant populist vehicle, Reform UK, won an unprecedented 14 percent of the vote. With Labour still struggling to rein in immigration, Reform's popularity could grow further in the future.

There is strong evidence that concerns about immigration are linked to support for populist movements in Europe. However, public opinion data take us only so far, as individual motivations are difficult to disentangle. As with economic factors, looking at data at the geographic level helps us understand how identity politics and populism are related.

Usually, because immigrants may be drawn to places where they are viewed favorably, it is difficult to measure the causal effect of immigration on public opinion. In some cases, however, immigrants come to settle within a destination country for quite arbitrary reasons. In the same way that we can assess the effects of exogenous, or externally caused, local economic declines on populist voting, we can see how sub-national changes in immigration affect populist support.[19]

Exploiting the fact that some Greek islands lie closer to the Turkish coast than others and as a result are more likely to receive asylum seekers crossing into the EU by boat from Türkiye, one study shows a sharp increase in support for the populist far right in Greece in exactly those places. Research also shows that Silvio Berlusconi's Forza Italia gained support in regions with higher immigration, and that immigration had a positive effect on the vote share of Jörg Haider's far-right Freedom Party (FPÖ) in Austria. The far right also gained in French presidential elections from 1988 to 2017 in places with more immigration. Yet another study shows that exposure to refugee transit routes in eighteen countries in Central and Eastern Europe decreased trust in political institutions and increased anti-migrant sentiments. My own research showed an increase in support for Griffin's BNP in British localities that had higher rates of asylum-seeker immigration.[20]

Even though not all research is in agreement, on balance, it seems that immigration, and growing ethnic diversity more broadly, leads to an increase in support for populism. Why does this relationship exist? Unless populism is equated with nativism or ethnic chauvinism by definition, it remains unclear why ethnic diversity or even domestic threats to the social status of once-dominant ethnic groups should show up as an increased demand for populism per se. Immigration appears to have little effect on support for left-wing populists, suggesting that it is a party's specific views on immigration that matter, rather than its populism as such. More fundamentally, although group prejudice seems to come naturally to humanity, it is far from clear that it is an "uncaused cause." Ethnocentrism, racism, or nativism may be correlated with support for populist leaders like Trump, but this raises the question of what causes those prejudices.

There is good reason to believe that material conditions are at the bottom of it. Although some research ostensibly shows that economic conditions cease to matter once views on identity and culture are measured, most of it relies on what is sometimes disparagingly called a "horse race" strategy. That is, a series of economic and cultural views or characteristics are included in a statistical model and those that have a statistically significant "effect" on the outcome are deemed to be causes; insignificant factors are deemed not causal. The validity of this approach depends on the implausible assumption that none of the factors in the model—income, education, perceptions of the economy, views on welfare, views on immigration—affect the others. Class, for instance, has been shown to affect all sorts of other attitudes. However, in standard models, if a person's social class affected support for Trump *only through* their cultural views, then we would erroneously conclude that class has no effect, when instead it has a strong *indirect* effect. Recent research in fact points in this direction, with class causing views on identity and these views in turn affecting support for Trump. European evidence also shows that the effect of education—a major component of class—on political preferences goes through ideological attitudes. In other words, views on cultural and identity issues may *mediate* the relationship between economic status and support for populism.[21]

How does anti-institutionalism affect the demand for populism?

There are deeper, more fundamental reasons that economic factors like class sometime seem to have inconsistent effects on support for populism. Much of this stems from the way we approach political behavior today. In the age of modern research methods—especially the survey, with its neat representative samples—we tend to think about political decisions as the sum of individual choices. But there is a compelling reason to believe that voting, at its core, is a collective, social act. It was Angus Campbell and his colleagues, who first illuminated this truth in their classic, *The American Voter*. Though the methods used are somewhat dated, the take-home point of the study remains valid six decades later: Voting is not a solitary act; it is an endeavor shaped by the groups we belong to. Our political preferences, *The American Voter* showed, are not born in a vacuum. We may not all be political sheep, blindly following the herd, but the fact is that people often do conform to the opinions of those around them. To buck the prevailing view of one's social circle may seem tempting to some, but for most, it leads to an internal struggle, known as cognitive dissonance. It is not just abstract ideas that people conform to, either. People who move for reasons unrelated to politics—say, for work or family—even find themselves switching political allegiances, abandoning their Republican or Democratic ties to blend in with the political majority of their new community. After all, as the saying goes, people do as Romans do. And so, election results follow a familiar pattern—geographically speaking. Even in the tightest of presidential races, individual precincts are rarely divided. More often than not, the votes in each precinct swing decisively in one direction or another, shaped not only by individual preferences but by the collective rhythms of the neighborhoods they belong to. It is not just about who votes. It's about who is voting together.[22]

Although more research is needed, my feeling is that the economy does affect the demand for populist candidates, but that it does so in an indirect way, which makes its measurement through surveys very challenging. Long-term economic decline or cost of living pressures may not have an immediate effect on an individual's welfare; yet these factors may precipitate a more diffuse decline in an individual's satisfaction with political institutions. In his recent book on left-wing populists in Europe in the 2000s, journalist Vincent Bevins describes the rise of an attitude that was "not just apathetic towards politics but actively opposed to all of its formal and institutional manifestations." That is, dissatisfaction with growing inequality, rising immigration, and cultural change was leading to a generalized distrust of the institutional status quo.[23]

There is growing evidence that institutional distrust is on the rise and that this is one of the main drivers of the populist surge. A 2024 poll revealed that across twenty-eight countries, including the United States, 61 percent of people believe "the system is broken" and 67 percent that "the political and economic elite don't care about people like me." How people feel about institutions also seems to affect how they interpret economic conditions. Research shows that trust in national and European institutions moderates the effect of economic insecurity on support for populist parties. An early, but unduly neglected, study of Latin American presidential elections showed that the aggregate level of institutional distrust in a country was a better predictor of populist performance than other factors such as economic crises. This finding is supported by more recent research at the individual level, with dissatisfaction with government institutions correlated with support for populist challengers. In the United States, tellingly, given that both arose as insurgent outsiders to their respective party establishments, institutional distrust is the best predictor of who supported either Trump or Sanders in 2016. Anger toward the government was associated with support for Trump, but no other Republicans, in the 2016 primary.[24]

No doubt, resentment is sometimes directed against particular "elites." Jewish billionaire financier George Soros is a perennial bogeyman of the Eastern European populist right. Yet this personification is far from universal. Rather, when resentment is made specific, institutions, if not organizations, take the brunt of it: affirmative action, Title IX, the European Union, NATO. . . . Of all institutions, however, political parties are perhaps the biggest offenders. Political parties are among the least trusted and liked institutions in the world. Voting for populists represents a rejection of the political establishment. And in turn, this opposition to institutions, including parties, acquires a kind of identity in its own right. As Didier Eribon writes in his moving memoir of life in his working-class home city of Reims in northern France, "Voting for the National Front must be interpreted, at least in part, as the final recourse of people of the working classes attempting to defend their collective identity, or to defend, in any case, a dignity that was being trampled on—now even by those who had once been their representatives and defenders [the Communist Party]." Viewing populism as a manifestation of institutional distrust—especially of political parties—helps explain why populism can be on the left or the right. Eribon continues: "Right or left, there's no difference; they are all the same, and the same people always end up footing the bill." The system is broken. Little wonder that people are willing to take a chance on something new. The evidence suggests that these anti-party views are only growing. While around two-thirds of Americans trust the military and the police, and about three in ten trust Congress, only 17 percent trust political parties. Research shows that distrust of politicians is associated with support for populist parties across multiple waves of European elections.[25]

Here, the destructive power of geographically concentrated economic decline becomes clearer. As I've pointed out, job losses from outsourcing or automation set off a chain reaction, a cascade of destruction that can ravage entire communities. The first blow comes when the loss of jobs reduces demand for local services—stores close, small businesses shutter their doors, and vacancy rates climb. Property values plummet, and with them, the quality of life. Social services, from healthcare to education, suffer. In communities already under strain, mental health deteriorates, drug use rises, and despair takes root. Populists frame the loss of jobs, the collapse of industries, as part of a larger, shadowy conspiracy, turning the cultural fears and prejudices that come with economic decline into political capital. In this way, economic decline, cultural tension, and institutional distrust feed into each other, creating a vicious cycle in which populists thrive. It may not be the case that losing a job causes a person to prefer a populist candidate like Trump. But it may be that the closure of a factory can cause a whole town to turn in that direction.

These anxieties, critically, play out at a community level, even more than a national one. *Regions* within Europe that have experienced local economic and industrial decline due to globalization, along with having higher unemployment and a less educated workforce, display less support for the European Union and greater support for Eurosceptic populists. Research indicates that the contemporary populist European right, including parties like the Sweden Democrats, have support that is geographically concentrated. Going back further, there is longstanding evidence that populist movements during the Great Depression similarly had their greatest success in rural regions where farmers were the first to feel the economic strains. In a context of economic malaise, resentment is directed toward a failing system.[26]

All of this is suggestive of the key role that institutional resentment plays in the surging support for populism. Populist supporters feel that the system is broken. Irredeemably so. There is no point in voting for the mainstream opposition because they too are part of that system. Only a real outsider can be trusted to bring it down. At present, we lack the psychological and experimental research to determine how deep this anti-institutional mindset goes. Is it situational, dependent on real or perceived institutional failures? Having ebbed away, can it ever return? We'll return to some of these questions in the concluding chapter. Ultimately, however, we'll see in Chapter 5 that institutional distrust, or any other belief, is insufficient as an explanation for the rise of populism. The demand side, by itself, tells us only so much.

Notes

1. Philip Wegmann, "Trump's Spending on Trucker Hats Helps Illustrate Why He's Losing," *Washington Examiner*, October 26, 2016, https://www.washingtonexaminer.com/opinion/986373/trumps-spending-on-trucker-hats-helps-illustrate-why-hes-losing/.
2. For county-level change, see Stephanie Muravchik and Jon A. Shields, *Trump's Democrats* (Brookings Institution Press, 2020). For working class voters, see Stephen L. Morgan and Jiwon Lee, "Trump Voters and the White Working Class," *Sociological Science* 5, no. 10 (2018): 234–245.
3. R. Michael Alvarez and Jonathan Nagler, "Economics, Issues and the Perot Candidacy: Voter Choice in the 1992 Presidential Election," *American Journal of Political Science* 39, no. 3 (1995): 714–744, https://doi.org/10.2307/2111651, accessed August 28, 2023.
4. On the relationship between economic hardship and populism, see Barry Eichengreen, *The Populist Temptation: Economic Grievance and Political Reaction in the Modern Era* (Oxford University Press, 2018); Dani Rodrik, "Populism and the Economics of Globalization," *Journal of International Business Policy* 1, no. 1 (2018): 12–33; Sergei Guriev and Elias Papaioannou, "The Political Economy of Populism," *Journal of Economic Literature* 60, no. 3 (2022): 753–832.
5. Economic crises reduce support for the market: C. Graham and S. Sukhtankar, "Does Economic Crisis Reduce Support for Markets and Democracy in Latin America? Some Evidence from Surveys of Public Opinion and Well Being," *Journal of Latin American Studies* 36, no. 2 (2004): 349–377, https://doi.org/10.1017/S0022216X0400745X.
6. T. Ferguson, B. I. Page, J. Rothschild, A. Chang, and J. Chen, "The Roots of Right-Wing Populism: Donald Trump in 2016," *International Journal of Political Economy* 49, no. 2 (2020): 102–123, https://doi.org/10.1080/08911916.2020.1778861; Walter Bossert et al., "Economic Insecurity and Political Preferences," *Oxford Economic Papers* 75, no. 3 (2023).
7. Wendy K. Tam Cho, James G. Gimpel, and Daron R. Shaw, "The Tea Party Movement and the Geography of Collective Action," *Quarterly Journal of Political Science* 7, no. 2 (2012): 105–133; David Autor, David Dorn, Gordon Hanson, and Kaveh Majlesi,

"Importing Political Polarization? The Electoral Consequences of Rising Trade Exposure," *American Economic Review* 110, no. 10 (2020): 3139–3183.

8. Anne Case and Angus Deaton, *Deaths of Despair and the Future of Capitalism* (Princeton University Press, 2021).
9. Ivan T. Berend, *Against European Integration: The European Union and its Discontents* (Routledge, 2019), 10–11.
10. Giray Gozgor, "The Role of Economic Uncertainty in the Rise of EU Populism," *Public Choice* 190, no. 1–2 (2022): 229–246. But see Kai Arzheimer and Carl C. Berning, "How the Alternative for Germany (AfD) and Their Voters Veered to the Radical Right, 2013–2017," *Electoral Studies* 60 (2019): 102040; Kai Arzheimer, "The Electoral Breakthrough of the AfD and the East-West Divide in German Politics," in *Contemporary Germany and the Fourth Wave of Far-Right Politics*, pp. 140–158 (Routledge, 2023); L. Guiso, H. Herrera, M. Morelli, and T. Sonno, "Economic Insecurity and the Demand for Populism in Europe," *Economica* 91, no. 362 (2024): 588–620; Y. Algan, S. Guriev, E. Papaioannou, and E. Passari, "The European Trust Crisis and the Rise of Populism," *Brookings Papers on Economic Activity, 2017* (2), 309–400; Rui Silva, "Well-Being Foundations of Populism in Europe," *European Journal of Political Economy* 81 (2024); D. Ferrari, "Perceptions, Resentment, Economic Distress, and Support for Right-Wing Populist Parties in Europe," *Politics and Governance* 9, no. 3 (2021): 274–287, https://doi.org/10.17645/pag.v9i3.3961; Nils D. Steiner, "Economic Inequality, Unfairness Perceptions, and Populist Attitudes," Gutenberg School of Management and Economics & Research Unit, "Interdisciplinary Public Policy" Discussion Paper Series, no. 2203, version 30, September 2021, https://download.uni-mainz.de/RePEc/pdf/Discussion_Paper_2203.pdf; L. Guiso, H. Herrera, M. Morelli, and T. Sonno, "Global Crises and Populism: The Role of Eurozone Institutions," *Economic Policy* 34, no. 97 (2019): 95–139; Chase Foster and Jeffry Frieden, "Crisis of Trust: Socio-Economic Determinants of Europeans' Confidence in Government," *European Union Politics* 18, no. 4 (2017): 511–535; Marcel Lubbers, Mérove Gijsberts, and Peer Scheepers, "Extreme Right-Wing Voting in Western Europe," *European Journal of Political Research* 41, no. 3 (2002): 345–378; Geertje Lucassen and Marcel Lubbers, "Who Fears What? Explaining Far-Right-Wing Preference in Europe by Distinguishing Perceived Cultural and

Economic Ethnic Threats," *Comparative Political Studies* 45, no. 5 (2012): 547–574.

11. Larry Bartels, *Democracy Erodes from the Top: Leaders, Citizens, and the Challenge of Populism in Europe* (Princeton University Press, 2023), 158. On Eastern Europe, S. Hanley and A. Sikk, "Economy, Corruption or Floating Voters? Explaining the Breakthroughs of Anti-Establishment Reform Parties in Eastern Europe," *Party Politics* 22, no. 4 (2016): 522–533, https://doi.org/10.1177/1354068814550438.
12. Yann Algan, Sergei Guriev, Elias Papaioannou, and Evgenia Passari, "The European Trust Crisis and the Rise of Populism," *Brookings Papers on Economic Activity* (2017): 309–382; Cameron Ballard-Rosa, Allison Carnegie, and Bryan Schonfeld, "The Geography of Democratic Discontent," *British Journal of Political Science* 53, no. 2 (2023): 366–386; Sascha O. Becker, Thiemo Fetzer, and Dennis Novy, "Determinants of Populist Voting: Who Voted for Brexit? 1." *Ifo DICE Report* 15, no. 4 (2017): 3–5; Kai Arzheimer and Theresa Bernemann, "'Place' Does Matter for Populist Radical Right Sentiment, but How? Evidence from Germany," *European Political Science Review* (2023): 1–20. J. Lawrence Broz, Jeffry Frieden, and Stephen Weymouth, "Populism in Place: The Economic Geography of the Globalization Backlash," *International Organization* 75, no. 2 (2021): 464–494; Helen V. Milner, "Voting for Populism in Europe: Globalization, Technological Change, and the Extreme Right," *Comparative Political Studies* 54, no. 13 (2021).
13. Sean McElwee and Jason McDaniel, "Economic Anxiety Didn't Make People Vote for Trump, Racism Did," *The Nation*, May 8, 2017, https://www.thenation.com/article/archive/economic-anxiety-didnt-make-people-vote-trump-racism-did/; Chauncey Devega, "It Was the Racism, Stupid: White Working-Class 'Economic Anxiety' Is a Zombie Idea That Needs to Die," *Salon*, January 5, 2017, https://www.salon.com/2017/01/05/it-was-the-racism-stupid-white-working-class-economic-anxiety-is-a-zombie-idea-that-needs-to-die/. For more in-depth analyses, see John Sides, Michael Tesler, and Lynn Vavreck, *Identity Crisis: The 2016 Presidential Campaign and the Battle for the Meaning of America*, (Princeton University Press, 2019); Tyler T. Reny, Loren Collingwood, and Ali A. Valenzuela, "Vote Switching in the 2016 Election: How Racial and Immigration Attitudes, Not Economics,

Explain Shifts in White Voting," *Public Opinion Quarterly* 83, no. 1 (2019). See also Diana C. Mutz, "Status Threat, Not Economic Hardship, Explains the 2016 Presidential Vote," *PNAS* 115 (19) E4330–E4339, (2018).

14. David Goodhart, *The Road to Somewhere: The Populist Revolt and The Future of Politics* (Penguin, 2017).
15. For example, see Roger Eatwell and Matthew Goodwin, *National Populism: The Revolt against Liberal Democracy* (Penguin, 2018).
16. Reny, Collingwood, and Valenzuela, "Vote Switching in The 2016 Election"; Brenda Major, Alison Blodorn, and Gregory Major Blascovich, "The Threat of Increasing Diversity: Why Many White Americans Support Trump in the 2016 Presidential Election," *Group Processes & Intergroup Relations* 21, no. 6 (2018): 931–940; D. N. Smith and E. Hanley, "The Anger Games: Who Voted for Donald Trump in the 2016 Election, and Why?" *Critical Sociology* 44, no. 2 (2018): 195–212; John Sides, Michael Tesler, and Lynn Vavreck, *Identity Crisis: The 2016 Presidential Campaign and the Battle for the Meaning of America* (Princeton University Press, 2019); John Sides, Lynn Vavreck, and Chris Tausanovitch, *The Bitter End: The 2020 Presidential Campaign and the Challenge to American Democracy* (Princeton University Press, 2023); John R. Hibbing, *The Securitarian Personality: What Really Motivates Trump's Base and Why It Matters for the Post-Trump Era* (Oxford University Press, 2020), 104.
17. Sheridan Stewart and Robb Willer, "The Effects of Racial Status Threat on White Americans' Support for Donald Trump: Results of Five Experimental Tests," *Group Processes & Intergroup Relations* 25, no. 3 (2022): 791–810.
18. Luis Noe-Bustamante, "Latinos' Views on the Migrant Situation at the U.S.-Mexico Border," *Pew Research Center*, March 24, 2024, https://www.pewresearch.org/race-and-ethnicity/2024/03/04/latinos-views-on-the-migrant-situation-at-the-us-mexico-border/. Shane Goldmacher, "How Donald Trump Has Remade America's Political Landscape," *New York Times*, May 24, 2025, https://www.nytimes.com/interactive/2025/05/25/us/politics/trump-politics-democrats.html.
19. On public opinion of immigration and populist support, see, e.g., Eric Kaufmann, *Whiteshift: Populism, Immigration and the Future of White Majorities* (Penguin, 2018); Steven M. Van Hauwaert and Stijn Van Kessel, "Beyond Protest and Discontent: A Cross-National

Analysis of the Effect of Populist Attitudes and Issue Positions on Populist Party Support," *European Journal of Political Research* 57, no. 1 (2018): 68–92; James Dennison, "How Issue Salience Explains the Rise of the Populist Right in Western Europe," *International Journal of Public Opinion Research* 32, no. 3 (2020): 397–420.

20. E. Dinas, K. Matakos, D. Xefteris, and D. Hangartner, "Waking Up the Golden Dawn: Does Exposure to the Refugee Crisis Increase Support for Extreme-Right Parties?" *Political Analysis* 27, no. 2 (2019): 244–254; Sascha O. Becker and Thiemo Fetzer, "Does Migration Cause Extreme Voting?" Center for Competitive Advantage in the Global Economy and the Economic & Social Research Council, Working Paper Series No. 306, 2016, 1–54; P. Vertier, M. Viskanic, and M. Gamalerio, "Dismantling the 'Jungle': Migrant Relocation and Extreme Voting in France," *Political Science Research and Methods* 11, no. 1 (2023): 129–143; G. Barone, A. D'Ignazio, G. De Blasio, and P. Naticchioni, "Mr. Rossi, Mr. Hu and Politics. The Role of Immigration in Shaping Natives' Voting Behavior," *Journal of Public Economics* 136 (2016): 1–13; Martin Halla, Alexander F. Wagner, and Josef Zweimüller, "Immigration and Voting for the Far Right," *Journal of the European Economic Association* 15, no. 6 (2017): 1341–1385; P. D. Kenny and C. Miller, "Does Asylum Seeker Immigration Increase Support for the Far Right? Evidence from the United Kingdom, 2000–2015," *Journal of Ethnic and Migration Studies* 48, no. 7 (2022): 1629–1646; N. Ajzenman, C. G. Aksoy, and S. Guriev, "Exposure to Transit Migration: Public Attitudes and Entrepreneurship," *Journal of Development Economics* 158 (2022): 102899.
21. Stephen L. Morgan, "Status Threat, Material Interests, and the 2016 Presidential Vote," *Socius* 4 (2018): 1–17; Michael McQuarrie, "The Revolt of the Rust Belt: Place and Politics in the Age of Anger," *British Journal of Sociology* 68(S1) (2017): S120–152; L. Morgan Stephen and Lee Jiwon, "The White Working Class and Voter Turnout in U.S. Presidential Elections, 2004 to 2016," *Sociological Science* 4 (2017): 656–685; Morgan and Lee, "Trump Voters and the White Working Class";Diana C. Mutz, "Status Threat, Not Economic Hardship, Explains the 2016 Presidential Vote," *Proceedings of the National Academy of Sciences*, 2018, retrieved June 25, 2018, http://www.pnas.org/content/pnas/early/2018/04/18/1718155115.full.pdf.

22. On switching parties, see Betsy Sinclair, *The Social Citizen: Peer Networks and Political Behavior* (University of Chicago Press, 2012).
23. Vincent Bevins, *If We Burn: The Mass Protest Decade and the Missing Revolution* (Public Affairs, 2023), 192.
24. David Brooks, "We Haven't Hit Peak Populism Yet," *New York Times*, May 23, 2024, https://www.nytimes.com/2024/05/23/opinion/populism-trump-elections.html; Andrés Rodríguez-Pose, Javier Terrero-Davila, and Neil Lee, "Left-Behind Versus Unequal Places: Interpersonal Inequality, Economic Decline, and the Rise of Populism in the USA and Europe," *Journal of Economic Geography* 23, no. 5 (2023): 951–977; David Doyle, "The Legitimacy of Political Institutions: Explaining Contemporary Populism in Latin America," *Comparative Political Studies* 44, no. 11 (2011): 1447–1473, Joshua J. Dyck, Shanna Pearson-Merkowitz, and Michael Coates, "Primary Distrust: Political Distrust and Support for the Insurgent Candidacies of Donald Trump and Bernie Sanders in the 2016 Primary," *PS: Political Science & Politics* 51, no. 2 (2018): 351–357; N. Wiesehomeier, S. Ruth-Lovell, and M. Singer, "Conditional Populist Party Support: The Role of Dissatisfaction and Incumbency," *Latin American Research Review*, published online 2025: 1–20. https://doi.org/10.1017/lar.2025.1.
25. T. Rudolph, "Populist Anger, Donald Trump, and the 2016 Election," *Journal of Elections, Public Opinion and Parties* 31, no. 1 (2019): 33–58, https://doi.org/10.1080/17457289.2019.1582532; Didier Eribon, *Returning to Reims* (Penguin, 2019), 122, 126; L. F. Stoetzer, J. Giesecke, and H. Klüver, "How Does Income Inequality Affect the Support for Populist Parties?" *Journal of European Public Policy* 30, no. 1 (2021): 1–20, https://doi.org/10.1080/13501763.2021.1981981. On Germany, see Pascal D. König, "Support for a Populist Form of Democratic Politics or Political Discontent? How Conceptions of Democracy Relate to Support for the AfD," *Electoral Studies* 78 (2022): 102493.
26. Matthew Rhodes-Purdy, Rachel Navarre, and Stephen M. Utych, "Populist Psychology: Economics, Culture, and Emotions," *Journal of Politics* 83, no. 4 (2021); E. D. Knowles and L. R. Tropp, "The Racial and Economic Context of Trump Support: Evidence for Threat, Identity, and Contact Effects in the 2016 Presidential Election," *Social Psychological and Personality Science* 9, no. 3 (2018): 275–284, https://doi.org/10.1177/1948550618759326; Johnpeter Horst Grill, "The Nazi Party's Rural Propaganda

Before 1928," *Central European History* 15, no. 2 (1982): 149–185, http://www.jstor.org/stable/4545955; Charles P. Loomis and J. Allan Beegle, "The Spread of German Nazism in Rural Areas," *American Sociological Review* 11, no. 6 (1946): 724–734; Susanne Wallman Lundåsen, "Rurality and Discontent: Unraveling the Context Effects of Living in Rural Districts in Local Elections on Support for Sweden Democrats," *Journal of Rural Studies* 106 (2024); J. Rickardsson, "The Urban–Rural Divide in Radical Right Populist Support: The Role of Resident's Characteristics, Urbanization Trends and Public Service Supply," *Annals of Regional Science* 67 (2021): 211–242, https://doi.org/10.1007/s00168-021-01046-1.

5

THE SUPPLY SIDE

What do populists have to offer?

In the years after the 2007 fall of Lehman Brothers' investment bank, the United States avoided an economic collapse as deep as the Great Depression of the 1930s, in part thanks to the hundreds of billions of dollars provided by the government to bail out the nation's ailing financial institutions. However, while bankers and corporate lawyers continued to receive huge bonuses, regular Americans with growing mortgage, tuition, and credit card debt saw little relief. As President Obama remarked in early 2009, "What gets people upset—and rightfully so—are executives being rewarded for failure, especially when those rewards are subsidized by U.S. taxpayers." There was deep frustration and anger at the status quo across the political spectrum. On the one side, followers of the Tea Party, who objected to federal taxation (and the welfare state it funded), dusted off the Revolutionary-era Gadsden Flag and its "Don't tread on me" motto. On the other, those in the Occupy Wall Street movement at Zuccotti Park in New York's financial district in late 2011 did some historical appropriation of their own, taking a slogan from the populist era of the 1890s: "We are the 99 percent!"[1]

In many respects, the Tea Party and Occupy could not have been more different. One focused its ire on feckless borrowers, the other on greedy lenders. One saw government as the problem, the other saw it as the solution. Yet the common separation of populist movements into right and left, exclusionary and inclusionary, can be deceiving. Despite the extreme political polarization in the contemporary United States, populist voters on the left and right are surprisingly united in their distaste for the neoliberal institutional consensus on trade, finance, and even immigration. Similarly in Europe, populist supporters of all stripes object to unaccountable bureaucracies and courts, supranational organizations like the EU, and a financial system that has produced mounting inequality. Populism is a rejection of the institutional status quo, of the rules of the game itself. As the radical Slovenian philosopher, Slavoj Žižek, put it in a speech at Occupy Wall Street, "The problem is *the system*." Tea Partiers could only have agreed.[2]

Although Trump would build on the legacy of the Tea Party to win the Republican Party nomination and the US presidency in 2016, Bernie Sanders's campaign of that year faltered at the primary stage, when he lost the Democratic race to Hillary Clinton. One puzzle, given the remarkable energy of Sanders's campaign, is why Sanders lost but Trump won. An even bigger enigma, perhaps, is why neither Trump nor Sanders, nor anyone like them for that matter, made similar inroads in 2012. Although the activity of the Tea Party and Occupy movements was nearer their respective peaks in 2012, populists received approximately zero percent of the primary vote, compared to over 50 percent four years later (including both Trump and Sanders). The answer to the second puzzle is that the Tea Party and Occupy lacked charismatic leaders in 2012, but had them in 2016. The answer to the first is that Trump faced a divided party establishment in the Republican primary, while Sanders faced one cohesively lined up behind his Democratic primary opponent, Hillary Clinton. The explanation for both problems, in short, can't found in voters' preferences. As we noted in Chapter 4, voters' support for both Trump and Sanders was driven by institutional distrust. The differing outcomes, between 2012 and 2016, and between Trump and Sanders, tell us more about the *supply* of populism than they do of its *demand*.[3]

This chapter turns to what political scientists call the "supply side" of populism. If the demand side—the focus of Chapter 4—centers on the motivations of voters, the supply side is about something different: the choices those voters are given. It is about the politicians. The parties. The people who decide what options to put before the electorate. It raises a fundamental question: Why do some leaders and parties offer populism in the political marketplace? And beyond that, what does it really mean to "supply" populism?

At one time, the answers to these questions might have seemed straightforward. Populism was a political program—a set of policies, including higher taxes on corporations, aimed at leveling the playing field between ordinary people and the economic elite. As we've seen, this was the central message of the original Populist Party of the 1890s, which advocated for the interests of small midwestern and southern farmers over those of the wealthy owners of railroads and banks. For many Americans, the word "populism" still carries that meaning. Elsewhere in the world, populism has followed a very different course. In Latin America and Asia, populists have been just as likely to come from the economic right as the left. And in the West today, populism is less about economic policies than about immigration, national identity, and cultural conflict. It is unclear which, if any, of these sets of policy offerings are "populist" ones. Populism does not follow a consistent ideological path. Instead, it follows public opinion. It gravitates toward the anti-establishment position, whatever that may be in a given time and place.

More problematic still for the argument that populism is a set of economic or cultural policies is that mainstream parties seem perfectly capable of supplying the same options. Even if populists, as political outsiders, can offer fringe (or heterodox) policies in a way that establishment parties *initially* cannot because of their commitments to various interest groups, mainstream parties are nothing if not adaptable. Despite their long-standing support for the free movement of labor, center-right parties across the West have moved along with their electorates toward immigration restriction. Tellingly, even center-left parties have begun to shift their policies in the same direction. Populists can shake up political alignments, but as political scientist Carles Boix argues in *Democratic Capitalism at the Crossroads*, in this sense they may be no different from normal new parties, like the Green parties that emerged to advocate for environmental protection in the 1970s. Ultimately, it is difficult to sustain the argument that populists are *supplying* different policy offerings.

Another way populists set themselves apart is not through what they say but how they say it. In this view, populism succeeds not because of the policies it offers but because of the way those policies are packaged. It is not just a political position—it is a performance. A style. A way of speaking, of acting, that breaks the rules of conventional politics. "I don't have time for political correctness," said Trump—one statement that his busy fact checkers could have no problem with. Populism, in this sense, thrives on transgression. It is a deliberate rejection of the polished, careful language of the political establishment. It is raw, direct, often shocking—and that is precisely the point. By flouting the norms of traditional politics, populists signal to their supporters that they are different, that they are outsiders, that they are on the side of the people against an out-of-touch elite. Yet it's unclear how obviously *elite* billionaires and media moguls like Italy's Silvio Berlusconi or Thailand's Thaksin Shinawatra fit into this schema. Trump himself would explicitly flout this logic, boasting about just what an elite he was: "I always hear about the elite. You know, the elite—they're elite? I went to better schools than they did. . . . I live in a bigger, more beautiful apartment. . . . I think we're the elites. They're not the elites." Certainly, populists seek to show that they are on the side of the people, but the question of how they *credibly* do so remains unanswered.[4]

In Chapter 4, we saw that populist voters want a leader who will break the status quo. But here lies the problem: speech, style—these alone are weak signals of who is truly an outsider. If authenticity were just a matter of word choice, tone, or even clothing, it could be easily imitated. And in an age where images, voices, and videos can be fabricated, the ease of imitation is greater than ever. In economic terms, these are *costless signals*—gestures that carry little risk, and therefore little meaning. A signal is only perceived as "honest" if it *costs* something.

Consider an example from nature. A gazelle being stalked by a lioness would prefer to communicate a simple message: *Don't waste your time on me—go for someone slower.* If speedier gazelles had evolved, say, an extra black stripe as a visual cue, the slower gazelles would have adapted by copying the signal. Just as harmless frogs mimic the bright colors of their poisonous cousins, a slow gazelle could develop similar markings, erasing the value of the signal. But that's not how nature works. Instead, fast gazelles perform a unique display—a sudden, high, bouncing leap called a *stott* or *pronk*. It serves no immediate purpose beyond one: signaling strength. Stotting takes energy that could otherwise be saved for escape. But because only the strongest gazelles can stott the highest, it functions as a costly, effective signal to the lioness—a message that says: *You won't catch me.*

And so it is in politics. A signal is only credible if it comes at a cost. The most successful populists do not just talk like outsiders; they act in ways that impose real risks to their careers, their standing, even their personal fortunes. They burn bridges. They defy institutions in ways that establishment figures—no matter how well they imitate the rhetoric—cannot. That is the difference between a costless performance and a genuine signal. And in populist politics, just like in the wild, only the costly signals truly matter.

There is another flaw in most so-called supply-side explanations of populism: They assume that supply naturally and effortlessly adjusts to meet demand. In economic terms, they assume that the supply of populism is *perfectly elastic*. But reality is more complicated. To understand why, consider how economists think about supply and demand. Take oil. When a cold snap hits, demand for heating fuel surges, and with it, the price. When temperatures rise and demand falls, so does the price. In a perfectly elastic market, supply would adjust instantly—producers would pump more oil when demand rises and scale back when it drops, keeping prices steady. But the oil market doesn't work that way. Because bringing new oil fields online is expensive and slow, supply often lags behind shifts in demand. When demand rises faster than production can keep up, prices stay high; when demand collapses, a glut keeps prices low. This is what economists call *inelastic supply*.

The analogy to populism is to say that the supply of populism is elastic when changes in the demand for populism result in a rapid adjustment of its supply. Perhaps, if we understood populism merely in terms of speech, or even policy, we could imagine that political entrepreneurs would quickly adapt what they do to offer populist rhetoric and policy positions. But if voters need a more credible signal than mere words, adjusting the supply of populism is not so straightforward. What most made Trump and Sanders different from the American political mainstream was that each launched personalist campaigns in opposition to the political establishment and its institutions. Understood in this more fundamentally anti-institutionalist way, populism faces barriers to entry that change over time and context. It is not perfectly elastic with respect to demand—if it were, a populist candidate would surely have made inroads in 2012. Somehow the supply of populism relative to its alternatives is sticky, taking time to adjust to voter preferences. Understanding populism as a different *form* of political movement, we can gain a better appreciation for when it will be supplied.

History suggests the supply of populism adjusts, but only slowly. Anti-institutionalist parties or movements do not thrive simply because they are demanded. In Britain in the 1970s, for example, there was substantial resentment with the institutional status quo. Inflation was soaring and mass immigration from Britain's former Asian, African, and Caribbean colonies had become a major political issue. Yet no populists came to power, or even came close. This was not for the absence of a suitably charismatic leader; Enoch Powell and Tony Benn aptly fit the profile on the right and left, respectively. Yet the structure of Britain's parliament, first-past-the-post electoral system, and the way in which party elites tightly controlled the leadership selection process precluded a direct, populist route to power. Just like the United States in 2012, voters didn't choose a populist; there was a demand for it, but it wasn't supplied as an option.

Populist movements have historically been rare, not because the demand for them didn't exist, but because the political landscape was dominated by two other powerful forms of organization: programmatic and clientelist parties. Populist leaders are fundamentally different from the leaders of these more traditional political organizations. Political parties, or at least stable factions, have always been a feature of democratic and republican systems. But the highly organized, bureaucratic model that defines most Western parties today is a relatively recent development—a creation of the twentieth century. These programmatic parties are structured, hierarchical institutions. They have formal rules for candidate selection and advancement. They maintain permanent offices, professional staffs, and a level of institutionalization that allows them to endure across elections, leaders, and even ideological shifts. Their presence extends far beyond election season. They operate constituency offices. They build deep networks within society, forming alliances with labor unions, churches, business groups, and nationalist organizations. For leaders of programmatic parties, political strategy is about more than personal charisma or media spectacle. It is about organization. They rely on party infrastructure, on professional staffers and allied institutions, to engage voters, mobilize their base, and turn out support when it matters. They are not insurgents railing against the system; they *are* the system. And for much of modern democratic history, that system left little room for populists to break through.

Prior to the formation of the programmatic party, clientelist or patronage-oriented parties sought to capture government at the national and local level and use this as a base from which to distribute the rewards to their followers. "To the victor belong the spoils," claimed William Marcy, Democratic machine politician and ally of US President Andrew Jackson in the 1830s. The clientelist arrangement is an explicit quid pro quo. Politicians get votes; supporters get the goods. Although less formal than with the bureaucratic party, the relationship between voters and the leadership remains heavily mediated under clientelistic parties. In clientelist parties, leaders—or patrons—win power by buying votes through a network of urban bosses and rural elites to connect with their eventual clients, the voters. We call these middlemen brokers; we'll see that they play a critical role in the rise and fall of clientelist parties.

Why do some aspiring political leaders choose the populist path rather than the programmatic or clientelist one? If you've read one of my previous books, you already know my answer. If not, the rest of this chapter will distill more than a decade of my research on the subject. My background is in economics and that is the lens through which I approach the populist strategy. Every choice we make comes with costs—not just the money or effort spent, but the opportunities we give up by choosing one path over another. The money I spend on a gym membership is money I *can't* spend dining out. The evening I spend with friends is time I *don't* spend fixing up my house. In economics, these are called *opportunity costs*—the price of doing one thing is the benefit given up of not doing another. The same principle applies to politics. Every strategy for mobilizing voters—whether programmatic, patronage-based, or populist—comes with its own costs, risks, and potential rewards. The programmatic approach requires deep institutional networks, the clientlistic one access to the state and loyal party machines. Populism, by contrast, is the path taken by those without access to either. It is not simply a preference but, for some, a necessity—a political strategy born out of the constraints and opportunities that leaders face in their pursuit of power.

When the programmatic or clientelistic strategies of connecting with voters through intermediary structures are cost-effective, they crowd out the populist option; when instead, the populist strategy of directly mobilizing voters through mass communication is more efficient, it is the programmatic and clientelistic approaches that are driven out of the market. Even if some mixing of the populist, programmatic, and clientelistic strategies is possible, an investment of resources in one type of strategy means forgoing their use in others. In other words, politicians must choose if they're going to be populist or not. From a supply-side perspective, populism is less a question of ideas than of an implicit strategic calculation. To understand why political leaders choose one approach over another, we need to grapple with the costs involved in the clientelist, programmatic, and populists strategies, respectively.

Why is populism a cost-effective strategy?

Costs matter critically for success in any marketplace—the political one should be no different. In the political marketplace, the "buyers" are politicians while the "sellers" are voters. Political leaders, like entrepreneurs in a marketplace, want to grow their share at the lowest cost. The more cheaply a politician can win votes, the more successful he'll be. Costs come in two distinct forms, which can be best understood with an example from the world of manufacturing. The first type, the *direct* costs of production, are easiest to comprehend: These are the costs of the raw materials, component parts, and labor that go into making an end product. The second type, the *indirect* costs, or transaction costs are somewhat harder to grasp, but they turn out to be very important to understanding the trade-offs among different political strategies. In economic terms, transaction costs include the *search costs*, *bargaining costs*, and *enforcement costs* incurred as part of an exchange between buyer and seller. The time spent finding an appropriate supplier of a component, negotiating an acceptable price with them, and then ensuring that the product is delivered as ordered all incur costs on a business.[5]

Although we don't usually think of politics in these terms, the process of getting votes carries enormous costs. These costs are easiest to illustrate for clientelist parties. Often called "money politics" or simply "vote buying," this kind of strategy is a classic transactional exchange. It involves doling out cash or goods in return for votes. Providing jobs in the public sector was how the legendary Tammany Hall political machine in New York maintained its power, with a third of Democratic voters holding a Tammany job in the 1910s. Similarly, as late as the 1960s, Chicago Mayor Richard Daley's Cook County—or Crook County—organization traded votes for some 30,000 public sector jobs. On election day in contemporary Indonesia, politicians launch the "morning attack." They, or rather their local agents or brokers, distribute t-shirts, badges, and even envelopes of cash to prospective voters. These are direct costs: Cash = votes.

The buying of votes under clientelism also entails an indirect or transaction cost, which can also affect the viability of this strategy. Every time a politician seeks to buy a vote, he must incur transaction costs. Voters have to be located (search costs), an amount must be agreed upon (bargaining costs), and then, most tricky of all, a means has to be devised to ensure that the voter delivers his end of the bargain (enforcement costs). All of this requires a team, or a network of vote managers, or brokers, who mediate between the politician and the voters. The costs involved in this kind of operation vary over time and from place to place.

Clientelism tends to be especially common in new democracies, before programmatic parties of the sort described in the following paragraphs have become organized. In these early stages of democratization, clientelism is a relatively cheap option. Coming out of the oligarchy-dominated systems of the Ancien Régime, or out of the foreign-controlled systems of colonial rule, voters have modest expectations. Votes can be bought for a few dollars—or a treat of rum and sandwiches, as was common practice in George Washington's day. What's more, when the resources for these bribes can be bilked from public funds, say, by supplying voters with state ration cards, fuel subsidies, or public sector jobs, this obviously reduces the personal cost to any given politician. But this depends on incumbency, or at least on having a very good prospect of winning and being able to deliver the spoils in the future. There is thus an obvious status quo bias in clientelism, as voters have more confidence that the incumbent machine will deliver. The result is that parties like Italy's Christian Democratic (DC) Party and the Indian National Congress (INC) Party can often maintain a state of near one-party rule for decades. Yet the costs of this system tend to ratchet up over time. Even though incumbents have an advantage, this doesn't stop opposition parties from making grand promises to increase those bribes *if* they are elected. Even entrenched incumbents are thus often compelled to spend more and more to secure the votes of their clients.

What about the costs of the programmatic strategy? This approach does not involve directly buying votes. Of course, programmatic parties appeal to class, regional, and ethnic groups by tailoring fiscal and other policies to their material needs. Money spent to benefit one group cannot be spent on another. This is not, however, the main sort of cost that determines the viability of the programmatic strategy. The main costs facing programmatic parties are of the indirect, transactional type. Having policies that meet the needs of a broad range of social groups is one thing; actually getting these groups to vote for you is another.

One of the ways that programmatic parties seek to mobilize voters is by institutionalizing their relationship with voters. Some of the earliest mass parties—especially those on the left—did this by introducing formal memberships. Membership gave voters a stake in the party's operations and fostered a sense of identification with it. But getting people to *pay* for the privilege of membership was no small challenge. Why would they do it? In theory, people join parties when they believe that people like them have real influence over the party's direction. But just as an individual vote has only a marginal effect in an election, a single person joining a party hardly shifts its course. The calculus changes, however, when people join *as a group*—when ten, a hundred, or a thousand members from a shared background enter together. This is where civil society organizations come in. In the age of industrial capitalism, workers joined unions to protect their rights and improve their conditions. From there, it was a short step to incorporate these organizations—whose interests were already aligned—into formal political coalitions. This is how parties like Labour in Britain and the Social Democrats in Germany emerged: not just as political organizations, but as extensions of the professional and civic institutions that shaped people's daily lives.

People rarely joined churches, nationalist groups, or service clubs for explicitly political reasons. Their purpose was religious, cultural, or social. But that didn't mean they couldn't be drawn into politics. Just like unions, these organizations could be co-opted by political parties—turned into powerful engines of voter mobilization. Britain's Conservative Party pioneered the construction of a nationalist social association and incorporated voters through it. Other conservative and nationalist parties would draw on veterans' associations, especially between the world wars. However, for many center-right parties across Western Europe, the churches and their related associations performed this role. In part in reaction to the rise of union-aligned socialist parties, which often advocated secular education, organized traditional and conservative forces typically emerged through churches. This phenomenon was evident in both Catholic countries and regions and in Protestant ones. Christian democratic parties became the dominant force on the center-right in the second half of the twentieth century in Italy, Austria, West Germany, Belgium, the Netherlands, and Luxembourg. But the importance of the church extends well beyond these confessional parties. Even without direct advocacy of policy positions from the pulpit, churches have the very basic function of bringing people together in public spaces. As sociologist Robert Putnam has noted, churches have long accounted for the lion's share of civil society activity for most individuals in the United States. Although American churches tend to be segregated by ethnicity, they are traditionally a place where rich and poor have rubbed shoulders. Political engagement, even the social pressure to vote, is associated with church membership.

The populist strategy mitigates the costs of either having to manage the needs of rival interest groups within a complex bureaucratic organization or of having to share the spoils to keep the competing factions in a patronage party satisfied. The modern populist strategy certainly requires some hard cash; direct communication, especially through television and social media advertising, can be costly; even public rallies require a great deal of staff, incur administrative and regulatory fees, and so on. It is no coincidence that some of the best-known populists—Thaksin, Berlusconi, and of course, Trump—were already fabulously wealthy when they turned to politics. When, early in his career, Julius Caesar put on lavish public games to win over the Roman crowds, the costs were nearly crippling.

For Caesar, Trump, and Co., this was all money well spent. When all the direct and indirect costs of bureaucratic or patronage-based party building are considered, populism is a relatively low-cost political strategy. Relying on personalist political organizations and direct mass communication, populism, Nadia Urbinati writes, "is an *affordable* politics." Especially for politicians with some pre-existing name recognition—successful generals, mayors, or even celebrities—populism provides a uniquely cost-effective route to power. Ukraine's president, Volodymyr Zelinsky, was the country's most famous comedian before he ran for office in 2019; the same was true of Guatemala's Jimmy Morales, who became that country's president in 2016; Italy's Beppe Grillo, also a famous comedian, led his Five Star Movement into government in 2018. Trump's own fame had been boosted largely by his decade-long stint as the star of NBC's *The Apprentice*.[6]

Populism involves minimal expenditure on organization and avoids the costs of having to monitor agents and brokers. Critically, populists reduce the in-house costs of seeking votes by avoiding the expense of building a national rule-based party infrastructure (programmatic incorporation) or using intermediaries to buy votes on their behalf (patronage incorporation). Trump twice won the presidency, despite being substantially outspent by his rivals, Clinton and Harris, in 2016 and 2024, respectively; in fact, he spent about half of what they did for each vote received. The only other American president to pull off the feat of winning as an outsider while spending less in recent times? Jimmy Carter, another populist. Populists operate relatively lean and low-cost organizations that seek to do one thing well—the exploitation of unmediated mass communication—thereby lowering the transaction costs involved in getting a vote and ultimately, buying power.

Why have parties become inefficient?

If the programmatic, patronage, and populist strategies each have a distinctive set of costs and benefits, the obvious question is what conditions make the populist strategy more effective than its alternatives? The populist strategy will be more efficient when conditions increase the cost of winning votes through distributing patronage or incorporating voters through a programmatic structure and/or conditions that decrease the cost of direct mobilization through mass communication. Factors that affect the cost of the clientelistic strategy include the size of the franchise and the extent of political decentralization; those that affect the cost of the programmatic strategy include the prevalence of mass civil society organizations like unions and churches; factors that directly affect the cost of the populist strategy include communication costs and the share of voters that is unaffiliated with an existing party.

Although patronage-based parties like Mexico's Revolutionary Institutional Party (PRI), Japan's Liberal Democratic Party (LDP), and the Indian National Congress (INC) party have retained power for decades at a time with this strategy, for several reasons it becomes more difficult for a clientelistic party in power to keep up its end of the bargain over time. As the number of clients that have to be served in this way goes up, the clientelist strategy becomes increasingly expensive. Periodic extensions of the franchise—such as happened in nineteenth-century Britain when the wealth threshold to vote was lowered to include the middle and eventually working classes—are one way this can occur. Politicians in late nineteenth-century Britain constantly complained about the costs of electioneering, by which they meant the amount of money they had to hand over to the hundreds or thousands of voters whose support they needed.

More gradual, but over the long run just as important, population growth can have a similar effect. The growth of the US population in the early decades of the nineteenth century and the creation of several new western states meant that the electorate outstripped the ability of the nascent party machines to keep up. Populist candidate Andrew Jackson's emergence on the national scene in 1824 was the result. Of course, clientelism is still common in densely populated places like India,

Indonesia, and the Philippines. Yet the evidence shows that vote buying is much more common at lower levels than in national elections. National, especially presidential, elections have become effectively detached from the local clientelistic system, even in places where it has been endemic. Economic development exerts other pressures on clientelism. As people become better off, the size of the payment needed to buy their vote also goes up. Thus, at a certain point, as electorates become larger and richer, buying votes becomes inefficient. These long-term shifts account in part for the development of programmatic parties across the late nineteenth-century West. Bureaucratic party mobilization began to attain a relative cost advantage.

Patronage-based parties are also subject to variable, shorter-term rises in costs. In addition to paying their voters, the leaders of clientelist parties are at the mercy of their brokers. The role of these brokers means that the costs of clientelism can rise precipitously, even in the absence of any change in the size or income levels of the electorate. As I argued in my first book, *Populism and Patronage*, there is a steeply increasing cost involved in managing the patronage racket. Unlike most of its former colonial counterparts, India remained democratic for more than two decades after independence, thanks to a combination of carrots and sticks that the country's first prime minister, Jawaharlal Nehru, used to keep in check the vast new nation's regional elites. With Nehru's death in 1964, however, these regional power brokers were able to assert their control. In effect, the leaders of just a handful of India's largest states chose the next prime minister, an unobtrusive man by the name of Lal Bahadur Shastri. The elderly Shastri lived only until 1966, so the regional leadership group, ominously known as The Syndicate, installed Nehru's daughter, Indira Gandhi, in the top job. Mrs. Gandhi chafed under The Syndicate's overbearing control, but because these regional power brokers effectively controlled the huge vote blocs of the INC in their states, she seemed to have no choice but to comply. It turns out that The Syndicate made a gross miscalculation. Mrs. Gandhi decided to cut out the regional elites by "going once more direct to the people," as she put it. In 1971 she embarked on a populist strategy that split the INC and set her on a path to prorogue democracy altogether in 1975.[7]

Why is it that brokers become so powerful in these patronage-based systems? Brokers have distinct interests from their patrons, leading to what is called a principal–agent dilemma. Political leaders (the principals) want votes at the lowest cost; brokers (the agents) in contrast, aim to maximize the fee they can extract for delivering those votes. Brokers are often disloyal, ever willing to sell their votes to the highest bidder. If brokers are tightly constrained from above, patronage is often a cost-effective strategy. However, the cost of maintaining a winning coalition of factions tends to rise over time, as brokers exploit their pivotal position for personal gain. In patronage-based polities as diverse as India and Italy, Venezuela and Japan, when political brokers—the powerful middlemen who control blocs of votes—gain more autonomy (e.g., separately elected mayors and governors) and more control over the purse (e.g., fiscal decentralization), the more expensive it becomes to buy them off. This makes it much more difficult for national leaders to keep their parties together through the distribution of patronage alone. Patronage-based costs have a kind of ratchet quality, almost always tending upward unless more authoritarian measures are used to cut the brokers down to size. These rising costs create an opening for low-cost populist challengers. There is strong evidence that decentralization in patronage-based political systems is associated with higher subsequent vote shares for populist leaders.[8]

Although programmatic politics was hegemonic during the industrial era, it too has gone into decline. Evidence from across the world shows that direct party membership and the size and scope of major civil society organizations has collapsed in recent decades. As a result, the bureaucratic strategy has become more expensive. As noted earlier, these parties were built on the back of a dynamic civic society. In the United States, the period from the end of the nineteenth century through to the midway point of the twentieth was the era of the mass civic-society organization; in addition to unions there was the Rotary Club, the Knights of Labor, and other such organizations. In-person socialization in clubs and associations was entertainment. However, socioeconomic and technological shifts have considerably changed the way people organize work and leisure today.

The decline of industrial employment in the West, particularly since the 1980s, has led to a precipitous fall in union membership. The United States leads the way in the fall of its unionized workforce, but such changes are prevalent even in the social democratic heartlands of Western Europe. Putting aside for the moment the contested effect of unions on wages and employment, the collapse of unions has had profound social and political consequences. In the mid-twentieth century, unions not only fought for improved wages and conditions for their workers but also provided members with a profound sense of common identity. Unions were also community institutions, with associated social clubs and social service provision. In factory towns, workers also lived in close proximity, while by the end of the century, residential dispersion was more common. This reduced workers' regular interactions in churches, union halls, and neighborhoods. Today, even when people are employed they are more isolated. In the gig economy, they don't even have coworkers.[9]

Just as unions are in retreat across the West, church membership and religious belief itself have been in decline for decades. Non-belief is particularly high in Scandinavia, but rates of religious belief and church attendance are declining everywhere. Although the United States was long an exception to the secularization trend, it is now finally heading in the same direction. Congregation size is declining and churches across the United States, especially in more sparsely populated areas, are shutting their doors. Most of the decline here has come from mainline Protestant churches, especially in the Northeast. Yet even evangelical churches, despite the impression of a rise in cultural conservatism, are also in decline. This growing secularization has critical implications for politics. If congregations once formed an interface for politicians to meet with and engage with people, this venue has all but disappeared in much of Western Europe and is on the wane even in the United States.

Here the relationship between church membership and support for Trump is both nuanced and fascinating. Although we know Evangelicals eventually rolled in behind Trump as the Republican candidate, there is abundant evidence that the nonreligious were among Trump's core early supporters. These are people who claim religious belief but are not members of a church or who do not attend religious services. Indeed, some evidence shows that the less frequently people attend church, the more they preferred Trump. Although populists including Trump utilize religion in their appeals, they increasingly speak in terms of a civilizational religion, one that speaks more to traditional cultural values than to matters of spirituality. Populists like Trump target the unattached, including the religiously unattached.[10]

The broader decline in civil society organization may also be significant as it makes engaging with constituents more difficult and more expensive for politicians. Instead of relying on social pressure from within communities to do the work for them, they must contact and mobilize voters through other means. With the advent of television in the postwar era, as Putnam documented in *Bowling Alone*, civil society in general went into a long retreat. Again though, we shouldn't think of the problem in terms of formal organizations alone. As sociologist Émile Durkheim argued in his classic study, *Suicide*, religious membership prevented social malaise and suicide primarily by embedding people in a community. Contrary to the folk view that suicide was due to a person being overwhelmed by the burdens of life, Durkheim argued that the risk "decreases when these burdens become heavier." The problem is not having too many dependents but too few. Tragically, people today are more likely to be socially isolated, unhealthy, addicted to drugs, and generally unhappy than at any time since records began. For the first time on record, younger cohorts are even less happy than older ones, suggesting that things are likely to get worse.

It is no wonder, given this epidemic of misery, that people are resentful of the status quo. Political parties, those organizations that have presided over this social decline, become the subjects of resentment and find it increasingly difficult to attract and retain engaged members. When party attachments are no longer reinforced by personal relationships forged through unions, churches, and community networks, they weaken considerably. Detachment from civil society and unhappiness both increase the likelihood of an individual voting for a populist party.[11]

The decline of unions, churches, and other mass membership associations has meant that today's programmatic parties are increasingly reliant on using expensive election campaign structures to appeal to voters. Advertising costs, especially around election time, have reached staggering proportions. In 2016, some $6.4 billion was spent on election campaigning, a third of this total on the presidential campaign alone. By 2024, the figure rose to nearly $16 billion. Former New York mayor Michael Bloomberg reportedly spent over a billion dollars of his own money contesting the 2020 Democratic presidential primary. Campaigns also require a functioning party machine of managers and workers. Consider that in late nineteenth-century America, some 5 percent of the entire adult male population were party workers, each of whom dedicated about ten to fifteen hours to party activity each week. More recently, Obama's 2008 campaign made use of the "free" labor of over 2 million volunteers. Campaigns also require teams of pollsters, speechwriters, policy experts, and other officials. Between elections, parties must maintain constituency offices that provide a range of services to voters. This investment of time and organization is not money going directly to voters but is another indirect cost of mobilizing their support. The costs of building and maintaining these kinds of parties is hard to calculate, with much of their capital embedded in intangibles like their brand, historical political loyalties, and their functional experience as actors in government. But however it's reckoned, the programmatic strategy has become increasingly expensive.[12]

A key condition for populist success is the availability of voters who aren't already enmeshed in richer relationships with other parties. Amid the gradual erosion of clientelist bonds and the fading allure of programmatic party loyalties, a new constituency emerges—a pool of voters now *available* for populist mobilization. In the void left by the erosion of these traditional linkages, populism offers a swift, if superficial, remedy for those disenchanted with an entrenched institutional order. At its helm stands the charismatic figure fwho casts a wide net of anti-establishment appeals, searching for the message that will strike a chord in the shifting light of public sentiment. In practice, this means that populists set aside the steadfast union member and habitual church goer, and the public employee whose career is safeguarded by the party machine. Impersonal mass communication seldom shatters these enduring, often social, bonds. Yet, where voters are relatively unattached, populist mobilization can amass widespread support with modest effort. Still, mere availability alone does not guarantee success. Populists must be able to reach these voters.[13]

Why do the costs of communication matter?

One political scientist has joked that Trump won in 2016 because he was the only baby boomer who knew how social media worked. It's a statement that may exaggerate, yet it underscores an essential truth: The populist leader depends on the availability of inexpensive, pervasive means of mass communication. As detailed in Chapter 3, a charismatic leader must first capture the attention of his followers, a feat achieved through the varied channels of public oratory, television advertising, or the immediacy of social media. The lower the cost of these channels, the more efficient and widespread the populist strategy becomes. In times past—consider Ancient Greece, when the sole method of public engagement was to address a gathering of all adult males in the Assembly or agora—the options were limited. Today, a diverse array of direct communication tools is at hand. Public speaking and mass rallies still hold a power all their own, for nothing quite replicates the immediacy of a physical encounter, as the enduring appeal of live music attests. When open forums were the only avenue available, populism was confined to the city-state, where sufficiently large assemblies could be mustered. With the gradual expansion of democratic states, however, populists have had to turn to a suite of new technologies—the printing press, the postal system, the road, and later the rail network—to reach an ever-growing audience.

Radio and television eventually emerged as formidable new instruments in the populist's arsenal. Radio, in particular, ushered in a revolutionary possibility: A politician could now deliver a single speech that resonated not with thousands, but with millions. Initially, though, politicians found radio a problematic medium. The prepared monologues that dominated early forms of political communication were boring. In 1924, both John W. Davis (Democrat) and Calvin Coolidge (Republican) bought advertising time for their speeches, with Coolidge spending about three times the amount on advertising that Davis did. Although Coolidge won, there's no evidence that radio advertising had any impact. Attempts to replay public speeches revealed an inherent flaw: The projection and vitality of a live speaker simply did not translate over the airwaves. Much like the elusive "weave" of Trump—whose intricate gestures defy understanding outside their proper context—the true power of oratory often resides in its live performance, where presence matters above all.

But radio would eventually find more adept users. Being a natural speaker certainly helped. FDR's "fireside chats" in 1933 and 1934 have acquired a legendary status. His insight was to speak to people, not like they were in an audience, but as if they were next to him, engaged in a one-on-one conversation, *present*. People could imagine, for the first time, being invited to share an intimate discussion with the president. Yet fear and hate translated just as well over the airwaves as warmth and hope. FDR's contemporary, Father Charles Coughlin, shot to national celebrity with a radio show that reached tens of millions. Coughlin, the "Radio Priest," fused Catholic social rhetoric with fascist flirtations and overt antisemitism, serving as the rhetorical hinge between the nativist revival of the 1920s Ku Klux Klan and the isolationist surge of the late 1930s that coalesced around Charles Lindbergh's America First Committee.

Radio, and curiously enough, low-tech AM radio, remains an important means of political communication. Local radio is often significant, but many of the most popular shows, not least in the United States, are syndicated national programs. This sort of political radio is, above all, entertainment. And it gives those hosts with a natural charisma of their own, a combination of humor and outrage, a key role as gatekeepers. Rush Limbaugh came to prominence in the 1990s first and foremost as an entertaining shock jock, closer to the equally politically incorrect and irreverent Howard Stern than to the pundits and writers of earlier generations like Walter Lippman. Limbaugh was not a kingmaker exactly, but he could wield enormous influence by controlling a vital channel of communication between aspiring political hopefuls and a core of influenceable voters. Glenn Beck, Sean Hannity, Mark Levin, and others do the same kind of thing. The way these shows allow a politician to sit in on an intimate conversation, to be a passenger in millions of cars, a guest in millions of kitchens, is a major development in the field of political communication. The problem for the politician is that radio intermediaries like Limbaugh,

Hannity and others become mediators with the power to make or break a career. This is not the kind of direct access to voters that populists crave.[14]

Television's political effects have been even better documented than those of radio. And its gatekeeping function is even more evident. In the case of television too, its impact has been less to persuade the uninformed with facts and formulas than to develop an image, or to use a marketing term, to increase brand awareness. The simple facts are that people are more likely to buy a product they've heard of, and they are much more likely to vote for a candidate whose name they know. Even Nixon, unnatural as he was on the screen, knew how much television mattered in creating an image. His defeat to the irritatingly handsome John F. Kennedy had taught him that. As much as a policy wonk as Nixon was, he told his campaign manager and later chief of staff, Bob Haldeman, "Speech is obsolete as a means of communication." Image, in other words, matters more than substance. And in terms of developing and promoting a brand, television remains king.

Until Trump came along, few American politicians had greater appreciation for the power of television than Newt Gingrich, the former Republican Speaker of the House. He realized early that a couple of minutes on the evening news was worth more than many hours of paid advertisements. Not only was this coverage free, but it came with the imprimatur of journalistic endorsement. This meant that controversy was as important as substance. "Conflict equals exposure equals power," Gingrich would say. The populist multi-term Alabama governor, George Wallace, also focused on major local media appearances rather than the more typical Southern press-the-flesh retail politics. According to one biographer, his strategy was to get "more exposure in more places in less time for less money by making one or two high-profile public speeches in each town to provide a news 'peg,' and then make as many appearances as possible on radio and television interview programs and call-in shows" to magnify the impact of the initial appearance. These were lessons Trump mastered intuitively.[15]

The Trump we saw on *The Apprentice* was no more a reality than one of the characters in the Emmy-award-winning drama, *Succession*. Trump, in reality, is not that decisive. Despite his "You're fired!" catchphrase on the show, Trump doesn't like face-to-face confrontations. But millions of viewers developed an impression of Trump as a man who could make hard decisions, good decisions; a man who was successful and powerful; and, no less important in the present age of celebrity worship, a man who was rich and famous.

Venezuela's Hugo Chávez similarly mastered the medium of television to create his brand. As president he launched a live television weekly program called *Hello President* that ran for hours at a time. Chávez televised government proceedings, inviting regular Venezuelans to be flies on the wall in the process of policymaking. He would take phone calls from citizens, showing off his natural capacity to connect, listen, and be present. Chávez sometimes took major policy decisions on air, including ordering troops to the border in a conflict with neighboring Colombia. In assuming control over Venezuela's national oil company, PDVSA, in 2001, Chávez fired its executives on air. In a real-life version of *The Apprentice*, Chávez would call out a name, and then say: "Thank you very much. You, sir, are dismissed!" For effect, he'd then blow a referee's whistle.[16]

Political leaders can communicate directly with voters through traditional mass media like radio and television, whether via paid advertisements, or better yet, unearned media (e.g., news coverage, interviews), but they also can now message their supporters directly at any time through a wide range of social media. As with the bifurcated television landscape, the main goal of internet advertising is not to convince or persuade new voters but to turn out those who are already sympathetic. The overlapping digital world reinforces this process. As Jennifer Stromer-Galley shows in her book,

Presidential Campaigning in the Internet Age, where the internet is particularly effective is as an advertisement delivery system.

Google, Facebook, and Amazon collect inordinate amounts of data on their users. What websites you look at. How long you look at them. What things and groups you like. What you buy. These data can be packaged and paired with voting records (that you voted, not how you voted), tax records, credit history, supermarket loyalty cards, and multiple other databases. Voter profiles can be developed with extraordinary precision. Single mothers, minority students, veterans. Google and Facebook can target these groups specifically with tailor-made ads. If you're a Republican strategist and want to get the working class out to vote, craft a message about how Hillary is in bed with corporate cronies and media elites. If you're working for Biden and want to maximize the Latino vote, stoke fears of repression by a nativist like Trump.

The importance of social media cannot be overstated. It's no surprise that one of the few politicians Trump himself has a grudging respect for on the Democratic side is progressive icon Alexandria Ocasio-Cortez. A millennial at ease with social media, AOC has something, as Trump puts it. Social media is the ideal means of communication for a populist, given its low barriers to entry. Tools from Facebook to Twitter to TikTok allow political leaders to speak instantly and directly with millions of potential supporters at almost no cost. There is even statistical evidence that the proliferation of 3G coverage—and with it access to these applications—increased the vote share of populists.[17]

The advent of YouTube seems to have been particularly significant, bridging the visual impact of television with the immediacy and intimacy of social media. Britain's Nigel Farage was one of the first to benefit from YouTube as a means of generating publicity. While speeches in the European Parliament were systematically ignored in the mainstream media, Farage would upload short monologues that often went viral. In 2010, Farage greeted the selection of Belgian prime minister Herman Van Rompuy as the inaugural president of the European Council with disdain: "You have the charisma of a damp rag, and the appearance of a low-grade bank clerk. . . . Who are you? I've never heard of you. . . . Who voted for you? . . . We don't know you; we don't want you, and the sooner you're put out to grass the better." Unlike the typical European Parliament speech, this one has been viewed millions of times.[18]

Not all of these services are cheap. Facebook charges an arm and a leg for its highly targeted advertisements and content placement. The Trump 2016 campaign demonstrated, however, that in a world of scarce resources, dollars could still be well spent here. In 2016, Trump devoted more than half his budget to social media. Through its American offshoot, Strategic Communications Laboratories (SCL), Cambridge Analytica alone ran over 5,000 individual ad campaigns with 10,000 modified iterations of each ad. Coupling this with the free distribution of Twitter, the celebrity candidate Trump had an unprecedentedly inexpensive megaphone to communicate with the masses. It is not mere coincidence that in the years prior to Trump's candidacy, Twitter usage in the United States exploded. While just one in three members of Congress had Twitter accounts in 2011, just two years later, every single representative had one. Trump's following grew from just 300,000 in 2011 to 4.3 million by the time he launched his candidacy in 2015.

The impact went well beyond his immediate followers, as his most outrageous Tweets were quickly repeated through mainstream media channels. Twitter is hardly a medium for a detailed policy debate. It is tailored to the soundbite, the slogan, the quip, the insult—precisely Trump's forte. With a massive, free assist from Russian hackers who stole terabytes of emails and other private data from the Democratic National Committee, Trump relentlessly propagated stories of alleged Clinton corruption. In the October before the election, he tweeted 164 times about the WikiLeaks data dumps. This was cheap, dirty, and highly effective campaigning. Trump himself said that Facebook and Twitter "helped him win." Of course, social media favors those with existing name recognition, as they have larger networks and followers to begin with, so its use as a mobilization strategy may not be available to everyone.[19]

In 2024, Trump proved to be the great innovator yet again. This time around, Trump was forced to work outside a mainstream media rejected him following his incendiary role in the Capitol Riot of January 6, 2021. He turned to the world of celebrity podcasts and the livestreaming channel, Twitch. Trump made some fourteen appearances on shows such as *The Joe Rogan Experience*, Logan Paul's *Impaulsive*, and Theo Von's *This Past Weekend*. These videos racked up an astonishing 68 million views. These appearances targeted a particular demographic where Trump had to, and did, win big: young men. Although often among Trump's biggest supporters, this group is notorious for failing to turn out on election day. Trump shifted this dynamic, getting previous non-voters to come and support him. Exactly, as we have seen, the strategy of the populist leader.[20]

However, even though direct communication can be effective, its results are conditional. A populist candidate, like any other, could win the vote of any given citizen; but for most voters, choosing a political leader is not like choosing takeout. While we might order Thai food one week and pizza the next, our political choices are not so changeable. Politics is more like a team sport, if not a religion, than it is an ethnic cuisine. Typically, once we develop a political affiliation, something that usually happens during our early twenties, we remain loyal to it. Simply seeing a tweet or hearing an interview is not going to be enough to persuade a partisan to switch sides. When voters are attached to a party through a dense web of social and professional ties, they are unlikely to switch loyalties in response to mass communication alone. Mere speech simply doesn't move the needle.

Thus, we should be skeptical of arguments that rely too heavily on the power of communication to shift votes. It is only when voters are detached from political ties that this kind of verbal persuasion comes into play. The decline in party membership has aided populists enormously. Populism just wasn't a viable strategy in the party heyday of the 1960s. Even wildly popular demagogues like George Wallace and Enoch Powell couldn't make political inroads in the face of entrenched party networks in the United States and Britain, respectively. In other places, where democracy is newer, political parties are less well established. In countries where parties are weak, loyalties are less ingrained. In these situations, more voters are available for the quick and direct populist mode of mobilization. In short, to explain populist success, we have to look beyond communication to understand the deeper social and economic sources of political attachment.

How do supply and demand interact?

The rise of populism is, at its core, a matter of supply and demand. On one side, there is the disenchanted voter—alienated from institutions, distrustful of elites, searching, however vaguely, for an alternative. There must be a *demand* for populism, a demand born out of economic frustration, declining social status, a sense that the system—both political and economic—no longer works for *people like us*. But populism is not inevitable. For it to take hold, discontent alone is not enough. There must also be a supply, the populist outsider—the charismatic figure who positions himself against the entrenched political class in every sense. This leader can harness the resentment, channel the frustrations, articulate the grievances in a way that feels authentic, urgent, undeniable. Critically, for this leader's message of change to cut through, there must be an opening—a failure of the political mainstream to contain or absorb the challenge. Where established parties succeed in maintaining a *cordon sanitaire* around the extremes, walling off the insurgents, keeping the challengers at bay, populism struggles to break through. Discontent simmers, but with no viable outlet, it remains politically inert.

As we have seen in this chapter, populism is not a constant. It is not a fixed feature of political life. It rises and falls with the political context, shaped by the ability of mainstream institutions to either accommodate or suppress it. Populism arises when the political mainstream fractures, when faith in existing structures erodes. Sometimes, this collapse is sudden and dramatic. Italy's First Republic crumbled in the early 1990s amid corruption scandals and economic turmoil, clearing the way for the rise of new populist challengers. Elsewhere, the process is slower, more insidious. In the Netherlands and Sweden, once-dominant political parties, some tracing their origins to the nineteenth century, have watched their voter bases wither, creating openings for insurgent movements. In the United States and Britain, the party names remain unchanged, but the institutions themselves have been hollowed out, their internal structures weakened. The old mass-membership parties—anchored by unions, churches, and civic organizations—have withered, leaving parties vulnerable to capture from within. In systems where third-party breakthroughs are rare, populists do not form their own parties; they take over existing ones. Trump. Johnson. Corbyn.

Why do voters turn to these outsiders? As we saw in Chapter 4, many feel the system is rigged against them. In the West, the losers from the global economy, the less educated, the less networked, struggle to get ahead while others—sometimes the wealthy, sometimes those they see as undeserving—appear to reap the rewards. Their resentment is not simply directed at individuals but at the system itself. When mainstream parties retain a strong grip on power, these voters have few options. But when social ties fray—when unions shrink, church pews empty, civic life disintegrates—voters become unmoored, adrift, open to something new. In the developing world, where party loyalty has historically been transactional, rising living standards have made old systems of clientelism too costly to sustain. Here, too, mainstream parties lose their hold, their promises dismissed as hollow. Voters become disgusted with rampant corruption, which now seems to serve only the already connected and wealthy.

Yet despite these sources of discontent, resentment often remains latent. Populist voters, in the beginning, do not engage. They withdraw. Their resentment festers. They may hear mainstream politicians speak of helping "the people," but they do not believe them. The credibility of the political class is gone. A small number will cast protest votes, but most will simply stay home. Abstention rises. Then, a leader appears. A leader who understands how to use the dominant media of the era to speak to these voters. The charismatic leader's ability to connect with voters who share this sense of threat, and to project himself as the potential savior of that group, is key to the populist dynamic. Relying primarily on mass communication rather than a party machinery, the charismatic leader signals his distance from the status quo.

At first, most of these detached voters remain indifferent. But a few listen. A few are drawn in, persuaded by the signals of leadership ability that charisma conveys: stature, confidence, success. They become the first devotees of the cult. The very growth of the movement provides evidence of the leader's ability. Divine providence, perhaps. The rallies grow louder. The media attacks intensify. The fights with the political establishment become part of the spectacle, reinforcing the leader's credibility as an outsider, as the man who just might be willing to tear it all down.

Empirical research on the role of charisma in the political arena remains thin, in part because it is so difficult to measure. But in one recent study on Rodrigo Duterte in the Philippines, we found a plausible way to capture it. Instead of deciding ourselves whether Duterte was considered charismatic, we asked Filipinos to describe then-president Duterte in their own words. We then let ordinary people—not academics, not students—determine whether Duterte was being described as a charismatic leader or not. We told our amateur coders: A charismatic leader is seen as extraordinary, heroic, even infallible, while a regular leader is judged by competence, policies, achievements. This is not the only way to measure charisma, but its main virtue is that it measures how people feel about a leader rather than scholars' perceptions of a leader's personality traits. The consensus among our coders was remarkable, and the results clear. Those who saw Duterte as charismatic were far more likely to support him—and his policies—than those who saw him as merely competent or effective.[21]

Critically, the demand here is not, at its core, for authoritarianism. It has become common to argue that populism is driven by people with an authoritarian personality who are displaced by the stresses of modern, capitalist society and find emotional satisfaction by subordinating themselves to a strong leader. Even if this theory makes some sense, the evidence is mixed. Some studies have found positive correlations between support for Trump in 2016 and measures of authoritarianism; other research finds no such relationship. Part of the issue is that these studies employ different measures of authoritarianism. Studies that use more distant measures of authoritarianism related to child rearing find no relationship, while those that use something more proximate like right-wing authoritarianism, social dominance orientation, and explicit preferences for dictatorship do find one. Here we have the problem of conflating authoritarianism with attitudes toward other groups.[22]

The same confusion appears in studies outside the United States, where attitudes toward other groups—ethnocentrism—are conflated with the wish to be controlled by a strong leader. In the Philippines, only a minority of Duterte's supporters showed any support for reinstituting the "martial law" regime of the Ferdinand Marcos era. Most simply saw Duterte as a strong leader who would take on the status quo, but one who was democratically elected nonetheless. My intuition is that people do not seek domination, submission, the kind of masochistic subordination that Freud and his disciples once imagined. What they seek is something older, something hard-wired: a leader. Someone who stands above the rest—not for himself, but for them. A leader willing to break the system. And if that leader is a bully? Then he is *their* bully.

Notes

1. Obama remarks February 4, 2009, https://obamawhitehouse.archives.gov/realitycheck/the-press-office/remarks-president-barack-obama-executive-compensation-with-secretary-geithner.
2. "the problem is," Slavoj Žižek, "Occupy Wall Street: The Wake Up Call," *ABC News*, October 11, 2011, https://www.abc.net.au/news/2011-10-11/zizek-occupy-wall-street-the-wake-up-call/3496710; More generally on this point, see David Leonhardt, "A New Centrism Is Rising in Washington," *New York Times*, May 19, 2024, https://www.nytimes.com/2024/05/19/briefing/centrism-washington-neopopulism.html.
3. J. J. Dyck, S. Pearson-Merkowitz, and M. Coates, "Primary Distrust: Political Distrust and Support for the Insurgent Candidacies of Donald Trump and Bernie Sanders in the 2016 Primary," *PS: Political Science & Politics* 51, no. 2 (2018): 351–357, doi:10.1017/S1049096517002505.
4. Michèle Lamont, Bo Yun Park, and Elena Ayala-Hurtado, "Trump's Electoral Speeches and His Appeal to the American White Working Class," *British Journal of Sociology* 68 (2017): S153–S180. "I always hear about the elite," quoted in Michael Sandel, *The Tyranny of Merit: What's Become of the Common Good* (Penguin, 2021), 83.
5. R. H. Coase, "The Nature of the Firm," *Economica* 4, no. 16 (1937): 386–405. On search, bargaining, and enforcement costs, see Carl J. Dahlman, "The Problem of Externality," *Journal of Law and Economics* 22, no. 1 (1979): 141–162.
6. "affordable politics," Nadia Urbinati, *Me the People: How Populism Transforms Democracy* (Harvard University Press, 2019), 178.
7. "going once more," in Paul D. Kenny, *Populism and Patronage: Why Populists Win Elections, in India, Asia, and Beyond* (Oxford, 2017), 1.

8. On some of the downsides of patronage as an election strategy, see Carolyn M. Warner, "Political Parties and the Opportunity Costs of Patronage," *Party Politics* 3, no. 4 (1997): 533–548.
9. Lainey Newman and Theda Skocpol, *Rust Belt Union Blues: Why Working-Class Voters Are Turning Away from the Democratic Party* (Columbia University Press, 2023).
10. For evidence that non-practicing Christians tend to support Trump in higher numbers, see Tobias Cremer, *The Godless Crusade* (Cambridge University Press, 2023); for a contrary view, see Gregory A. Smith, "5 Facts about Religion and Americans' Views of Donald Trump," *Pew Research Center*, March 15, 2024, https://www.pewresearch.org/short-reads/2024/03/15/5-facts-about-religion-and-americans-views-of-donald-trump/.
11. Émile Durkheim, *On Suicide*, trans. Robin Buss (Penguin, 2006), 214; World Happiness Report, 2019, chapter 3, "Happiness and Voting Behavior," https://worldhappiness.report/ed/2019/happiness-and-voting-behavior/; Robert Booth, "Young People Becoming Less Happy Than Older Generations, Research Shows," *The Guardian*, March 20, 2024, https://www.theguardian.com/society/2024/mar/20/young-people-becoming-less-happy-than-older-generations-research-shows; Adam Nowakowski, "Do Unhappy Citizens Vote for Populism?" *European Journal of Political Economy* 68 (June 1921): 101985, https://doi.org/ 10.1016/j.ejpoleco.2020.101985. https://www.sciencedirect.com/science/article/pii/S0176268020301336; Annika Lindholm, Georg Lutz, and Eva G. T. Green, "Life Dissatisfaction and the Right-Wing Populist Vote: Evidence from the European Social Survey," *American Behavioral Scientist* (2024): 00027642241240334; Tito Boeri, Prachi Mishra, Chris Papageorgiou, and Antonio Spilimbergo, "Populism and Civil Society," IMF Working Paper WP/18/245, November 2018, https://www.imf.org/-/media/Files/Publications/WP/2018/wp18245.ashx.;
12. For the 2016 election: "Cost of Election," OpenSecrets.org, https://www.opensecrets.org/overview/cost.php; for Bloomberg, see Jason Lange, "Bloomberg Bows Out of Presidential Contest but His Money Will Stay," *Reuters*, March 5, 2020, https://www.reuters.com/article/us-usa-election-bloomberg/bloomberg-bows-out-of-presidential-contest-but-his-money-will-stay-idUSKBN20R2AJ;

13. On the importance of voter "availability" in explaining populist support, see esp. Kurt Weyland, "Clarifying a Contested Concept: Populism in the Study of Latin American Politics," *Comparative Politics* 34, no. 1 (2001): 1–22; Michele F. Margolis, "Who Wants to Make America Great Again? Understanding Evangelical Support for Donald Trump," *Politics and Religion* 13, no. 1 (2020): 89–118, https://doi.org/10.1017/S1755048319000208; Jessica Martínez and Gregory A. Smith, "Trump Has Benefited from Evangelicals' Support, but He's Not the First Choice of the Most Committed," *Pew Research Center*, April 4, 2016, https://www.pewresearch.org/short-reads/2016/04/04/trump-has-benefited-from-evangelicals-support-but-hes-not-the-first-choice-of-the-most-committed/; David E. Campbell, Geoffrey C. Layman, and John C. Green, *Secular Surge: A New Fault Line in American Politics* (Cambridge University Press, 2020), ch. 9; Cremer, *The Godless Crusade*.
14. On conservative talk radio, Brian Rosenwald, *Talk Radio's America: How an Industry Took over a Political Party That Took over the United States* (Harvard University Press, 2019).
15. "Conflict equals exposure equals power," in Julian E. Zelizer, *Burning Down the House: Newt Gingrich, the Fall of a Speaker, and the Rise of the New Republican Party* (Penguin Press, 2020), 67. "more exposure in more places," Stephen Lesher, *George Wallace: American Populist* (Perseus Publishing, 1994), 267.
16. "Thank you very much," quoted in Roy Carroll, *Comandante: Hugo Chávez's Venezuela* (Penguin, 2013), 73.
17. Ekaterina Zhuravskaya, Maria Petrova, and Ruben Enikolopov, "Political Effects of the Internet and Social Media," *Annual Review of Economics* 12, no. 1 (2020): 415–438.
18. Farage's speech is available at: https://www.youtube.com/watch?v=dranqFntNgo.
19. "helped him win," Rich McCormick, "Donald Trump Says Facebook and Twitter 'Helped Him Win,'" *The Verge*, November 14, 2016, http://www.theverge.com/2016/11/13/13619148/trump-facebook-twitter-helped-win; Jennifer Stromer-Galley, *Presidential Campaigning in the Internet Age*, 2nd ed. (Oxford University Press, 2019); Joshua D. Potter and Johanna L. Dunaway, "Reinforcing or Breaking Party Systems? Internet Communication Technologies and Party Competition in Comparative Context," *Political Communication* 33, no. 3 (2016): 392–413.

20. Maxwell Model, "US Election Shows How Podcasts Are Shaping Politics—and What the Risks Are," *The Conversation*, November 20, 2024, https://theconversation.com/us-election-shows-how-podcasts-are-shaping-politics-and-what-the-risks-are-243325.
21. Paul D. Kenny and Ronald Holmes, "A New Penal Populism? Rodrigo Duterte, Public Opinion, and the War on Drugs in the Philippines." *Journal of East Asian Studies* 20, no. 2 (2020): 187–205.
22. For supportive evidence, see Matthew C. MacWilliams, "Who Decides When the Party Doesn't? Authoritarian Voters and the Rise of Donald Trump," *PS: Political Science and Politics* 49, no. 4 (2016): 716–721, http://www.jstor.org/stable/26359708; J. Womick, T. Rothmund, F. Azevedo, L. A. King, and J. T. Jost, "Group-Based Dominance and Authoritarian Aggression Predict Support for Donald Trump in the 2016 U.S. Presidential Election," *Social Psychological and Personality Science* 10, no. 5 (2019): 643–652, https://doi.org/10.1177/1948550618778290; S. Feldman, "Authoritarianism, Education, and Support for Right-Wing Populism," in *The Psychology of Populism* (New York, Routledge: 2021), 348–364; S. Talaifar, M. Stuetzer, P. J. Rentfrow, J. Potter, and S. D. Gosling, "Fear and Deprivation in Trump's America: A Regional Analysis of Voting Behavior in the 2016 and 2020 U.S. Presidential Elections," *Personality Science* 3 (2022): 1–57, https://doi.org/10.5964/ps.7447; Karen Stenner and Jonathan Haidt, "Authoritarianism Is Not a Momentary Madness, but an Eternal Dynamic within Liberal Democracies," in Cass R. Sunstein, ed., *Can It Happen Here? Authoritarianism in America* (Harper Collins, 2018); John W. Dean and Bob Altemeyer, *Authoritarian Nightmare: Trump and His Followers* (Melville House, 2020); Christopher M. Federico and Agnieszka Golec De Zavala, "Collective Narcissism and the 2016 US Presidential Vote," *Public Opinion Quarterly* 82, no. 1 (2018): 110–121; J. Knuckey and K. Hassan, "Authoritarianism and Support for Trump in the 2016 Presidential Election," *Social Science Journal* 59, no. 1 (2020): 47–60, https://doi.org/10.1016/j.soscij.2019.06.008; for the alternative view, see John R. Hibbing, *The Securitarian Personality: What Really Motivates Trump's Base and Why It Matters for the Post-Trump Era* (Oxford University Press, 2020); J. Eric Oliver and Wendy M. Rahn, "Rise of the Trumpenvolk: Populism in the 2016 Election," *ANNALS of the American Academy of Political and Social Science* 667, no. 1 (2016): 189–206; T. Wood, "Racism

Motivated Trump Voters More Than Authoritarianism," April 17, 2017, Retrieved from http://www.washingtonpost.com/news/monkey-cage/wp/2017/04/17/racism-motivated-trump-voters-more-than-authoritarianism-or-income-inequality/?utm_term=.2efc69ae6622. On the effect of measurement choice, see David Norman Smith, "Authoritarianism Reimagined: The Riddle of Trump's Base," *Sociological Quarterly* 60, no. 2 (2019): 210–223. Outside of Europe, see Armin Schäfer, "Cultural Backlash? How (Not) to Explain the Rise of Authoritarian Populism," *British Journal of Political Science* 52, no. 4 (2022): 1–17.

6

POPULISM AND DEMOCRACY

What do populist governments do?

When monetary policy works—when prices, wages, and interest rates remain stable—it is all but invisible. It provokes little debate, little urgency. But when it fails, it dominates everything. Hyperinflation erodes savings, deflation crushes wages, both shaking the foundations of economic life. In extreme cases, the mismanagement of monetary policy unravels the social order. Today, central banks control monetary stability, insulated from political pressure. But this is new. For most of history, money itself was a political battleground. Before central banks gained independence—before the Federal Reserve was created in 1913—monetary policy was fought over in Congress, on campaign trails, by populists eager to shape it to their ends.

After the economic chaos of the Napoleonic Wars—and after the US government let the First Bank of the United States expire—the country's financial system seemed to find stability with the creation of the Second Bank in 1816. At first, it worked. The Bank restored much needed confidence to the market. In fact, so optimistic were investors that the return of easy credit soon led to a speculative land boom, especially in the new South and the vast midwestern region that had only recently been acquired with Jefferson's 1803 purchase of the Louisiana territory from France. Then, in 1819, as the Bank sought to curb risk by restricting the circulation of currency, the bubble burst. For two long years, farmers—big and small—drowned in debt. They blamed the eastern moneymen. One of those who lost heavily was a man who never forgot it, a man who would ride that resentment all the way to the White House: Andrew Jackson.

Jackson cast himself as an outsider, a champion of the people against the Virginian and New England elite that had long ruled American politics. In 1828, he mobilized a rapidly expanding electorate to win the presidency. When the opportunity for Jackson to take revenge on the Bank arose, he grabbed it with both hands. The Second Bank's charter was up for renewal in 1836, which would give Jackson veto power over the Bank if he could secure re-election. Sensing the threat, the Bank's president, Nicholas Biddle, forced the issue early, pushing for recharter in 1832—turning that year's election into a referendum on the Bank itself. Then, in an effort to demonstrate its power and undermine Jackson, the Bank cut lending, triggering a minor recession. Jackson saw it as a fight to the death. As he put it to his vice president, Martin Van Buren, "The Bank is trying to kill me, Sir, but I shall kill it!"

On July 20, 1832, Jackson vetoed the recharter. In his message to the Senate, he denounced "the rich and powerful" who "too often bend the acts of government to their selfish purposes." He did not promise equality of wealth—nor did he believe in it. But under the law, he declared, "every man is equally entitled to protection" and none to "exclusive privileges" that serve only "to make the rich richer and the potent more powerful." The political and economic establishment—even many in his own party—opposed him. But the people backed him. That November, they delivered Jackson a resounding victory, securing his second term and sealing the fate of the Bank.[1]

To date, far more attention has been paid to the effect that populists in power have on the institutions of democracy themselves than on the more mundane aspects of forming and executing public policy. The effects of populism on democracy are important—Jackson, for instance, was not someone to let something like a Supreme Court ruling get in his way—and we'll examine them in detail in the next chapter. But for many citizens, the mechanics of democracy matter less than the policies that directly affect their lives. This is why the appeals of populists' opponents to "save democracy" so often fall flat. We need to understand what populists do with the power they win at the ballot box.

Jackson's Bank War matters less for what it reveals about monetary policy than for what it tells us about the link between populist policymaking and democracy. First, while it's easy to view policies like Jackson's war on the Bank as personal crusades, there is growing evidence that populists act as they do not just out of conviction but because they are highly responsive to public opinion. Jackson had no opinion polls to guide him, but as a man of modest means in his youth, he understood instinctively that many Americans shared his resentment of the Bank's monopoly on financial power. The evidence suggests he was right. Far from being autocrats who impose their will unchecked, populists may be even more dependent on public approval than traditional party leaders with institutional backing.

Second, populist policy is distinctly heterodox—it defies accepted norms. Attempts to find a consistent ideological direction in populism have often failed. Some populists push policy left, others right. What remains constant, however, is their opposition to the status quo. Jackson's Bank War was opposed by nearly every establishment figure of his time. But that was the point. Populists rise to power because their supporters are dissatisfied—resentful of the way things are, whether in trade, immigration, or finance. And once in office, they often deliver on their promise to upend the system, dismantling the agreements and institutions that defined their predecessors' rule.

Third, Jackson's assault on the Second Bank reveals another defining trait of populist governance: a willingness to break legal and ethical norms to force the institutional change their supporters demand. Few progressive readers will mourn the wealthy shareholders whose property rights Jackson trampled in the Bank War. But Jackson's disregard for established rules went far beyond monetary policy. In open defiance of Supreme Court rulings, he promised his base—and delivered—the ethnic cleansing of Native tribes from east of the Mississippi. Populists do what their supporters want, even when it means violating the law. Whether overriding domestic statutes on commerce or defying international agreements on war and human rights, they act first and justify later—if at all.

The institutional protections that safeguard minority political rights—press freedom, judicial independence—are essential to democracy, even in its minimalist sense. As I'll argue in Chapter 7, when leaders weaken these protections enough, they are no longer populists but dictators. But what about rights that don't directly affect free and fair elections? The picture becomes less clear. Do women's reproductive rights fall under the same democratic protections? Do transgender individuals have a right to access public spaces that don't align with their sex at birth? Do smokers, drinkers, and opioid users have a right to self-destruction—especially when the cost falls on taxpayers? Do criminals and terrorists have an inviolable right to due process? Do non-citizens have a right to equal treatment under the law?

These are the fault lines where populism collides with liberal democracy, where the definition of rights—and who deserves them—is fiercely contested. These are not just legal questions but moral and political dilemmas, ones on which reasonable people will disagree. Democratic governments will draw these lines differently, at different times, without undermining their legitimacy—so long as they can still be voted out of office. In theory, these decisions reflect both domestic and international norms as well as public opinion. But part of the problem—part of what is fueling resentment of the status quo—is the growing disconnect between contemporary institutions and the views of the average voter. Populist policies may clash with established institutions, but that does not mean they contradict democracy itself. In many cases, they embody it.

All populists rail against the institutional status quo, but the content of that status quo can vary dramatically. As a result, there is no coherent set of populist policies. One of the things we'll see in this chapter is that populist policy is diverse. One area where populists often seem to have a consistent policy is the economy. In the first section of this chapter, I challenge this idea, finding little by way of consistent populist economics.

A similar pattern emerges in international economic policy. While populists may differ on domestic issues, they are often seen as champions of economic nationalism—populism, in this view, stands in direct opposition to globalism. But populism is not inherently anti-globalist. In eras when the institutional status quo was protectionist, populists were the free-trade rebels. Their allegiance is not to a fixed economic ideology but to opposition itself—wherever the establishment stands, they take the other side. Although research on the relationships between populism and other aspects of international relations are less well established, there is reason to expect that populist policy follows a distinctly unorthodox pattern in this domain too.

I next examine several other policy issues said to be distinctive to populist government. Most of these revolve around the treatment of minorities, such as immigrants and criminals. Central to the popular turn toward a charismatic leader is an intensification of group solidarity. While that group can be defined in class terms, more often, it is an identity grounded in ethnicity, language, or religion.

On average, populists appear more willing and able to override institutional protections for the rights of minorities—however defined—than conventional democratic leaders. This can take the form of the exclusion of certain groups from the polity. Anti-immigration sentiment has been on a steady rise in the West in recent decades with populists like Orbán and Farage spectacularly delivering. For the most part the goal of populists has been to keep immigrants out, but for some, like Trump, it has been to expel those already present.

Others target not ethnic or national outsiders, but so-called social deviants—drug addicts, sexual minorities, criminals. Penal populists have found deep wells of support in pursuing harsh law and order policies. In the Philippines, Rodrigo Duterte waged a brutal drug war. In El Salvador, Nayib Bukele cracked down on gangs with mass arrests and military force. Both maintained approval ratings above 80 percent. Still others, like Italy's Giorgia Meloni and Argentina's Javier Milei, have followed their base in challenging institutional norms on women's reproductive rights and gender nonconformity. Whether through immigration, crime, or culture, the populist impulse is the same: Redefine who belongs—and who does not.

In the final section of this chapter, I examine what these patterns reveal about the relationship between populism and democracy. Populists are pragmatists, not ideologues. Beyond their desire to stay in power, they are programmatically flexible—even on major issues. Their policies vary because public priorities shift across time and place. In this sense, populist policymaking aligns with democracy. If anything, their ability—and willingness—to deliver what mainstream parties will not exposes the failures of the existing democratic order. Populists do not create dissatisfaction with institutions; they exploit it. And in doing so, they reveal its depth.

Yet, as sociologist Michael Mann has argued, democracy has a "dark side"—one in which even ethnic cleansing can be popular. Populists, by playing on group identity, make the exclusion or persecution of minorities more likely. Andrew Jackson could only so brazenly violate the rights of Native Americans because his social Darwinist beliefs were not his alone—they were widely shared by his southern and western supporters. The populist imperative to satisfy the demands of the majority often comes at the expense of liberal safeguards for the minority. This collision—between populism and democracy's pluralist requirements—is where the story picks up in Chapter 7.[2]

What is populist economic policy?

Political thinkers have long recognized the link between democracy and the distribution of wealth. In Aristotle's classic formulation, because "as a fact the rich are few and the poor many," democracy—rule by the *demos*—essentially means government of the poor. Modern political economists build on this idea, arguing that democracy should be more redistributive than authoritarianism. The logic is straightforward: The typical voter benefits from policies that shift resources downward. And because populists rely on mass support, they should, in theory, champion the poorer majority.

History offers many examples of this kind of populism in action. The original Populists of the 1890s pushed for a range of progressive economic policies that would have redistributed wealth from rich to poor—at least if they were white. In the 1930s and '40s, populists like Huey Long in the United States and others worldwide revived these themes, championing debt relief, job programs, and protectionist measures to aid struggling workers. In mid-twentieth-century Latin America, populist leaders defied ideological labels but consistently expanded the welfare state while pursuing state-led industrial policies. In Argentina, Juan Perón built his base among poor urban migrants in Buenos Aires. In Colombia, Jorge Eliécer Gaitán never reached the presidency—his assassination cut his rise short. But his overwhelming support from the poor made many suspect that was precisely why he was killed. Brazil's Getulio Vargas—"Father of the Poor"—railed against big business and large landowners.

Writing from the perspective of the failure of these import substitution industrialization (ISI) policies of the 1960s and 1970s, macroeconomists were among the first to argue that populism's chief characteristic was its unsustainable promises of fiscal largesse. Right on cue, the 1990s saw the emergence of another "Pink tide" in Latin America, epitomized by the neo-socialist policies of the Hugo Chávez regime in Venezuela. Having failed to take power in a botched coup in 1992, Chávez turned to an electoral strategy on his release from prison, and in 1998 he won the loyalty of poorer voters in Caracas and other major cities. Chávez quickly moved to nationalize Venezuela's oil operator, PDVSA, replacing half of its 30,000 employees and using the expropriated funds to launch a host of social programs. The Chávez regime reduced inequality and brought millions above the poverty line. As Chávez exported his Bolivarian Revolution abroad, a wave of nationalizations and increased welfare spending followed in Bolivia, Ecuador, and elsewhere in the region.

This progressive brand of populism would surge in the West in the aftermath of the global financial crisis of 2008. The collapse of Lehman Brothers and the insolvency of the American International Group (AIG) threatened to crash not just the American economy but also the global financial system. In the United States, Occupy Wall Street gave that anger a voice. In Spain, street protesters—the Indignados—rallied behind Podemos, a new populist party. In Britain, a decade of austerity fueled the rise of Jeremy Corbyn, who led the Labour Party's radical left turn in 2015. But nowhere was the backlash stronger than in Greece, the hardest-hit economy in Europe. There, the populist party Syriza came to power, pledging to resist the demands of "the Institutions"—the European Central Bank, the European Commission, and the IMF. The fight between populists and the financial establishment was no longer just in the streets. It was in government.

This characterization of populism as inherently progressive runs into a problem: In recent decades, many populists have been on the right. Because populism thrives on opposition to the institutional status quo, when that status quo leans left—particularly in social democratic systems—populist movements often emerge from the opposite direction. Latin America provides a striking example. At the end of the 1980s, the failure of statist and protectionist policies to shield economies from global market forces triggered a political realignment across the continent. In Argentina, Carlos Menem initially campaigned on the traditional left-wing platform of Peronism, but once in office, he executed a stunning volte-face, becoming the face of Washington Consensus neoliberalism. Menem was not alone. In Brazil, Fernando Collor de Mello; in Colombia, Álvaro Uribe; and in Peru, Alberto Fujimori all pursued similar paths. They abandoned economic nationalism in favor of radical liberalization, giving rise to a new label once thought oxymoronic: "neoliberal populism."[3]

Today's populists often draw more support from the middle class than from the poor. For these voters, inflation and asset (home) values are often more important than the unemployment rate or the minimum wage. Trump, for instance, made direct appeals to America's working class, but his economic policies were solidly conservative. His tax and regulatory agenda has overwhelmingly favored corporations over lower-income individuals. His first major legislative victory was a sweeping corporate tax cut, with only modest, temporary benefits for the working class. He also catered to oil and mining interests, gutting regulatory agencies like the Environmental Protection Agency and opening protected national lands—both onshore and offshore—to exploitation. His populism spoke the language of the people, but his policies served the interests of capital.

This is not merely a feature of populism in wealthy states like the United States. Coming to power in 2016, the Philippines' Rodrigo Duterte was especially sensitive to inflation—and to the cost of rice in particular. The only period in which his approval rate dropped below 80 percent was when inflation began to creep up to 7 percent. Duterte rapidly introduced a new rice tariffication law that brought rice prices back down to their 2014 levels. Rice farmers weren't happy, but with a majority of Filipinos living in urban areas, Duterte's rice-consuming base was. As we'll examine in more detail below, middle class and urban Filipinos were precisely those who were most concerned about being victims of property crime or seeing their loved ones get involved in drugs. Brazil's Jair Bolsonaro, El Salvador's Nayib Bukele, and Argentina's Javier Milei all similarly adopted economic policies that favored corporate and middle-class economic interests, even while they benefited from the support of lower-class groups.[4]

It probably should not come as a surprise that overall, populist governments have not been any more likely than non-populist ones to reduce inequality. Indeed, economic inequality increased at an accelerating rate under Trump. Two separate studies examining the effect of populist rule on inequality in Latin American and the Caribbean have found no evidence that it reduces inequality. Critically, the lack of impact on inequality applies even when we examine the records of left-wing populists alone. The most comprehensive global analysis also finds that populist government has no impact on inequality or on workers' relative share of national income compared to investors.[5]

Even though populism has done little to reduce inequality, it has not been without economic consequences. The old assumption that populists are inherently fiscally irresponsible—recklessly expanding the welfare state in the style of Chávez—no longer holds. But the evidence does suggest that populist governments tend to preside over weaker economic performance. The reason, I argue, is not their specific policies, but their anti-institutionalism. Their impact on growth and stability is not just about what they do, but what they dismantle.[6]

Populist policy, even if popular, is often bad policy, at least when it comes to the economy. Populists, as we'll see in Chapter 7, consistently erode the rule of law. This has implications for democracy, of course, but it also directly impacts the economy. Populists are far more likely to undermine the very institutions that keep an economy functioning efficiently. Confidence in the law is essential to the business world. Investors need to know that the contracts they sign with borrowers are worth the paper they're printed on. They also need to know that the state will respect their property rights, which may be less secure under populist government. I've shown across a multi-regional sample that populists, especially those on the left, are more likely to nationalize property and to redistribute land without compensation. The perception of populist governments as a greater expropriation risk casts a long shadow over investment. When capital holders fear their assets could be seized or devalued by political fiat, they hesitate. The result? A chilling effect on economic growth, deepening the very crises populists claim to fix.[7]

Consider again Andrew Jackson. He took his landslide 1832 re-election as a mandate to crush the Bank and immediately withdrew the Treasury's deposits from the Bank, placing the funds in a network of state banks instead. Dubbed Jackson's "pets" because they were under the control of his Democratic allies, the banks suffered from an acute moral hazard problem. Unlike an independent central bank, the Jackson government was unlikely to withdraw its funds from politically connected banks, however risky their lending. When global credit tightened in 1837, Jackson's pet banking system left the United States mired in recession for almost the entire presidency of Jackson's anointed successor, Martin Van Buren. The economic fallout of Jackson's war on the Bank lasted far beyond his time in office. Populist economic policy can cast a long shadow, a fact that is especially worrying in light of Trump's second-term policies on trade—an issue we turn to in the next section.

Are populists anti-globalists?

Trump has flip-flopped on a lot of issues, from abortion to marijuana legalization; he was even once even a registered Democrat. But his mercantilist view of global economics has remained constant since the 1980s. Even as his fellow New Yorkers on Wall Street were then giddily embracing the acceleration of globalization, Trump called for tariffs on imported goods, especially from Japan: "We don't have free trade right now," he complained, because of other countries' use of domestic subsidies and other non-tariff barriers. Today Trump continues to repeat the mantra that "we don't have fair trade," or as he put it on another occasion, "we want balanced trade that is both fair and reciprocal." It's notable that Trump had substituted the word "free" for "fair" over the years, and that by 2016 his attention had shifted away from Japan. China—his main target—he says is "killing us with unfair trade deals." Even longtime allies have been designated cheats. The EU, according to Trump, was "formed to screw the United States." While most economists tend to see trade as a positive-sum game, for Trump, a win for China or Europe is a loss for America and vice versa.[8]

These views are not unique to Trump. Running for president in 1992, Ross Perot famously warned that the passage of the North American Free Trade Agreement (NAFTA) would create "a giant sucking sound" as US employers moved south to take advantage of lower wages in Mexico. More broadly, international institutions, such as free-trade agreements, play a crucial role in popular attitudes toward globalization. Trump's contemporary brand of populism explicitly opposes international institutions like the World Trade Organization (WTO), NAFTA, and the aborted Trans-Pacific Partnership (TPP) as unfair and illegitimate.

Trump's anti-institutionalism lands with voters because the positive role played by the organizations that govern global trade, finance, and industry are often hidden. We take for granted the ability to walk into a store or click a button online and gain immediate access to a vast array of goods sourced from every corner of the globe. Why wouldn't a consumer in New York purchase an iPad designed in California, assembled in China, using microprocessors from Taiwan, cobalt from the Democratic Republic of Congo, and rare-earth minerals extracted in Australia? Why wouldn't companies structure production across continents, linking the low-cost labor of Bangladesh to the design expertise of Italy, and the agricultural output of Brazil to the consumer markets of Europe? People appreciate the cheap goods this system delivers—electronics, clothing, cars, the everyday products that fill their homes and lives. But the institutional machinery that makes these goods so abundant, so readily available, operates at a scale so vast and distant from ordinary citizens that it is poorly understood, and often deeply distrusted.

The folk understanding of trade is that it resembles a simple barter system. Australia exports gold and iron ore to China and imports mobile phones and electric cars in return. But an efficient trading system requires that parties can make exchanges using credit—goods are usually shipped before they are paid for. In turn, a system of credit requires *trust*. At one time this trust was often provided by international networks of financiers related by kinship—the Jewish traders of the Maghreb are the classic example. But if contracts can be enforced in a court of law, the circle of trust can grow exponentially larger.

In the domestic economy, a creditor can summon a delinquent borrower before a local magistrate, a process governed by laws that, however imperfectly, remain within the reach of those they affect. International trade operates on a different scale. By design, the laws, rules, and institutional features needed to maintain international trade and finance are not controlled locally. From their inception, the architects of the international economic order sought to shield these institutions from political pressure. The first of them, created in the aftermath of World War I—the League of Nations and the Bank for International Settlements—were deliberately constructed to be beyond the influence of national electorates. And when, after World War II, the more powerful institutions of Bretton Woods were established, they followed the same model. Decisions that shaped the global economy would be made not by elected legislatures but by technocrats, central bankers, and financial officials operating behind closed doors.[9]

To those governed by these institutions, this distance from democratic control is not theoretical. It is real, and it is resented. The rules that determine economic winners and losers, that dictate currency values, trade flows, and financial policy are written by those who are neither elected nor easily held accountable. And so, to many, the institutions that govern globalization do not merely seem undemocratic. They seem illegitimate.

Outside of institutions like the WTO is another even less accountable system upon which the international trading system relies. WTO rules specify minimal regulations regarding tariff and non-tariff barriers. Beyond this, states are free to negotiate arrangements with one or more other states in the form of bilateral or multilateral agreements. As of 1990, there were some 290 bilateral investment treaties in force worldwide. This shot up to 1,415 a decade later, and today there are more than 2,000 such agreements in place.[10]

When an aggrieved commercial party wants to make a legal challenge to a foreign government's interference with the conduct of their business, they register what is called an investor-state dispute settlement (ISDS). If, for example, the US government follows through with its banning of the Chinese social media and video sharing platform, TikTok, on national security grounds, the company would likely sue the government not in an American court, or even a Chinese one, but in an international tribunal made up of a small panel of private arbitrators.

By design, these tribunals operate beyond the jurisdiction of any single country. Their rulings are final, not subject to appeal, and are enforceable against sovereign governments. The massive TPP, negotiated under Obama but later spiked by Trump, would have included just such an ISDS mechanism—one that, like those in other free-trade agreements, empowered corporate interests to challenge national regulations before panels of unelected arbitrators. Such mechanisms are efficient, insulated from political interference, and designed to ensure stability in global markets. But it is precisely this insulation that makes them so far removed from public influence that they lack even the pretense of democratic legitimacy.

Decisions with sweeping consequences—rulings that can override environmental protections, labor laws, or national tax policies—are made not by elected legislatures but by technocrats, lawyers, and economists whose authority derives not from any popular mandate, but from the very institutions they serve. If domestic institutions are sometimes viewed as unresponsive or unaccountable, international systems—from the World Trade Organization to the Bank for International Settlements—are more than that. They are obscure, opaque, unreachable. To the populist, they are not merely undemocratic, but inherently suspect—symbols of an elite order that operates above and beyond the will of the people.

In 2006, Ecuador's Rafael Correa, a former economics professor, ran for president promising to extricate his country from what he labeled oppressive and unfair international institutions. Under pressure from Correa, the Ecuadorian government expropriated the assets of US oil firm Occidental. Correa became president that October and refused to back down as Occidental filed a number of ISDS claims to recover its losses. Finding Ecuador in breach of its trade treaty with the United States, the arbitrators awarded Occidental $2.3 billion in compensation. Correa withdrew from the International Centre for Settlement of Investment Disputes (ICSID), the dispute-settlement institution embedded in most modern free-trade agreements, and severed bilateral investment treaties (BITs) with a host of trading partners including El Salvador, Uruguay, and Romania. Correa left office in 2014 with a 60 percent approval rating, and his example had spread. Bolivia's populist leader, Evo Morales, also withdrew from the ICSID in 2006, while Chávez took Venezuela out in 2012.

These anti-globalist views might make sense for the left-wing leaders of states with weaker international bargaining power, but why do free-market conservatives from wealthy countries, like Trump and Perot in the United States, also adopt them? Against the backdrop of a highly globalized institutional status quo, populist policy almost inevitably represents a nationalist rejection of it. But just as with domestic policy, populism is not defined by a particular set of international economic policies. It espouses not simply a change of policy but a change of the system itself. In the context of today's era of globalization, it is more likely that populists will be anti-globalist in economic outlook. Moreover, because the rules governing international trade and finance are not determined domestically, because they are not subject to the democratic will in a direct way, the institutions that set them are especially susceptible to accusations of illegitimacy and unfairness. Such international institutions are often also implicated in domestic socioeconomic disruptions. Even the speculative boom and bust that nearly broke Andrew Jackson, and set him on his path to power, was partly due to the sudden halt in capital inflows from London. The financial crises faced by Weimar Germany in the 1920s and early 1930s so well exploited by Hitler were inseparable from the restoration of the Gold Standard, Germany's reparations debts from World War I, and the interwar restrictions on global trade.

However, populist policy should not be understood as being inherently opposed to globalization. Rather, it is heterodox—running against the accepted institutional status quo. At times, that order has been protectionist, built on tariffs, quotas, and rigid trade barriers. And when that was the case, it was populists who championed open markets. But to see this, one must look beyond the present, beyond the recent decades, which have been synonymous with deregulation and free trade—because history shows that populists are not rigid anti-globalist ideologues. They have adapted to the moment to overturn the system, whatever it may be.

Following the Congress of Vienna that brought the Napoleonic Wars to an end in 1815, the British Empire was the most extensive ruling body in the world. Even though it had lost some of its North American colonies, it retained possessions throughout the Western Hemisphere, Asia and the Pacific, and the Middle East. The century preceding the outbreak of the First World War has become known as the Pax Britannica: British naval power underwrote the rapid growth of the international trading system. The industrial revolution within Britain that went along with this new global order wrought tremendous social disruption. The masses of workers who operated mines, mills, and factories in Britain needed cheap food. Although much new wealth was generated by industrialization, the landholding aristocracy remained prominent among the elite—not least in the House of Lords, the upper chamber of parliament. The people demanded free trade to lower tariffs on food imports that had been introduced in 1815, primarily the Corn Laws; the elite sought to retain these protectionist tariffs to preserve their wealth.

The Anti–Corn Law League agitated on behalf of Britain's working and middle classes to repeal the tariffs. Although often associated with Richard Cobden, the movement's intellectual godfather, just as critical was John Bright. Entering parliament only in 1843, Bright shot to fame as the free-trade movement's most celebrated speaker. Bright spoke not only in parliament, where his influence was limited, but at mass meetings throughout the country. Along with the contemporary Chartist Movement—about which more later—the drive for free trade was one of the largest mass movements in nineteenth-century Britain (see Figure 6.1).

Largely because of their interests as consumers, the British people remained firmly committed to free trade. Toward the end of the nineteenth century, while Joseph Chamberlain advocated the introduction of imperial preference in trade, he was vigorously opposed by the populist Lord Randolph Churchill. Although an aristocrat himself, Churchill led what

Figure 6.1 Populists for Free Trade: The Anti–Corn Law League

he called the "Tory Democrat" wing of the Conservative Party. He sought to challenge the Liberals' popularity among the masses and appealed directly to people's interests on free trade and reform to become one of the most charismatic politicians of the era. His son, Winston Churchill, too, would make his name as a staunch free trader, one of the few political constants throughout his shapeshifting career. Interestingly, British populism continues to have this strongly internationalist streak—with respect to trade if not the movement of people. Nigel Farage distinguished himself from the far-right British National Party leader, Nick Griffin, by declaring, "I believe in free trade and globalism."[11]

The younger Churchill, like many European statesmen in the interwar period, understood the dangers in rising protectionism. He saw not just an economic trend but a force with political consequences—a force that was reshaping the world. The 1920s and 1930s were a time when the great economic powers, battered by war and instability, retreated behind trade barriers, each step reinforcing the next. The Smoot-Hawley Tariff Act, passed by the US Congress in 1930, raised duties by nearly 20 percent on imported agricultural and industrial goods. It was meant to protect American industry. Instead, it triggered retaliation. America's trading partners, unable or unwilling to absorb the blow, imposed tariffs of their own. Trade collapsed. Markets that had once been open were suddenly closed. And across Europe, nations turned inward, their economies increasingly isolated.

Hitler's pursuit of autarky—his vision of a Germany that could sustain itself without reliance on international trade—is often remembered as a policy born of ideology. But it was just as much a response to the reality of a world closing in around Germany. After World War I, the Allied powers did not integrate Germany into the global economy; they excluded it. Germany was denied free access to external markets. It was denied the colonial empire that other great powers had used to secure raw materials and captive consumers. And so, when Hitler promised Lebensraum in the East, he was not merely offering conquest. He was offering what seemed, to many Germans, the only economic alternative left. Even then, Hitler's rise was not inevitable. Through the 1920s, most German voters, though embittered, still placed their faith in the political center. It was only after the Great Depression, when unemployment soared and desperation deepened, that they abandoned the center for Hitler's radical, racially pure autarky.[12]

What can we conclude overall on the relationship between populism and the global economy? One important study, which uses the ideational approach to classify populist governments, finds that populist leaders are on average more protectionist than non-populist ones. Populist governments raise tariffs, reduce the share of international trade in the economy, and decrease financial openness more than alternative regimes. However, not all research is in agreement on this point. Another analysis, employing a different dataset of populist governments, finds that populist rule per se has no systematic effect on various measures of trade openness. Some populists, especially those on the left like Ecuador's Rafael Correa and Venezuela's Hugo Chávez, tend to reduce trade openness, while others on the right, including Argentina's Carlos Menem, Peru's Alberto Fujimori, and Japan's Junichiro Koizumi, increase trade liberalization.[13]

On balance, contemporary populists are more likely to be anti-globalist. But this is not because they are driven by an absolute ideological commitment. It is because populism, by its nature, defines itself in opposition to the prevailing order. And for the last four decades—the very period in which populists have been most likely to rise to power—that order has been a globalized one: trade agreements negotiated behind closed doors; capital flowing across borders, beyond the reach of national governments; factories shuttered in one country, reopened in another. These have been the defining economic realities of the modern era, and so, it is against these developments that populists have directed their fire. But if globalization had not been the dominant force, if instead the economic order had been protectionist, then populists could well have positioned themselves as champions of free trade. Because at its core, populist economic policy is not bound to a single doctrine. It is not globalization or protectionism, not free markets or state control. It is heterodoxy—the rejection of orthodoxy, whatever that orthodoxy happens to be. And in that, populism's defining characteristic is not any specific economic belief, but its relentless opposition to the status quo.

Are populists a threat to the international order?

When Trump adopted the "America First" slogan as his own, he was promising a more robustly nationalist foreign policy that went well beyond trade. Along with his frequent diatribes against unfair trade deals, Trump constantly railed against America's military allies, who, he said, took advantage of America's security guarantees. NATO—the North Atlantic Treaty Organization—set up at the dawn of the Cold War, is a persistent Trump bugbear, and he has frequently threatened to withdraw from it or to refuse to abide by the requirement to join in the fight with a fellow member if it is attacked. Trump believes that America bears too much of the responsibility in terms of men and money to keep everyone else safe, declaring that "the United States should pay its fair share, not everybody else's fair share." Germany, for instance, spends well under the 2 percent of its GDP on its military required as part of its NATO membership. For Trump, this is money that Germany "owes" to NATO, if not to the United States directly.[14]

Other US allies—Japan, South Korea, Taiwan—have faced the same withering criticism. To Trump, their security is not an obligation of American leadership, not a strategic necessity, but a financial transaction. If they want US military protection, they must pay for it. And if they refuse, he has made clear that he is willing to leave them to their fate. His reasoning is blunt. If China moves against Taiwan, if North Korea launches an attack, it will not be American cities that burn, not American lives that are lost. It will be theirs. And so, in Trump's view, the burden should fall not on Washington, but on Tokyo, Seoul, and Taipei. It is a worldview that upends decades of US strategy, one that reduces alliances to balance sheets and security guarantees to mere leverage. And in doing so, it forces America's allies to confront a question that, for generations, they had never been forced to ask: whether, when the moment of crisis comes, the United States will still be there at all.

In other respects, Trump's foreign policy has been even more disruptive. He taunted North Korea's Kim Jong-un as "Little Rocket Man." He scrapped the Obama administration's Joint Comprehensive Plan of Action (JCPOA), the treaty designed to curb Iran's nuclear ambitions. He seemingly gave tacit approval of Russia's aggressive annexation of parts of Ukraine. But for all the confrontational rhetoric, for all the upheaval in diplomatic norms, one fact distinguishes Trump from every president since Reagan: During his four and a half years in office to date, he has initiated no new wars.

The tools of American power remained in use. The drone strikes that had become a signature of US counterterrorism policy under Bush and Obama continued, but their scope did not widen. When Trump ordered the assassination of Iran's top general, it was an escalation—but one that did not provoke the wider conflict many had feared. Iran, despite its bluster, backed down. Trump's words were provocative. His actions were aggressive. But in the ways history typically measures the use of American force—new conflicts, large-scale military interventions—his impact was muted. Trump talked a big game, but in the end, the wars that so often defined his predecessors were absent from his presidency.

What about other populists? There is evidence that populist leaders are more likely to criticize and withdraw from international institutions like the International Criminal Court (ICC). Rodrigo Duterte, for one, withdrew the Philippines from the ICC, openly defying its opposition to his brutal war on drugs.

Yet these actions fall well short of posing a dire threat to the international order. Militarized conflicts are rarer than trade or legal disputes, and so are less susceptible to large-scale statistical study. Wars, interventions, strategic alliances—these unfold in ways that defy easy categorization, shaped by forces far beyond any single leader's control. And so, populism's effect on international security remains harder to discern—more elusive, more dependent on context, and ultimately, more difficult to predict.[15]

As a result, attention is often drawn to the most visible cases of alleged populist aggression—moments that seem, at first glance, to mark a break with the existing order. Venezuela, under Hugo Chávez, sought to extend its influence across Latin America, leveraging not just ideology but sheer economic power. With oil prices soaring to nearly $150 a barrel in the mid-2000s, Chávez wielded Venezuela's resource windfall as a geopolitical weapon, funding allies, undermining adversaries, and threatening military action when it suited his aims. In 2008, when Colombian President Álvaro Uribe—a different kind of populist, one aligned with neoliberal economics—ordered the killing of a leftist guerrilla leader in neighboring Ecuador, Chávez responded with force, sending troops to the border with Colombia. It was a show of strength, meant to signal Venezuela's willingness to defend its allies, to reshape the region on its own terms. Elsewhere, the same dynamics played out. In the lead up to the 2019 elections, India's Narendra Modi ordered airstrikes on an alleged jihadi terrorist training camp in Pakistan. No targets were hit, but the saber rattling was a fillip to Modi's then sagging approval ratings. Yet, in the end, the status quo remained intact.

This is not to say that the rules are never broken. Few leaders have gone as far as Hitler in seeking not just to challenge but to completely rewrite the international order. His opposition to the Versailles Treaty was not a passing grievance—it was a constant, unyielding theme of his political campaigns throughout the 1920s and early 1930s. Versailles, in Hitler's telling, was not merely a settlement but a humiliation, a straitjacket imposed by Germany's enemies to ensure its permanent subjugation. And from the moment he took power in 1933, he moved to dismantle it. His first act was immediate. Germany withdrew from the League of Nations, rejecting outright the international framework that had been designed to prevent its resurgence. Soon after, he repudiated Germany's international debts, directly defying the financial obligations Versailles had imposed. But these were only preliminary steps. The real test came in 1936, when Hitler sent German troops into the Rhineland—a region that Versailles had declared a demilitarized buffer zone, meant to separate Germany from France and ensure that a future war could never be launched from German soil.

The move was not just a violation of a treaty. It was a calculated gamble. The German military was not yet ready for war; Hitler knew that if France responded with force, his position would be untenable. But France did not move. The League of Nations, already weakened, took no action. And so, in an instant, Versailles was no longer just defied—it was exposed as an agreement that no one was willing to enforce. From that moment forward, Hitler understood what was possible. The international order, as it had been imposed on Germany, was not unbreakable. It could be rewritten—not through negotiation, not through diplomacy, but through bold, unilateral action. And step by step, he would do exactly that, bringing Austria within the German Reich, followed by the German-speaking territories of Czechoslovakia—the Sudetenland. Hitler's costless diplomatic victories massively boosted his popularity and weakened the hand of any military Cassandras who might have opposed him.

In recent years, Vladimir Putin has similarly pushed back on what he believed was the illegitimate eastward expansion of NATO in the wake of the Soviet Union's collapse. After brutally repressing the insurgency in Chechnya in 1999–2000, first as prime minister and then as president, Putin exploited the continued unrest in the Georgian-held territories of South

Ossetia and Abkhazia in the Caucasus to occupy the breakaway republics in 2008 and advance into Georgian territory. Having seen his Ukrainian ally, Viktor Yanukovich, overthrown in a popular revolution in early 2014, Putin sent Russian forces—without their insignia—into Ukrainian territory to occupy the Crimea, a strategically significant peninsula, about the size of West Virginia, that juts out into the Black Sea. On this occasion, Putin barely concealed his revisionist intentions, arguing that Crimea was really Russian, Former Soviet premier Nikita Khruschev having only "gifted" the territory to Ukraine in 1954. A swift and relatively bloodless victory only emboldened Putin, as he came back for a bigger bite of Ukrainian territory in 2022. Although Russian forces failed to take the capital, Kiev, at the time of writing it appears that Putin will get much of what he wanted—a non-NATO Ukraine, acceptance of the annexations to date, and a reduction of American forces in Europe. Time will tell how this ends.

These cases of populist aggression are important, but they are exceptional for at least two reasons. First, both Germany and Russia, even if not dominant global powers at the moment their leaders launched their revisionist assaults on the international order, possessed the military capacity to fight and win multi-front wars. That distinction is crucial. Because this is not true of most states where populists have risen to power. Ecuador, Greece, the Philippines, even Indonesia—these are not countries capable of reshaping the global order through force. Their leaders, no matter how bold their rhetoric, no matter how defiant their stance, do not set the terms of international security. They accept them. In this arena, they are price takers, not price makers. Even where populist leaders of middle powers—figures like Modi in India or Chávez in Venezuela—have adopted aggressive postures, the pattern remains clear. The threats, the military gestures, the nationalist rhetoric—these serve political ends. They rally supporters, intimidate adversaries, reinforce the image of strong leadership. But they do not, in the end, overturn the order they claim to challenge. Because force, not words, is what ultimately shapes the structure of global power. And in that realm, most populists, no matter how loudly they speak, lack the means to act.

Second, by the time Hitler and Putin began their revanchist military adventures, they had long since crossed the threshold to dictatorship. This is another vital distinction. Populists rely on their popularity in a way that is not true of dictators. They may manipulate institutions, bend the rules, tilt the playing field in their favor—but they can still lose elections. Dictators like Hitler and Putin cannot. This difference is essential to understanding the effect—or lack of effect—of populism on international security. War-mongering may play well with a nationalist electorate. The rhetoric of strength, the promise of restoring lost greatness—these can be persuasive themes in elections. But wars themselves, the real ones, with their casualties and costs, are rarely popular for long. Both in Nazi Germany and in modern Russia, public opinion was initially sympathetic to their leaders' revisionist ambitions. People approved—enthusiastically, even—so long as the gains came without sacrifice, so long as their lives remained untouched by the true cost of war.

But when the bodies began to pile up, the enthusiasm faded. In Nazi Germany, support for the war effort remained strong so long as victory seemed assured. But by 1943, after the Allied firebombing of major cities including Hamburg and Dresden, and the Wehrmacht's defeat at Stalingrad by the Soviets, the illusion of Nazi invincibility was shattered, and national morale plummeted. Today, in Russia, the same pattern is emerging. What began as a demonstration of strength has become a slow, grinding war of attrition—one that has tested the limits of popular support. And yet, both Hitler and Putin could keep their countries at war—not because their people demanded it, but because by the time war came, public opinion no longer mattered. They had already dismantled the mechanisms that could have restrained them. They had already ensured that there would be no electoral consequences, no public reckoning. And that, more than any ideological commitment, is what separates dictators from populists. A populist leader, no matter how aggressive his rhetoric, is ultimately constrained by the need to win elections. A dictator is not. And when it comes to matters of war and peace, that distinction makes all the difference.

Populists oppose the institutional status quo with the result that international treaty commitments, and indeed, the international "order" more broadly conceived, carries little truck with them. However, while we might expect populists to cause trouble in international institutions, to withdraw from international agreements, and even to rattle their sabers, their dependence on popular opinion seems to prevent them from going much further.

Does populism always exclude?

With populist policy straddling the traditional left–right economic spectrum, many scholars now argue that what truly distinguishes it from establishment politics is not economics, but culture. A growing body of scholarship insists that populism is inherently nationalist, ethnocentric, even racist. Here I propose a different explanation: Just as populists defy economic orthodoxy, rejecting globalization when it is dominant and championing free trade when protectionism prevails, they do the same in the cultural sphere. Populists, by this reasoning, are not ideological purists. They are reactive. They do not dictate public sentiment—they channel it. And when the status quo is cosmopolitan, multicultural, and inclusive, they define themselves in opposition to it. The institutional approach I outlined in Chapter 3 suggests that populist movements are invariably based on collective, or group-based, resentments of the status quo. The leaders of these movements, the charismatic figures who embody their demands, do not set the terms of the debate. They respond to them. And if their base demands exclusionary policies, they are likely to pursue them.[16]

Although my incorporation of charismatic leadership of the group in explaining populism's tendency toward exclusion is new, the idea that populist movements are bigoted is not. Already by the late 1950s, the established idea of populism as a kind of proto-progressivism was coming under challenge. In his Pulitzer Prize–winning *Age of Reform*, historian Richard Hofstadter argued that the populism launched in the 1890s had a deeply exclusionary streak. Writing at the time of Joseph McCarthy's virulent anti-communist crusade, Hofstadter argued that bigotry was the real driving force behind populism. Antisemitism and racism cut through the original Populists' rhetoric and policy, with big finance often implicitly, and sometimes explicitly, assumed to be Jewish. Even if the Farmers' Alliance had seen the wisdom in collaborating with former slaves to prevent poor white farmers being undercut in their battle against railroads and banks, electoral logic soon put this experiment to bed. Tom Watson, Populist Party candidate for vice president in 1896, was at one time an outspoken advocate of collaboration across the color line, but by the turn of the century he gave voice to the most virulent of white supremacist views.

As we saw in reviewing the demand side, feelings about immigrants and minorities provide some of the sharpest contrasts between supporters of populist movements and their opponents. Trump rose to political prominence as a backer of the "birther myth" that Barack Obama was not really born in America and hence not eligible to be president. He promised to build a wall to keep out Mexicans—vowing to make them pay for it too. All of this was red meat to Trump's populist supporters—attitudes on immigration and minority rights were highly correlated with support for Trump in 2016. Citing fears that terrorists were taking advantage of America's lax visa policies, one of Trump's first acts in office, Executive Order 13769, was to suspend immigration from seven predominantly Muslim nations on security grounds. The measure caused chaos at entry points around the country as citizens of Iraq, Syria, and other states were prevented from entering the United States, even if they had already set off on their journeys with fully approved visas. Trump had to walk back the ban because of legal objections, but he clearly signaled that he meant business when it came to immigration.

Building the wall between the United States and Mexico proved an even harder promise to keep. Congress balked at the projected $18 billion price tag of a steel barrier—a measure few immigration experts even believed would be effective. With his efforts to construct the wall held up, Trump moved against a different policy cherished by Democrats. The Deferred Action for Childhood Arrivals (DACA) policy was put in place by Obama to remove the threat of deportation for immigrants who had come to the United States illegally, but as minors. Trump at times seemed personally sympathetic to these law-abiding young immigrants who had spent virtually their whole lives in the United States. Yet a year after he took office, he rescinded DACA, with Immigration and Customs Enforcement (ICE) officials being instructed that those previously covered by DACA were now breaking the law.

In mid-2018, Trump dialed up the temperature further, adopting what he called a "zero tolerance" approach to illegal border crossings. While adult migrants attempting to cross the border could be detained while their cases are processed, children historically could not. The usual practice was thus for migrants with children to be temporarily released while their immigration case was pending. Trump's administration broke with this practice. It separated adults from their children and infants at the border, detaining the parents, and placing the children in government institutions or eventually into foster care. Although this family detention policy was unpopular with the population as a whole, it had a massive 20-point majority support of Republicans. In other words, it was popular with Trump's base.[17]

Immigration remained, with the economy, the defining issue of the 2024 election for Trump supporters. Doubling down on the policies of his first term, Trump promised an even more aggressive military roundup and deportation of immigrants without valid visas. The early weeks of his second administration saw a raft of new orders issued to federal agencies including ICE and the IRS—the nation's tax agency. Tens of thousands have been detained and deported so far, including those without criminal convictions. Agreements were quickly reached with several Central American states to take deportees of other nationalities. Some immigrants have even been deported to the US military detention site at Guantanamo Bay, Cuba. The main chokepoint to ramping up this system further seems to be a lack of detention space within the United States as deportation proceedings are conducted. Public opinion appears to be even more firmly on Trump's side: 6 out of 10 Americans approve of his efforts to deport those living in the United States illegally.[18]

With the surge in asylum seekers heading to Europe through Turkey and the Balkans in 2015, following the implosion of Syria and the rise of ISIS, Hungary's Viktor Orbán got one up on Trump, completing construction of a new razor wire fence along the state's whole eastern border. Interestingly, although Orbán has become a hero to nativist Europeans, he had little to say on the subject during his first term in power (1998–2002), or even in the first five years of his second stint in office (2010–present). It was only with the increased salience of immigration that it became a core part of Orbán's political identity. While Orbán became the face of restriction, Germany's Angela Merkel staked her legacy on opening Germany's borders. Although admired internationally for her policy of *Willkommenskultur*—welcome culture—the sudden inflow of 1.5 million desperate refugees provoked an instant backlash from the right. Although populism has been kept at bay, the anti-immigrant Alternative for Germany (AfD) continues to rise in the polls. Other states in Western Europe have taken note. Italy's Giorgia Meloni, leader of the right-wing Brothers of Italy party, has begun to make good on her campaign promise to curb immigration from Africa and the Middle East. After initially rising in 2022, immigration figures dropped by more than 50 percent in 2024. Skirting EU policies, Italy has signed separate agreements with Libya (2017) and Tunisia (2024) to staunch the flow of immigrants at the point of departure. More recently, it agreed with Albania that any male migrants that do make it to Italy would be held in detention in Albania while their claims are being processed.

Although many readers in the West will think of countries like India as sources of immigration, they are also destinations, with the result that immigration policy is also salient there. In India, Narendra Modi's Bahujan Janata Party (BJP) has long been the political front of Hindutva, or Hindu Nationalism. Accounting for about 85 percent of India's population, Hindus are the overwhelming majority. While divided into multiple castes, not just the *varna* familiar to most in the West but also into local clan-cum-occupational groups called *jati*, the Hindu community is not a naturally cohesive one. To make it so, critics argue, Hindu Nationalists have constructed Muslims as a malignant and alien other, which all Hindus should oppose. Although the BJP has not managed to convince every Hindu to vote for it, it has been the country's most popular party by a long way over three elections running. In 2019, the BJP passed the Citizenship Amendment Act, fast-tracking citizenship for immigrants from Afghanistan, Bangladesh, and Pakistan, but only if they are Hindu, Sikh, Buddhist, Jain, Parsi, and Christian, not Muslim.

Populists, in short, have been willing and active in imposing immigration restrictions that mainstream leaders have resisted. Populist leaders in the opposition have promised more of the same. However, in the majority of places where populists have come to power—mostly states in Latin

America, Asia, and Africa—immigration is just not politically salient. Overall, populists have been much more likely to be elected as president or prime minister in states with weaker party systems, and this in turn is correlated with those economic conditions associated with high rates of emigration, not immigration. Populists will act on immigration when it is a significant issue, when their base demands it. Should more populists gain sole office in the West, there is every reason to expect efforts to tighten immigration policy. Where immigration is not salient, it is a non-issue for populists.[19]

Of course, social exclusion is not always directed against immigrants. Returning to India, it has been India's Muslim citizens, rather than immigrants from its neighboring countries, that have borne the brunt of the BJP's exclusionary policies. As shown by the 2002 pogrom in the state of Gujarat—then run by Modi as chief minister—high levels of ethnic violence can be tolerated and aided by a democratic government. Many sources put the death toll at 2,000, the vast majority of whom were Muslims. As prime minister, Modi has distanced himself from such extrajudicial killings, but the anti-Muslim slant in government policy continues. In 2019, Modi removed the extraordinary constitutional status of the state of Jammu and Kashmir, then India's only Muslim-majority state. Modi downgraded its status as a state and split it into two new union territories: Jammu and Kashmir, and Ladakh. With Hindu immigration and property ownership now permitted in the state, many fear that this signaled an intention to Hinduize the contested territory. Prior to the 2024 elections, Modi consecrated the controversial new Ram Mandir temple, which was constructed on the grounds of a sixteenth-century Mughal mosque that had been torn down by Hindu nationalists in 1992.

Bad as this case may seem, social exclusion can sometimes take an even darker turn. Andrew Jackson owed his popularity more to his aggressive Indian policy than anything else. As a circuit judge and land speculator on the Tennessee frontier, Jackson developed a visceral animosity toward America's native population. With white settlement, much of it illegal, encroaching on Indian lands, bloody skirmishes were not uncommon. When the Red Stick faction of the Creek Indians launched an all-out attack on Fort Mims, which lies about forty miles north of Mobile, Alabama, the result was the bloodiest-ever Indian assault on America's settlers. Jackson was revolted by the deaths of some 250 white civilians and the same number of militia. As the leader of the Tennessee militia, Jackson got revenge at the Battle of Horseshoe Bend, slaughtering about a thousand Creek Indians. Jackson was authorized by the government to "negotiate" treaties with the defeated tribes, in which the latter were compelled to surrender vast tracts of land. Even though Jackson's tactics ran afoul of the Supreme Court, he continued his policy of Indian removal in office, eventually ethnically cleansing virtually the entire Southeast of its native Indian population.[20]

Few others have managed to pursue such a thorough persecution of a minority population while remaining even technically democratic. It is tempting here to refer to the most egregious case, that of Nazi Germany. On the one hand, few of the 37 percent of Germans who voted for Hitler in 1933 could seriously argue that they believed a Nazi government would be anything but hostile to the Jews. Even in the two months of Nazi government before the passage of the enabling act in March 1933, new research shows that the rights of Germany's Jews were being systematically violated. In the years before the outbreak of the war, Germany's Jews were discriminated against with the express purpose of removing them from the country. Yet Germany's transition to full-blown dictatorship under Hitler makes it difficult to evaluate the role of populism in the Holocaust. Other European dictatorships, including those in Poland and Hungary, which violently persecuted their Jewish populations even before Hitler came to power, show that anti-Semitism was not unique to Nazi Germany. Yet the near extermination of Europe's Jewish population was probably inconceivable but for the context of wartime authoritarianism.

Ethnic cleansing is possible under a populist government, but it seems more likely that exclusionary populist policies will fall short of this extreme. Moreover, the most flagrant cases of apartheid in nominally democratic states—Northern Ireland, South Africa, Israel—have all occurred without the impetus of populist mobilization.

As we saw in Chapter 3, the demand for populism is associated with a sense of group threat. Populism can, in some cases, be founded on an ethnic sense of identity that is not synonymous with that of the nation—Hindus only, whites only, and so on. However, it has been far more common for populists to claim to represent all the people in a nation. Although the source of that threat might be domestic, it has far more commonly been external. In Jacksonian America, Indigenous tribes were semi-sovereign nations, not citizens. Even in the case of Nazi Germany, Hitler built on the long-standing perception that Jews were not authentically German. When Wisconsin Senator Joseph McCarthy rode to fame as a communist fighter in the 1950s, the fears he played on were rooted in the emerging Cold War. At that time communism had a small domestic constituency in the United States. The fear McCarthy evoked was over Russian spying. On this basis, populist policy would seem more likely to target immigrants and foreign enemies than domestic minorities. But this is a question for future research.

Is populism a moral panic?

Populists elsewhere have developed signature policies on areas other than the economy and national identity. In a number of cases, populism has been associated with tough stances against crime and social non-conformism. In this case the threat to the group comes from those excluded as morally deviant. With the Philippines economy humming along well under incumbent president Benigno "Noynoy" Aquino in 2016, presidential candidate Rodrigo Duterte lashed the administration for its mishandling of crime and drugs.

Duterte drew on his reputation as the strong-man mayor of Davao City, vowing to rid the country of illegal drugs within six months of his confirmation. In early March 2016, he pronounced that if elected president, he would kill thousands of dealers and addicts, the funeral parlors would be packed, and he would dump 100,000 of the slain criminals in Manila Bay where the fish would grow fat. He was known for saying, "If you are not prepared to kill and be killed, you have no business being president of this country." He promised no mercy, saying "God will weep if I become president." After winning the election, he made good on his word, with thousands falling victim to police and vigilante killings in his first few months in office. Duterte made no apologies for the deaths, even likening himself to Hitler, saying that he was prepared to exterminate millions in his effort to wipe out drug dealers and users.[21]

Current president of the notoriously crime-ridden El Salvador, Nayib Bukele, made much the same promise. In 2018, the year before Bukele took office, El Salvador's homicide rate stood at 51 per 10,000; by 2023, this had fallen to just 2.4 per 10,000. Bukele locked up tens of thousands of gang members in a new mega-jail. His approval ratings were so high that he overrode the constitutional prohibition on serving a second term to win 83 percent of the vote in his 2024 campaign for re-election. Trump too, we shouldn't forget, made law and order a constant theme in his campaigns of both 2016 and 2024. He tapped into conservatives' fears, portraying inner cities—none of which, as a Republican, he had any hope of winning—as dystopian hellholes. Brazil's Jair Bolsonaro—the Trump of the Tropics—also campaigned heavily on the issue of crime, promising to use the military to eradicate heavily armed gangs. Before any of them, Peru's Alberto Fujimori and Colombia's Álvaro Uribe waged brutal counterinsurgency campaigns against their country's Maoist-inspired and drug-money-financed guerrilla armies. Populist policy, in this view, is more like a *mano dura* ("hard hand") policy of law and order.

Yet it is difficult to maintain the view that such policies are distinctive of populism. Richard Nixon was one of the first to ride the popular reaction to the increasing crime of the 1960s to power and popularity. In 1971, Nixon launched the "war on drugs," declaring the drug problem to be "public enemy number one." Nixon created the Office of Drug Abuse Law Enforcement (ODALE) in late 1971; over the following two years, the agency made 6,000 drug arrests, before being absorbed into a new larger agency, the Drug Enforcement Administration (DEA). Reagan would escalate the conflict, ramping up penalties for possession, especially of crack cocaine. The system of mass incarceration, largely of Blacks, famously called the "New Jim Crow" by author Michelle Alexander, did not depend on populism. Across the Atlantic, Margaret Thatcher too bemoaned the state of lawlessness in Britain when she took office in 1979. Marxist sociologist Stuart Hall would label Thatcher's hardline approach "authoritarian populism," but in truth it was neither authoritarian nor populist. Thatcher was popular, but she was no populist. She served not just at the pleasure of the electorate but of her party—as her unceremonious ouster in a party spill in 1990 made clear. In short, law-and-order policies are something that mainstream parties seem perfectly adept at satisfying.[22]

Another possibility is that populists are more likely to introduce reactionary social and sexual policies than non-populists. During his first term in office, Donald Trump instituted anti-trans policies across government departments, defining sex as sex-at-birth. In the closing weeks of his 2024 campaign against Harris, he appealed to conservative reaction against the gender self-identification movement, his team spending some $46 million pushing the slogan "Kamala is for they/them. Trump is for you." Trump promised that in his second term he would cut funding from schools that teach "radical gender ideology." In the early weeks of his return to office, he issued directives preventing trans-identifying youth from accessing puberty blockers and hormone treatments, and banning transgender women from competing in female sports. Majorities support these Trump policies.[23]

Nor are these populist culture wars unique to America. In Argentina, President Milei has spoken openly against abortion, transgenderism, and "cultural Marxism." In mid-2024, Milei dissolved the agency responsible for persecuting gender-based violence, and in February 2025, he implemented a ban on gender affirming care for minors. It Italy, in a blow to same-sex couples, Giorgia Meloni has instructed local councils to register only biological parents on a child's birth certificate. Brazil's Jair Bolsonaro once said, "A dead son is better than a gay one." In office, he criticized the Supreme Court's overturning of a ban on gay men donating blood.[24]

Yet not all populists line up together on this issue. The Netherlands' Geert Wilders has been a prominent advocate for LGBT rights. In fact, he stresses that Western Europe's individual rights in this domain makes it superior to Islam's intolerance toward sexual and gender non-conformity. Wilders is not alone. France's Marine Le Pen has also come out in favor of gay rights.

It is again important to stress that moral crusades are not distinct to populists. The war on drugs, along with the exponential rise in incarceration rates that took off with the crack epidemic of the 1980s, was hardly driven by populism. Moreover, it was supported not only by white Americans but also by urban Blacks. Although the latter were more likely to be incarcerated as a result, they were also more likely to have been victims of violent crime in the first place. However, this was hardly the beginning of the turn to tougher policing and sentencing. These policies, so often associated with Nixon, had already begun under his predecessor, Lyndon Johnson. Even then, the prohibition of alcohol in 1920, followed by the violent battles between police and armed gangs, who then peddled alcohol more than drugs, had already set a direct precedent for moral policing. Overall, there is as yet little systematic evidence that populists in office are more likely to adopt more aggressive forms of policing or to be especially reactionary on social issues such as trans rights.

Populists' rhetoric often seems to outdo what they achieve in practice. This is not to say that populist words are unimportant, but they can be distracting. Even though majorities of Brazilians oppose gay marriage and abortion, Bolsonaro's war on woke remained primarily one of words. The old quip about the contrast between Trump's supporters and his opponents has some resonance: While his followers take him seriously but not literally, his antagonists take him literally but not seriously. In other words, we need to pay more attention to what populists like Trump really do than to what they say. Populist policy tends to be unorthodox, but this alone doesn't make it undemocratic. Indeed, populist policy on issues from trade to trans rights is often very popular. As I discuss in Chapter 8, this is a fact that mainstream parties must deal with. Only by addressing the policy demands of voters will we be able to prevent the populist erosion of democracy associated with populism, the topic of Chapter 7.

Notes

1. "the rich and powerful," from "President Jackson's Veto Message Regarding the Bank of the United States," July 10, 1832, *The Avalon Project*, https://avalon.law.yale.edu/19th_century/ajveto01.asp. On the role of the state banks, see Harry N. Scheiber, "The Pet Banks in Jacksonian Politics and Finance, 1833–1841." *The Journal of Economic History* 23, no. 2 (1963): 196–214.
2. Michael Mann, *The Dark Side of Democracy: Explaining Ethnic Cleansing* (Cambridge University Press, 2005).
3. Kurt Weyland, "Neoliberal Populism in Latin America and Eastern Europe," *Comparative Politics* 31, no. 4 (1999): 379–401.
4. Aurora Almendral, "Duterte's Lustre Dulls as Rice Prices Soar in Philippines," *New York Times*, October 10, 2018, https://www.nytimes.com/2018/10/10/world/asia/duterte-philippines-inflation-rice.html.

5. Christian Houle and Paul D. Kenny, "The Political and Economic Consequences of Populist Rule in Latin America," *Government and Opposition* 53, no. 2 (2018): 256–287; Martin Strobl, Andrea Sáenz de Viteri, Martin Rode, and Christian Bjørnskov, "Populism and Inequality: Does Reality Match the Populist Rhetoric?" *Journal of Economic Behavior & Organization* 207 (2023): 1–17. On Trump, see David Cay Johnston, "You Can Thank Trump if You're Feeling Poorer Today," Inequality.org, June 8, 2021, https://inequality.org/research/trump-income-inequality/.
6. Manuel Funke, Moritz Schularick, and Christoph Trebesch, "Populist Leaders and the Economy," *American Economic Review* 113, no. 12 (2023): 3249–3288; István Benczes, "Taking Back Control over the Economy: From Economic Populism to the Economic Consequences of Populism," *European Policy Analysis* 8 (2022): 109–123, https://doi.org/10.1002/epa2.1134.
7. Paul D. Kenny, "'The Enemy of the People': Populists and Press Freedom," *Political Research Quarterly* 73, no. 2 (2020): 261–275.
8. "We don't have free," "we don't have fair" quoted in Charlie Laderman and Brendan Simms, *Donald Trump: The Making of a World View* (I. B. Tauris, 2017), 34, 41; "formed to screw," "Trump Vows 25% Tariffs on EU and Says Bloc Was 'Formed to Screw US'—Video," *The Guardian*, February 27, 2015, https://www.theguardian.com/us-news/video/2025/feb/26/trump-vows-to-slap-25-tariffs-on-eu-and-claims-bloc-was-formed-to-screw-us-video.
9. Jamie Martin, *The Meddlers: Sovereignty, Empire, and the Birth of Global Economic Governance* (Harvard University Press, 2022); Quinn Slobodian, *Globalists: The End of Empire and the Birth of Neoliberalism* (Harvard University Press, 2018).
10. Haley Sweetland Edwards, *Shadow Courts: The Tribunals that Rule Global Trade* (Columbia Global Reports, 2016).
11. "I believe," quoted in Michael Crick, *One Party After Another: The Disruptive Life of Nigel Farage* (London: Simon & Schuster, 2022), 201.
12. Tara Zahra, *Against the World: Anti-Globalism and Mass Politics Between the World Wars* (New York: W. W. Norton, 2023).
13. Kent Jones, *Populism and Trade: The Challenge to the Global Trading System* (Oxford University Press, 2021), 30; Funke et al., "Populist Leaders."

14. "the United States should," quoted in Kanishka Singh, "Trump Again Conditions US Help to NATO Allies on Their Paying 'Fair Share,'" *Reuters*, March 20, 2024, https://www.reuters.com/world/us/trump-again-conditions-us-help-nato-allies-their-paying-fair-share-2024-03-19/.
15. Erik Voeten, "Populism and Backlashes against International Courts," *Perspectives on Politics* 18, no. 2 (2020): 407–422.
16. J. Mostov, "Populism Is Always Gendered and Dangerous," *Frontiers in Sociology*, January 11, 2021, https://doi.org/10.3389/fsoc.2020.625385.
17. Dylan Matthews, "Polls: Trump's Family Separation Policy Is Very Unpopular—Except among Republicans," *Vox*, June 19, 2018, https://www.vox.com/policy-and-politics/2018/6/18/17475740/family-separation-poll-polling-border-trump-children-immigrant-families-parents; Catherine Rampell, "Americans Prefer Trump on Immigration. Just Not His Actual Policies." *The Washington Post*, March 12, 2024, https://www.washingtonpost.com/opinions/2024/03/12/trump-immigration-polls-policies/.
18. J. Baxter Oliphant and Joseph Copeland, "What Americans Think about Trump's Immigration Actions Early in His Second Term," *Pew Research Center*, February 7, 2025, https://www.pewresearch.org/short-reads/2025/02/07/what-americans-think-about-trumps-immigration-actions-early-in-his-second-term/.
19. James Dennison, "How Issue Salience Explains the Rise of the Populist Right in Western Europe," *International Journal of Public Opinion Research* 32, no. 3 (2020): 397–420.
20. On Jackson's Indian policies, see Alfred A. Cave, *Sharp Knife: Andrew Jackson and the American Indians* (Bloomsbury, 2017).
21. "Kill the Criminals! Duterte's Vote-Winning Vow," *Inquirer.net*, http://newsinfo.inquirer.net/774225/kill-the-criminals-dutertes-vote-winning-vow; Randy David, "Dutertismo," *Philippine Daily Enquirer*, May 1, 2016, http://opinion.inquirer.net/94530/dutertismo#ixzz554QleIXs; Jonathan Miller, *Duterte Harry: Fire and Fury in the Philippines* (London: Scribe Publications, 2018), 14; Karen Lema and Manuel Mogato, "Philippines' Duterte Likens Himself to Hitler, Wants to Kill Millions of Drug Users," *Reuters*, October 1, 2016, https://www.reuters.com/article/us-philippines-duterte-hitler/philippines-duterte-likens-himself-to-hitler-wants-to-kill-millions-of-drug-users-idUSKCN1200B9.

22. Michelle Alexander, *The New Jim Crow: Mass Incarceration in the Age of Colorblindness* (The New Press, 2010); Stuart Hall, "Authoritarian Populism: A Reply to Jessop et al." *New Left Review* 151, no. 1 (1985): 115–123.
23. "Americans Have Grown More Supportive of Restrictions for Trans People in Recent Years," *Pew Research Center*, February 26, 2025, https://www.pewresearch.org/short-reads/2025/02/26/americans-have-grown-more-supportive-of-restrictions-for-trans-people-in-recent-years/.
24. "gender ideology," "Javier Milei Claims Extreme Gender Ideology Is 'Child Abuse'," *UnHerd* January 23, 2025, https://unherd.com/newsroom/javier-milei-claims-extreme-gender-ideology-is-child-abuse/. "A dead son," quoted in Robert Tyler Valiquette and Yvonne Su, "The rise of Duterte and Bolsonaro: Creeping Authoritarianism and Criminal Populism," *New Mandala*, December 13, 2018, https://www.newmandala.org/the-rise-of-duterte-and-bolsonaro-creeping-authoritarianism-and-criminal-populism/.

7

POPULISM AND DICTATORSHIP

Why does populism undermine democracy?

Ratfuck [verb]: *to carry out dirty tricks and crafty maneuvers to sabotage an opponent's election campaign.* It was a young lawyer, Donald Segretti, who took the term, if not the practice, of ratfucking from USC campus politics to the White House. In his memoirs, Richard Nixon claimed not to have known Segretti, though ultimately, it doesn't matter. Nixon, "the ratfucker in chief," as one of his biographers called him, was already well versed in the strategy long before Segretti ever joined his campaign. In the run-up to the 1972 election, Nixon and his attorney general and campaign manager, John Mitchell, set up the Committee to Re-elect the President (CREEP) to gather intelligence on and undermine his political enemies. Watergate would be Nixon's undoing—unlike Mitchell, he'd avoid jail—but bugging the Democratic National Committee (DNC) headquarters in the famous Watergate Hotel was probably one of the *least* offensive black bag jobs that Nixon's team had planned. CREEP envisaged a vast program of clandestine activities—code-named GEMSTONE—that went well beyond bugging and robbery to include money laundering, kidnapping, and extortion.[1]

For a long time after Watergate, it remained a mystery as to why Nixon took the risk of sanctioning the spate of illegal operations that included the botched DNC job. A year out from the election, Nixon was an overwhelming favorite to retain the presidency. Only in recent years have we come to learn that Nixon's presidential high crimes and misdemeanors during the 1972 campaign were likely in the service of covering up a much more serious offense that occurred before he even came to office in 1969. In his quest for the presidency in 1968, Nixon conspired with Republican Party China lobbyist, Anna Chennault, to scuttle incumbent President Lyndon Johnson's peace talks with the Vietnamese, denying the Democrats a public relations coup. This was, bluntly put, an act of treason that could have put Nixon's head in a noose. CREEP was set up in part to cover his tracks in the Chennault Affair. Fearing that the leaker of the Pentagon Papers on the US war in Vietnam, Daniel Ellsberg, might disclose Nixon's treacherous activities, Nixon had his CREEP operatives break into the office of Ellsberg's psychiatrist in September 1971 in the hopes of uncovering dirt on him.[2]

Nixon was hardly the first or the only president to use devious and even illegal tactics to gain and retain power. With some justice, Nixon would accuse John F. Kennedy of stealing the election from him in 1960. By paying off a former Nixon associate and allegedly engaging in a burglary of its own, the Kennedy campaign team uncovered evidence of shady financial transactions by Nixon, which it leaked to the press to smear the then vice president just days before the election. In office, Kennedy, like Nixon eight years later, would name his campaign manager as attorney general, giving him undue influence over the operations of the Justice Department. Nixon, after losing the 1960 election by the slimmest of margins, privately fumed that the Kennedys were "the most ruthless group of political operators ever mobilized." And there was reason for his bitterness—credible evidence suggested that fraud in Illinois and Texas may have tipped the race. But in the end, Nixon, for all his resentment, accepted defeat. He did not challenge the results. He did not seek to use the machinery of the state to overturn them.[3]

Trump did. Even against America's long bipartisan history of political dirty tricks and interference in the justice system, the Trump campaign's efforts to overturn the results of the 2020 election are shocking. His outright refusal to concede the 2020 election sparked a constitutional crisis not seen since 1876, when rampant fraud and violence in several southern states led to a disputed result that had to be arbitrated by an ad hoc Election Commission created by Congress. Then, the crisis was resolved through backroom negotiation—a deal that handed the presidency to Rutherford B. Hayes while effectively ending Reconstruction. That case included, no American president has been as willing as Trump to use the legal and coercive apparatus of the state to override an election. Others have bent the rules. Others have tested the limits of institutional power. But no one—not Nixon, not any president before him—has so openly sought to dismantle the democratic process itself.

I began this book by proposing that the events of January 6, 2021, were a consequence of populism. Yet the story is complex. Populism is often a threat to democracy, but it is not necessarily so. As we saw in Chapter 6, populist governments often deliver what the people, or at least what a plurality of voting citizens, want. Moreover, as Chapter 8 will illustrate, when the status quo is authoritarian or even deeply unrepresentative, populism can have a positive effect on democracy, expanding the franchise and improving government accountability. In practice, however, populism in power is more likely to weaken democracy than to strengthen it. Yet simply applying labels like "democratic illiberalism" or "authoritarian populism" are unhelpful; they describe rather than explain why populism has this effect. Developing such an explanation is the goal of this chapter.

Before explaining why populism tends to weaken democracy on average, it is worth recalling again what we mean by democracy. I argued in the opening chapter that democracy is an either/or proposition. Either it is possible to remove the government through elections or it is not. But democratic regimes vary in terms of how easy this process is. Elections are necessary, but alone they are not sufficient to make a polity democratic. Press freedom, the rule of law, and a reasonably equitable system for translating votes into governmental power are also required. Elections are not free and fair if the opposition cannot publicize itself, if the government can manipulate electoral rules to give it a grossly unfair advantage, or if the leaders of the opposition are systematically repressed. If political competition is sufficiently limited, we say a regime has crossed the threshold into dictatorship. Some populists have managed to make this transition, but we'll see that it is rare, occurring in only 10 to 20 percent of instances of populist rule. For the majority of populist governments, although there is a departure from "perfect" scores on features of democracy like the rule of law and press freedom, they fall short of a transition to authoritarian rule. We'll examine why these transitions are so unusual.[4]

To understand populism's threat to democracy, this chapter focuses on its opposition to the institutional status quo. There are several elements to this. First, populist leaders have strong personal incentives to weaken democratic competition once they've gotten into power. For a populist, political survival means personal survival, not the survival of a movement or party. When a populist leader's popularity ebbs, he doesn't have a structured, loyal party base to fall back on. He needs other, less kosher, forms of insurance.

Second, populists come to power with an implicit, if not explicit, mandate to weaken the liberal institutions that protect minority rights. Populist leaders can take advantage of popular resentment of the status quo to gain control of additional institutions they may claim block this mandate; these might include the media, the judiciary, and the opposition in general.

Third, the absence of internal party constraints on a populist leader provides them with the opportunity to take measures that erode the quality of democracy. The constraints on democratically elected leaders are, on one level institutional, but on a second, and I think more important level, they are political. This is where the absence of party comes to the fore. Political parties constrain their own leaders. The absence of an organized party structure is part of the populist appeal to voters, but this also means that populists are free to undermine those rules that support the pluralism needed for democracy to work.

To see this logic in action, let's return to the Nixon–Trump comparison for a moment. Nixon's example makes clear that non-populists act in ways that are ethically and legally problematic. But the denouement of Watergate also suggests that non-populists may face greater constraints in undermining democracy than populists do. Why?

It's usually argued that the main restrictions on a power-hungry leader are institutional. Before the 2016 election, I coauthored an op-ed for the *Washington Post* based on my research on Latin American populism, anticipating that a Trump presidency could harm American democracy. The editors published our commentary but insisted that we tone down our alarmism. US institutions are "stronger" than their Latin American counterparts, making a presidential power grab unlikely, they argued.[5]

The US Constitution is sometimes criticized for being anachronistic, but its very longevity and immutability make its constraints, like those on term limits, difficult to evade. However, like all legal documents, the Constitution can be interpreted in more ways than one. The impeachment process is the classic example. While the US Constitution states that the president "shall be removed from Office on Impeachment for, and Conviction of, Treason, Bribery, or other high Crimes and Misdemeanors," it does not define any of these terms. Essentially, they are what a majority of the House and a supermajority of the Senate decide they are at any given time.

Ultimately, Nixon was compelled to resign because his own party elites abandoned him to save themselves. By the time he resigned, Nixon could count on the support of just a handful of senators, making impeachment a foregone conclusion. The very opposite scenario prevailed in Trump's case. More popular than the party elite, the latter had to save *him* to preserve themselves, not once but twice. In 2019, all but one of fifty-three Republican senators voted to acquit Trump on charges of abuse of power; in his second impeachment trial in 2021 on the charge of inciting an insurrection, still forty-three of fifty Republican senators voted to acquit the former president. As long as he retained his popularity among his base, Trump could violate the rules with virtual impunity.

The problem, and paradox, of populism today is this: People (or at least a bloc of them) feel that the institutional status quo is failing them. It is not that people do not support the democratic ideal of majority rule. Rather, it is that they oppose those institutions that preserve the special privileges of minorities: immigrants, tenured academics, the rich and powerful. They support the leader whose promises of change to this institutional status quo are most credible: the populist outsider.

However, the same autonomy from the constraints of a political party that makes a leader the most credible agent of change also makes him far more likely to damage the institutions that make his election possible. Eroding the protections for minorities to speak, seek justice, and get elected undermine the competitiveness of democracy. The more experienced populist leaders are, the better they can undermine those institutional safeguards. This chapter examines three institutions of crucial importance to the maintenance of democracy: press freedom, electoral integrity, and the rule of law. Then we'll examine how populists fully throw off these institutional constraints to become dictators.

What does populism do to press freedom?

As a celebrity, Trump has long had a love-hate relationship with the media. Television airtime is his oxygen, but being thin-skinned, he is intensely bothered by negative coverage. Making his mark as the heir to his father's New York real estate empire, Trump was a regular feature in the city's gossip columns. Although he frequently garnered the attention of the tabloid *New York Post*, what he really craved was the establishment approval of *The New York Times*. Almost from day one of his presidency, Trump found himself at war with the press, contesting media reports of his modest inauguration crowd. White House press secretary Sean Spicer said that Trump had the "largest audience to ever witness an inauguration—period—both in person and around the globe," but aerial images and public transport data blatantly undercut his claim. Trump campaign advisor, Kellyanne Conway, in an apparent attempt to clarify Spicer's comments, claimed that the press secretary was using "alternative facts." As the media continued to pile on, Trump excluded critical outlets, including *The New York Times*, from White House briefings.[6]

While Trump increasingly relied on Twitter and the amplification of his views through Fox News and sympathetic internet sources like Breitbart News, the US Constitution's First Amendment protections for free speech were so entrenched that short of a direct assault on the judiciary, there was little he could do to staunch the mainstream media criticism. He resorted instead to public attempts to undermine the authority of the press. He called journalists "among the most dishonest human beings on earth," claimed that he was in "a running war with the media," and denounced the press as "the enemy of the people."[7]

When the major television networks, including the usually sympathetic Fox News, called the 2020 election for Biden, Trump immediately pushed back. On election night, at 2.21 a.m., Trump appeared on national television, not to concede, but to announce "a fraud on the American public. . . . We were getting ready to win this election. Frankly, we did win this election. We did win this election." Trump appeared on Fox News again at the end of November putting forth conspiracies like mysterious "dumps of votes," and the alleged hacking or manipulation of voting machines run by the private firm, Dominion. "This is total fraud" he said, suggesting the FBI and Department of Justice could be involved. "This election was rigged," he claimed.[8]

Although we cannot be sure that Trump's relentless attacks on journalists have had a causal effect on public opinion of the press, the proportion of Americans who trust the national media hit a record low of 32 percent in 2016, a floor only breached in 2024, when it hit 31 percent. At one time he pondered silencing his critics by opening up libel laws so he could sue them as private individuals, but in the lead-up to his 2024 re-election bid, Trump went further, calling for the Federal Communications Commission (FCC) to revoke the licenses of "fake news" media outlets. This draconian option, clearly violating the spirit of the first amendment, might seem far-fetched. Yet the independence of the press can be suspended during a national emergency, a tactic that Trump has been willing to use in the past in other policy areas such as immigration, over the objections of Congress. Early in his second term, Trump has made good on his threat to open FCC investigations on mainstream networks, while also calling for Congress to defund the Public Broadcasting Service (PBS) and National Public Radio (NPR).[9]

Bad as this may seem, Trump's efforts to control the media during his first term still pale in comparison with populists elsewhere in the world. In May 2019, Volodymyr Zelinsky, a celebrity comedian, became president of Ukraine on the back of a mass rejection of the political status quo. Given his popularity, his political opponents kept their powder dry during the first year of his administration, but when Zelinsky's approval ratings dropped, they turned hostile. Zelinsky then banned the three television networks controlled by his political rival, and Russia sympathizer, Viktor Medvedchuk. When Russia launched a new military campaign in 2022, Zelinsky assumed almost total control of print and mainstream media.[10]

Although unconstitutional, Zelensky's actions might be justifiable on national security grounds. Yet this can be a slippery slope, with domestic political resistance justifying similar measures. Consider the actions of Türkiye's president, Recep Tayyip Erdoğan. In the two weeks following the failed July 15, 2016, military coup against his government, Erdoğan shut down more than 150 news outlets, including forty-five newspapers, twenty-nine publishing houses, twenty-three radio stations, sixteen TV stations, fifteen magazines, and three news agencies; hundreds of journalists were imprisoned. Although the threat has passed, Erdoğan fully controls the media in Türkiye and has "zero tolerance" for any criticism.

Even without the justification of national security, populists have proven more than willing to erode press freedom. Hugo Chávez began his presidency of Venezuela in 1999 with a radical overthrow of the legal structure of the old regime as we'll see later in this chapter. Chávez utilized the state broadcaster to air his *Hello President* show, often for three or more consecutive hours at a time. Most of the media, however, remained in private hands, and it poured out a withering barrage of criticism of the president. But Chávez had the authority to cut into any private network's broadcast to deliver "urgent" information, a threshold apparently met on average every three days.

After the failed 2002 coup against Chávez, which was supported by most of the privately owned media, they quietly curtailed their criticism of the government. Radio Caracas Televisión (RCTV), however, continued to be outspoken opponents of the regime. In 2007, RCTV lost its public broadcasting license. It continued as a niche cable network channel until 2010, when Chávez finally clamped down on it and the remaining media outlets aligned with the opposition. Globovisión too had been tactically permitted to continue its critical approach from the confines of the private cable network to give the illusion of a free press, but by 2010, it was also shuttered amid trumped-up charges of broadcasting antinational misinformation. Some thirty-four radio stations were closed at the same time, leaving Venezuela with a media environment about as free as that of Stalinist Russia.[11]

In the Philippines, Rappler, a news website and one of the harshest critics of President Rodrigo Duterte, had its certificate of incorporation revoked by the Securities and Exchange Commission in January 2018 on legally dubious grounds and it has since been charged with tax evasion. In June 2020, its co-founder and CEO, Maria Ressa, was convicted of libel and sentenced to jail. Despite the change in government, Ressa lost her appeal in July 2024 and still faces imprisonment at the time of writing.

In Hungary, Fidesz leader and prime minister, Viktor Orbán, created the Media Authority in 2010, giving the new regulator control over Hungary's media, telecommunications, and postal sectors. Fidesz has also used its control over government purse strings to apply economic pressure to media it perceives as hostile. In 2017, the party passed a law regulating billboards that forced the country's second largest firm in the sector—and a Fidesz opponent—out of business, leaving the field open to a company linked with the government. The state broadcaster also became a mouthpiece of the Orbán government, with one insider slamming it as "direct manipulation and lies." In 2024, the Orbán regime went further still, creating a new sovereignty protection office with a remit to discipline any media outlets or NGOs that might threaten the "sovereignty" of Hungary through its criticism of the government.[12]

I could go on. But the chilling effect of populist government on the press is evident beyond these well-known examples. In a study of populist rule across ninety-one countries from 1980 to 2014, I've shown that populist government is negatively associated with freedom of the press and freedom of expression more broadly. We know that press freedom is lower in dictatorships, so in assessing the effect of populism on press freedom, it is important to make sure that we are not accidentally capturing a dictatorship effect. This study shows that the negative relationship between populism and press freedom persists even excluding cases like those of Chávez and Fujimori who cross the threshold into dictatorship. Overall, the substantive negative effect of populist rule on various indicators of media freedom is about a third the size of that of authoritarian rule.[13]

It is also worth noting that not all populists are the same. Interestingly, I find that being on the right rather than the left moderates the negative effect of populist rule on press freedom. This is not likely due to a penchant for self-criticism from right-wing populists like Trump and Orbán. Although we can't be entirely sure, it is probably due to the right's preference for free markets and deregulation, which could mitigate the occurrence of state regulation in general. Left-leaning populist governments, in contrast, because of the greater likelihood that they will engage in the nationalization of private assets or other forms of state intervention in the market, may be more likely to erode the independence of private media. This interpretation is supported by an additional finding that left-leaning populist governments are more likely to engage in uncompensated land redistribution and to weaken the investment climate, outcomes we noted in Chapter 6. To be clear, though, populism of all stripes poses a substantial threat to press freedom.

Because populists, more than the leaders of better institutionalized movements, rely on the media to connect with voters, they are especially sensitive to media criticism. Even if only a fraction of the voting public pays close attention to policy debates, it is through the media that party leaders become known. The way in which populist parties are organized means that they have especially strong incentives to erode press freedom and freedom of expression more broadly. While other types of political leaders can rely on party membership, dense civil society organizations, or clientelistic linkages mediated by a network of party brokers to mobilize supporters, populists have little to go on but their personal connection with voters. If the media denies populists this link, or if it corrupts it by constantly providing negative imagery of them, populists feel forced into a corner and seem prepared to act accordingly.

What does populism do to electoral integrity?

Maintaining popularity by controlling public perceptions is one way to hold on to power. But those who study propaganda, who see in it an omnipotent force capable of shaping the masses' beliefs at will, often miss something fundamental. No amount of messaging, no barrage of carefully constructed falsehoods, can convince a population of a leader's virtues when the breadlines stretch around the block, or when hospital corridors overflow with the sick and dying. Even Joseph Goebbels, the Nazi master of the dark arts of social control, acknowledged that propaganda worked best not by changing minds but by reinforcing what people already believed. Persuasion was never its strength. And history has proven him right. The most enduring effects of Nazi propaganda on attitudes toward Jews were found not in places where people had been indifferent, but in those areas where antisemitism already ran deep. As the Nazi intelligence agency itself candidly admitted in an internal memorandum, "Our propaganda encounters rejection everywhere among the population because it is regarded as wrong and lying."[14]

In short, faced with a declining or stagnating economy, a national health emergency, or a military defeat, information alone is unlikely to save a populist from electoral defeat. No amount of rhetoric, no manipulation of perception, can withstand the force of reality indefinitely. Without an institutionalized base of support in the form of a loyal party membership, many populists have seen their soaring popularity plummet like an overvalued stock. In Peru, Alan Garcia began his first presidential term in 1985 with a 90 percent approval rating. He ended 1988 with just 13 percent backing his performance. Yet despite leaving office in 1990 with the lowest approval rating in Peruvian history, he was reelected president in 2006. The Philippines' Joseph "Erap" Estrada came to power in 1998 with the massive support of the Second People Power Revolution but found himself impeached halfway into his term of office as his popularity drained away. Public opinion is a fickle master. And so the populist, if he is to remain in power, learns something else—control of perception may not be enough. To ensure that he stays in power, the populist often seeks to control something far more concrete: the machinery of elections themselves.

One of the bluntest approaches to electoral manipulation is to simply count the votes until you get the outcome you want. Often this means placing pressure on electoral officials to miscount the true vote. Following the November 2020 election, Trump persistently raised doubts about the integrity of the election. During a January 2, 2021, phone call, he pressured Georgia's Republican Secretary of State Brad Raffensperger to "find 11,780" votes, the number by which Biden had won the state. Trump threatened Raffensperger that his refusal was "criminal" and a "big risk." Nor was this an isolated incident. Trump or his staff engaged in more than 200 acts to pressure public officials to overturn state election results. He pressured Acting Attorney General Jeff Rosen and Acting Deputy Attorney General Richard O'Donoghue to "just say the election was corrupt." In his speech at the Ellipse on January 6, 2021, Trump said, "When you catch somebody in a fraud, you're allowed to go by very different rules." Trump's efforts to "stop the steal" amounted to, in the words of US District Judge David Carter, "a campaign to overturn a democratic election, an action unprecedented in American history." It was "a coup in search of a legal theory." After his election defeat in 2020, Trump argued that massive vote fraud justified the "termination of all rules, regulations and articles, even those found in the Constitution."[15]

In the end, Trump failed. But where he fell short, other populists have succeeded. His mistake was one of timing. He waited until after the election to try to manipulate the outcome. The more effective strategy—the one that has worked for others—is to shape the process before a single vote is cast. There are many ways to do this. Ballots can be designed to confuse voters, with misleading layouts and ambiguous instructions. And once cast, those ballots can be subjected to rulings by government-appointed officials, whose decisions—seemingly technical, often arbitrary—can determine which votes count and which do not. Sometimes, these manipulations are overt. Other times, they appear accidental. Consider Florida in 2000. The now-infamous "hanging chads"—punch-card ballots that were only partially perforated—left thousands of votes in legal limbo. The election in the state was decided by just a few hundred votes. The dispute went to the US Supreme Court, where a Republican-majority bench shut down the recount, handing the presidency to George W. Bush. Analysts later estimated that Al Gore had likely received more votes. But by then, the result was irreversible. Trump tried to follow a different path. Rather than shaping the rules in advance, he sought to challenge them after the fact. He argued that postal ballots—where Biden had a decisive lead—were fraudulent. But even courts sympathetic to him found no legal basis for his claims. However, had the groundwork been laid earlier—had the legal uncertainties been baked into the process itself—he might have had, at the very least, the reasonable doubt needed to tip the outcome in his favor.[16]

One legal and highly effective way of doing this is to change the electoral system to give the winning party more seats. Countries often have minimum thresholds for parties to be able to take up seats in parliament. This approach is sometimes seen as necessary to limit the number of independents and micro-parties which can make forming a government difficult. This is often the case in proportional representation voting systems, where voting patterns tend to be more fragmented. However, this method can also be exploited to provide the leading party with extraordinary majorities. In Türkiye, Erdoğan's Justice and Development party (AKP) benefited from a remarkably high threshold of 10 percent until as recently as 2022—this disproportionality allowed the AKP to secure nearly two-thirds of the seats in parliament with just a little over one-third of the popular vote. Even as the threshold was reduced to 7 percent in 2022, Türkiye's continued use of the D'Hondt method for allocating seats still advantages larger parties like the AKP.

Another tactic is to politicize the drawing of electoral boundaries. This process determines not just who votes where, but, at the margin, who holds power. Nowhere is this more apparent than in the United States. Here, the task of drawing electoral boundaries is not entrusted to neutral commissions but to state governments themselves—governments controlled by politicians with a direct interest in the outcome.

In 1812, under pressure from the national leadership of James Madison's Democratic-Republican Party, Massachusetts Governor Elbridge Gerry approved a redistricting plan designed not to reflect the natural shape of communities but to ensure his party's continued dominance. The strategy, later known as *gerrymandering*, involved grouping together voters not by geography, but by political inclination—twisting districts into unnatural, contorted shapes that resembled, to critics, the sinuous form of a salamander. The goal of this operation was clear: to disperse the opposition's votes across multiple districts, diluting their influence, while consolidating Democratic-Republican strength where it mattered most. It was a crude but effective weapon—a way of tilting elections before a single ballot had been cast.

More than two centuries later, gerrymandering has not only endured but evolved. With the advent of computing technology and increasingly sophisticated voter data models, it has become a tool of extraordinary precision, allowing political operatives to carve up the electoral map with surgical accuracy. The consequences are striking. In the 2024 US congressional elections, 366 of the 435 House seats were effectively uncontested—not because of overwhelming public support for incumbents but because district lines had been drawn to make true competition all but impossible.

The gerrymander remains a legal—but profoundly unethical—means of ensuring that elections are decided not by voters but by those who wield the power to shape the map. Populists have been eager to take advantage. After returning to power in 2010, Viktor Orbán sought to ensure he'd never have to endure another period in opposition. His party quickly set about redrawing constituency boundaries. Unlike in the United States, Hungary allows for district populations to vary by up to 35 percent. This allowed Fidesz to cram opposition voters into more populous districts, while having their own supporters distributed across less populous ones. In 2010, Fidesz's electoral performance showed little variation between the country's least- and most-populous districts. But by the next election in 2014, after it had redrawn the electoral map to its advantage, the results told a different story. In districts with fewer than 70,000 eligible voters, its vote share was 6 percentage points higher than in those with at least 80,000. The impact was decisive. With just 45 percent of the vote, Fidesz secured a two-thirds supermajority in parliament, ensuring that it could govern with near-total control. In 2018 and 2022, the pattern was repeated. With a mere plurality of the vote, it once again claimed a supermajority in parliament.[17]

It's also easily forgotten that governments must appoint some kind of administrative entity to manage the running of elections. The responsibilities of these bodies include setting the location and hours of polling and the methods used in counting ballots. In Venezuela, the National Electoral Council created after the passage of the 1999 Constitution was fully controlled by Chávez. As a result, he and his successor, Nicolás Maduro, have had extraordinary leverage over the conduct of elections, including the ability to bar opponents, such as María Corina Machado, from running. When Edmundo Gonzales ran as a substitute for Machado in the 2024 elections, the Maduro-controlled electoral council and the nation's highest court announced that Maduro won, despite the tallies from individual polling stations that showed otherwise.

Governments can also tamper with electronic voting machines, steal or destroy the ballots of the opposition, stuff ballot boxes with votes for the government, or allow voter impersonation or multiple voting. These tactics carry risks, however, as they are more visible to the press, independent election monitors, and even citizens themselves. Some populists nevertheless use them, although usually when they are already on the threshold of dictatorship. In Türkiye, vote counters added an estimated 2.5 million votes to the 2017 referendum on a new constitution, which adopted a strong presidential system designed for Erdoğan to occupy. The amount of ballot stuffing was particularly egregious, being double the 51–49 percent margin of victory. Clearly, the referendum would have gone down had ballot boxes in AKP strongholds not been stuffed and numbers artificially added to the "Yes" vote. Officials also dumped the ballots of "No" votes in bins and on building sites. The outright manipulation of election results didn't stop there. When an Erdoğan surrogate lost the 2019 Istanbul mayoral election, the Supreme Electoral Council invalidated the result, prompting a do-over. Trump promptly congratulated Erdoğan on his actions, although he was peremptory. The runover election was also lost, a signal perhaps that Erdoğan's regime at least until then remained populist rather than authoritarian.[18]

Although the anecdotal evidence suggests a willingness on the part of populists to undermine the integrity of elections, unlike with press freedom or the rule of law, there have been no broader statistical studies on this question. The most widely used dataset of electoral integrity—the Electoral Integrity Project (EIP), based on expert surveys conducted after national elections—goes back only to 2010, so it misses many of the populist governments that have been in office during the twentieth century.

Using the dataset of populist governments based on the strategic approach described in Chapter 2, I examined whether there was an association between populist government and electoral integrity. To be on the conservative side, I first excluded any leaders that had crossed the threshold into dictatorship. Some of these regimes hold elections, but they are virtually meaningless. This leaves a total of 268 national legislative or presidential elections covered by the EIP, forty-three of which occurred in states under populist rule.

Among this subset of cases, populist government is associated with lower levels of electoral integrity. The results remain robust when controlling for a country's level of development—something likely to be associated both with populists getting elected and with electoral integrity. These preliminary results are suggestive, but we should treat them with caution. It is possible that there are other unobserved factors associated both with populists coming to power and with low-quality elections. Further research is needed, but there is reason to believe that populists do indeed degrade the quality of elections in ways designed to secure their hold on power.[19]

What does populism do to the rule of law and law enforcement?

In theory, democracy appears simple—a system in which the people rule. In practice, it is anything but. For democracy to function, it requires not just a cultural acceptance of the principle of popular sovereignty but an intricate framework of rules and laws to ensure that competition for power remains both free and fair. These rules define who can run for office, who can vote, how ballots are counted, and what mechanisms exist to resolve disputes. Yet rules, no matter how well-intended, are rarely immune to ambiguity. When gaps exist, they require interpretation. And when those in power gain the ability to define or reinterpret the very rules that govern elections, democracy's core promise—genuine competition over the reins of government—begins to erode. The distinction between democracy and autocracy is often framed as the difference between the rule *of* law and rule *by* law—a cliché, but a revealing one. Dictators dispense with pretense; they rewrite laws to suit their needs or ignore them altogether. The law is a weapon to be used against ones opponents. As Peruvian dictator (1914–1915 and 1933–1939) Óscar Benavides put it, "For my friends everything, for my enemies the law." Populists, constrained by the democratic framework they claim to uphold, cannot so easily eliminate opposition through brute force. But they can push democracy to its limits—manipulating election rules, tilting regulations in their favor, and weaponizing legal ambiguities to weaken their opponents.

For legal constraints on government to be effective, there must be an independent prosecutorial and judicial system. Indeed, it is a fundamental principle of the law that no man can sit in judgment of his own cause. Thus, a key component of democracy is the separation of powers. Republican thinkers since at least the Baron de Montesquieu have recognized that democratic constitutions require the existence of multiple independent centers of power. As James Madison put it in *The Federalist Papers*, "The constant aim is to divide and arrange the several offices in such a manner as that each may be a check on the other that the private interest of every individual may be a sentinel over the public rights." Often, as in the American case, this means a formal separation of executive (the presidency) and legislative (Congress) powers; but on a deeper level, it means a separation of the law-making from the law-enforcing arms of government.[20]

Legislation, and sometimes constitutions, determine how constituencies are to be drawn up, whether the electoral system will be proportional or first-past-the-post, and how much a candidate can spend in any given election. Yet whether the party of government is held to account for disobeying any of these regulations depends on there being a robust rule of law that is free from political interference at both the judicial and the enforcement stages. If members of the government cannot be found guilty of misconduct by a court, or if they can simply ignore the court's rulings, they can act with impunity. Simply put, if an incumbent president can violate the laws that preserve democracy at will, there are few institutional constraints on his holding on to power in perpetuity. Again, this doesn't mean a sudden turn to a police state. Political leaders who control the courts are free to take more subtle actions like censoring the media or prohibiting especially critical associations (such as NGOs that receive foreign funding). Reducing judicial autonomy is thus often a key step that populists take in securing their rule.

There are now many excellent books and investigative reports documenting populists' efforts to undermine the rule of law, some of which I refer to in the further reading section. A few examples from this body of research will suffice to make the point. Even though the 1961 Venezuelan Constitution had no provision for a Constituent Assembly, Hugo Chávez had built his campaign for the presidency in 1998 on a proposal to radically rewrite the constitution. Venezuela's constitution had provided the basis for one of Latin America's longest-lived democracies, but it also led to the entrenchment of a highly centralized, corrupt political duopoly that proved unable to address the country's slide into economic catastrophe in the late 1980s. Shortly after assuming office in 1999, Chávez issued a referendum on whether to hold an election for a new Constituent Assembly, reserving for himself the prerogative to draw up the assembly's electoral rules. The referendum passed with overwhelming support. However, opposition parties boycotted the subsequent assembly election, whose rules they disputed, and Chávez supporters won 90 percent of the seats in the assembly.

The new 1999 Constitution written by the assembly allowed that same body to arrogate the original constituent powers to act as a legislature in place of the recently elected congress. Its "temporary" authority included appointment power over all the other branches of the state, including the judiciary and the election council. The Supreme Court was closed and replaced by a new Supreme Judicial Tribunal. All of its new members served at the pleasure of government. There was no security of tenure. In effect, the heads of all major offices from the public prosecutor to the state comptroller could henceforth be appointed and removed by the president. In 2007, Chávez sought to entrench his regime further, but the proposals were rejected in a referendum. No matter. The congress simply passed most of the relevant measures by legislation or Chávez pushed them through by presidential decree. He thereby gained the ability to remain in office in perpetuity. All without "breaking" the law. After Chávez stacked the courts, his government won every one of over 43,000 rulings.

Similarly, in Hungary, just seven months after its election in May 2010, Orbán's Fidesz government had written and passed a new constitution, called the Fundamental Law. The document was drafted in secret and debated for only nine days. On April 25, 2011, it then passed a major constitutional reform without a referendum. Over the next dozen years, the Fundamental Law required ten further amendments. The new constitution enlarged the Constitutional Court, allowing Fidesz to secure a majority on it. The number of judges was increased from eleven to fifteen, and parliamentary consensus was no longer needed to make appointments to the bench. Seven Fidesz-loyal judges were appointed within a year. Cases were brought to the European Court of Justice, which ruled against the government on the forced retirement of judges at sixty-two, but it was a fait accompli by the time the rulings landed. At the same time, Fidesz limited public access to the court (to challenge the constitutionality of government action). A new standing order was passed that truncated the need for consultation prior to passing legislation. Around 100 acts were approved, none of which were challenged constitutionally. It also created a new National Judicial Office, which had powers over case selection and the assignment of cases across the judiciary. Péter Polt, a former Fidesz politician, was appointed chief prosecutor, and his term lengthened from six to nine years, and he was now removable only by a supermajority. The leaders of a variety of state institutions had their tenures extended to up to twelve years. As a result of these measures, the opposition has almost no legal recourse against Orbán's government.

Although this has been less well studied to date, populist encroachment on the autonomy of the judicial system goes beyond the courts. While control over courts, especially those that rule on the constitutionality of legislative and executive action, is critical to a leader's entrenchment in office, another string in the populist bow is to control the state's prosecutorial functions. If accusations of criminal misconduct need to be pursued by the justice department or a public prosecutor, then the autonomy of that office from the executive branch is essential. Moreover, if the public prosecutor can be not only deflected from investigating the government but directed toward hounding opponents, populist chief executives have yet another means of holding on to office.

Like Nixon's efforts to cover up the Watergate burglary nearly fifty years earlier, it was Trump's efforts to interfere with Justice Department investigations of suspected wrongdoing during the 2016 election that were a greater source of legal liability for him than the original offense. It's by now well known that the Russian government undertook "Active Measures" against the United States to undermine the 2016 election. Perceiving Hillary Clinton as likely to be the more hostile president, Russia ran at least two separate operations to hack into Democratic Party systems to uncover and release potentially damaging information on it, to spread misinformation that would benefit Trump and demobilize Clinton supporters, and actively undermine election systems including voter registration systems. Because of various contacts between Trump campaign members or surrogates and Russian operatives, the Justice Department was obliged to investigate.

Once in office, Trump immediately sought to pressure his attorney general, Jeff Sessions, to quash the investigation. Sessions, to his credit and much to Trump's annoyance, recused himself because of a conflict of interest and appointed a special prosecutor, Robert Mueller, to investigate. Although the Mueller Report failed to find smoking gun evidence of collusion between the Trump campaign and the Russians, Mueller would eventually prosecute over thirty members of Trump's team. Still Trump and his new attorney general, William Barr, declared victory. As bad as this was, things would get worse as I describe in the next section.

Beyond the United States and these other headline cases, there is systematic evidence of the populist erosion of the rule of law. In one of the earliest papers on this question, my coauthor Christian Houle and I found that populist governments in Latin America were much more likely to erode the rule of law and judicial autonomy than non-populist ones. To deal with the possibility that those places where the rule of law was already problematic were the ones in which populists are most likely to come to power, we conducted an additional comparison between those cases in which populists won compared to those where they won a substantial share of the vote, but just lost. Even then, we found that populism has a negative effect on the rule of law. This is not to say that the prior rule of law makes no difference. A recent paper using a global dataset of populist governments shows that populism undermines the rule of law, but it does so to a greater degree in places where the rule of law is already weak. In the next section, I examine how populists build on these processes to cross the threshold into dictatorship.[21]

When and how do populists become dictators?

Some scholars have used the behavior of leaders like Trump to argue that populists are inherently undemocratic. This notion draws in part on the constitutional approach to defining populism. If populism is by definition anti-pluralist or illiberal, then it axiomatically follows that it is inconsistent with democracy. If minorities, whether based on economic, ethnic, or political criteria are denied the ability to speak, organize, and otherwise behave in the same ways as the majority, what we have is no longer a democracy. As we'll see in this section, some populists do cross the threshold into dictatorship. These populist-dictators are leaders who came to power through free and fair elections, but who then closed political competition to entrench themselves in office.

The transition from populism to dictatorship is rare. In a recent coauthored study with Alex Baturo and Evren Balta, I found that these transitions occurred under only 10 to 20 percent of all the populist leaders who have come to power globally since 1945. The range depends on whether we limit the cases to those of fully free liberal democracies or if we include electoral democracies where some prior deficiencies are already evident. While the current number of authoritarian transitions is low, the significant potential for populist leaders' agency in eroding democracy is concerning. What distinguishes the much more typical case of first-term Trump, who ultimately left office after losing an election, from a rare "successful" populist like Chávez, who entrenched himself in power permanently?

One theory is that an acute social or economic crisis allows populist leaders to gain extraordinary popularity as "saviors." They can then exploit this status to sweep away constraints on their authority and gain dictatorial powers. As charismatic leaders, populists supposedly exploit a latent mass yearning for order, if not domination, that is heightened during times of crisis or change. Certainly, the sense of imminent group threat lies at the heart of charismatic authority. Adolf Hitler's assumption of decree powers in the wake of the Reichstag Fire of early 1933 is perhaps the most infamous example of a populist exploiting a threat to achieve permanence in power, but the process is far from unique. Chávez came to power with a mandate to overthrow the constitution after more than a decade of economic and social chaos that included the death of about 3,000 people in the 1989 anti-austerity Caracazo riots. Although it is difficult to test for the full range of "crisis" conditions that might facilitate a populist rolling back institutional limits on his power, we found that negative economic conditions do make it more likely that a populist makes the transition into dictatorship. Yet, this is unlikely to be the whole story. Populists like Orbán and India's Narendra Modi came to power under benign socioeconomic conditions, but each has managed to undermine constraints on their authority.

An alternative, increasingly prominent explanation is that populists become dictators when formal and informal institutions fail to perform their function as "guardrails" against democratic backsliding. One of the key problems Trump supposedly faced in 2021 was that whatever his personal willingness to break the rules and remain in office despite his election defeat, he could not overcome institutional resistance to his efforts. In theory, a variety of institutional rules and norms, including the separation of legislative and executive powers, judicial autonomy, a depoliticized military, and a robust civil society should hinder any executive power grabs. Where such institutions are weak, they cannot perform this role. Problematically, however, it is difficult to tell how "weak" an institution is until after it is challenged. An institution is defined as weak if compliance is not enforced or if the institution is easily changed. Institutional weakness is thus often only evident after the fact. Moreover, to the degree that institutions are weakened by continual assaults from within and without, weakness is part of the very process we want to explain.[22]

My answer to this puzzle is somewhat different. Indian political commentator, K. S. Komireddi, astutely observes that "institutions are not self-animating creatures. What they do is contingent upon those who people them." That is, when we talk about the strength of institutions to resist power grabs, we're talking about the capacity and the will of the people who staff the organizations that create, maintain, and enforce those institutions to act autonomously. To control institutions is to control the people that staff them. Populists who have effectively become dictators, like Hungary's Orbán, appreciate the importance of personnel. As Hungarian opposition politician, Zsuzsanna Szelény, writes, "Orbán trusts people, not institutions, and this is precisely why he has entrusted the most important state institutions to his own friends, who go back further than the foundation of Fidesz."[23]

Why didn't Trump, or indeed the four out of five other populist leaders who've come to power, seemingly recognize the need to occupy the institutions in this way? Simply, some leaders know better than others. Even if socioeconomic crises and prior institutional weakness provide opportunities for populists to break through the institutional guardrails of democracy, history suggests that leaders vary in the degree to which they can seize such openings. Institutional manipulation takes skill, even if it is in the political dark arts that more often earn condemnation than approbation. As historian Robert Caro has shown in his magisterial multivolume biography of President Lyndon Johnson, irrespective of background social conditions, even seemingly impotent institutions can be transformed into effective instruments of power by astute and ambitious political operators. The overthrow of democracy requires both an understanding of institutional rules and norms as well as the law, and the interpersonal skills to manipulate both allies and opponents who occupy nodal positions within the administrative and judicial entities that conrol key institutions.[24]

A deeper understanding of the operation of political institutions, and greater knowledge of how to assert their personal control over them, is strongly correlated with a leader's prior political experience. More experienced leaders understand which roles within political organizations need to be held by allies to control their agenda and direct their operations. In turn, such leaders also tend to be more able to draw from a longer bench of loyal supporters to make such important political appointments than are political novices. The related political psychology research generally supports this conjecture, finding that the learning, practice, and feedback received over time, such as from longer time in politics, in turn helps individuals to overcome various policy challenges with more competence. Crucially, the political experience of populists may be particularly potent when they operate under more malleable institutions governing appointments, where they are able to remove potential opponents from gatekeeper roles within state organizations more easily, and replace them with allies.

As the previous sections have shown, populists the world over are bad for democracy, but it is experienced populists that citizens should be most concerned about. Our research has found that transitions to dictatorship are more likely under populists who have more experience in politics. In addition, we found that the effect of experience is amplified when the rules on government appointments are informal. Encouragingly, among fully liberal democracies, such transitions are rare, with only Hungary experiencing a full breakdown in 2019. Notably, however, this democratic breakdown occurred under Orbán, a seasoned politician who had previously served as prime minister when he returned to power in 2010. Yet it is worth stressing that relatively few populists have come to power in liberal democracies in the first place, so these systems have rarely been tested in this way.

Consider instead the inexperienced populist leader. Trump's problem in 2021 was not the "strength" of institutions in an abstract sense but the fact that he didn't have any leverage or favor with the people who occupied key institutional roles. Back then, Trump had a very simplistic understanding of executive power and the institutional constraints on it, initially apparently assuming that merely issuing an order would be enough for it to be faithfully executed. Encountering resistance from the "deep state" to his various initiatives, Trump often could not understand how to circumvent it. Political novices, as Trump was in his first term, also tend to lack the deep network of allies required to make strategic appointments and attempt to capture the institutions necessary to overcome resistance to the concentration of power. He could call on only a very limited number of family members and reliable political cronies, and thus had to appoint people unfamiliar to him, who often proved unwilling to implement his decisions. In 2017, Trump appointed Republican stalwarts to key positions in the Justice Department (Attorney General Sessions) and the Department of Defense (James Mattis; replaced by Mark Esper), and as Director of National Intelligence (Dan Coats). These three institutions resisted Trump's efforts to prosecute rivals and to subvert the 2020 election. As I noted above, much to Trump's chagrin, Sessions recused himself from the Russia election-interference investigation, leading to the drawn-out probe of Robert Mueller. Even more ominously, while Esper refused to deploy the military during the Black Lives Matter protests in 2020, this was not a concern for Trump's second-term defense secretary, Pete Hegseth. In May 2025, Trump sent thousands of National Guard troops and 700 active-duty marines to Los Angeles in response to protests against the federal government's anti-immigration enforcement in the city. Hegseth and other loyalists only egged Trump on.

All in all, Trump managed to inflict only limited damage on American democracy during his 2017–2021 presidency. In 2024, however, while many pundits believe that Donald Trump is still the same novice he was in 2016, he is a much more seasoned politician than he was then. As Peter Baker of *The New York Times* recently summarized, "Trump learned from those experiences. When he first arrived at the White House, he had not spent a single day in public office and therefore often relied on people he did not know well. He returns eight years later with a much better understanding of how power works in the White House and a better sense of whom to trust." With eight years of experience leading the Republican Party, and four of those as president, this second Trump term looks to be posing a greater threat to democracy than the first. Just months into his second stint in office, the president is weaponizing the Justice Department against his enemies, and he has pardoned the convicted rioters of January 6. Law firms that opposed Trump have been threatened with prosecution, and mainstream media outlets with having their licenses revoked. Private universities like Harvard and Columbia are being strongarmed into compliance with the party line. On deportations, the government appears to be bypassing all legal restraint. Troops are on the streets.[25]

Although the future is difficult to predict, as this book goes to press in mid-2025, democracy remains intact. Trump has yet to overtly interfere with the machinery of elections. My expectation is that congressional elections will occur in 2026, and that they will be closely fought. Republican state governments may well seek to erode the competitiveness of the electoral process in the interim, but as in places like Poland, elections will be real; the opposition will be able to win.

Why is populism different from fascism?

In the run-up to the 2024 US presidential election, Trump's former chief of staff, General John Kelly, told *The New York Times* that his former boss "fitted the general definition of a fascist." This view was seconded by the chairman of the Joint Chiefs of Staff under Trump, General Mark Milley, who told author Bob Woodward that "Trump is a fascist to the core." When Kamala Harris was asked live on CNN whether she agreed that Trump was a fascist, her answer was unequivocal: "Yes I do." This was not merely a bit of political name calling. Serious scholars trotted out the F-word too. Jason Stanley, professor of philosophy, had been labeling Trump a fascist even prior to January 6, 2021. After the Capitol Riot, many others followed, including the doyen of fascism studies, historian Robert Paxton. Historian Federico Finchelstein also modified his opinion of Trump after January 6, putting him among a group of political leaders who at least had fascist tendencies, even if they were not yet full-blown fascists.[26]

By no means are all experts in agreement, however, in large part because there is so little agreement on what is meant by fascism. In one influential approach, historian of political thought Roger Griffin defines fascism as "a genus of political ideology whose mythic core in its various permutations is a palingenetic form of populist ultranationalism." Trump would certainly seem to meet the criteria of being both populist and hyper-nationalist, but Griffin asserts that Trump is not a fascist owing to his lack of ideological coherence. For those who understand both populism and fascism as a set of ideas, there is considerable difficulty in drawing the boundary between them. Griffin, like others, confusingly includes populism as a defining characteristic of fascism.[27]

As with populism, it remains contentious as to whether fascism is best understood as an ideology rather than as a political movement. Political scientist Sheri Berman cautions that while "Trump is undermining various norms and institutions of democracy . . . this doesn't make him a fascist, which means *much* more than these things." As with populism, I think we can better distinguish fascism from populism and other related concepts by examining what it does more than what it says. It is critical to remember here that fascism itself was even less ideologically coherent at the time than it appears in hindsight. As one historian of Fascist Italy puts it, when fascism burst on the political scene in the course of 1921–22, it was "characterised by ideological eclecticism and uncertainty," offering "no clear programme or ideology." The Italian Fascists developed a somewhat coherent doctrine only *after* they had got to power. Even then, when in 1927, five years after the March on Rome, Giovanni Gentile, an Italian political philosopher and member of Benito Mussolini's government, put forward a historical and philosophical account of Italian Fascism, he resisted the idea that fascism was a coherent "philosophy."[28]

Fascism shares with populism an association with charismatic authority; both rely heavily on the unmediated incorporation of the masses by a personalistic leader. This kind of political mobilization is strongly associated with the use of identity politics. It is when people believe themselves to be part of a threatened group that they are most likely to delegate power to a charismatic leader. Fascists too could be popular. Hitler's support continued to grow through 1940, long after any semblance of democracy in Germany had been extinguished. Mussolini, although he was never as electorally successful as Hitler, also attained a high degree of popularity. Critically, however, in the final analysis, the fascist's hold on power rests not on mass support or ideological persuasion, but on the actual or threatened suppression of the opposition.

If the key feature of populism as a type of politics is the personalistic mobilization of support through mass communication rather than the use of an institutionalized political party, fascism's essential quality is the use of violence. Historian of fascism, Stanley Payne, pointedly reminds us that "Hitler's place in history is not based on his remarks." The Nazis were extraordinarily violent, both on the way to power, and even more so once they got there. The same was true of Mussolini's Fascist movement, which unlike the Nazis, essentially came to power through a coup. As John Foot writes in his recent history of Italian Fascism, *Blood and Power*, "Having taken power through murderous violence, Italian fascism held onto it through further bloodshed and the occupation of the state." Foot continues, "Without violence. . . fascism would never have come close to power." It represented a new and still distinct way of doing politics, "a militia party, whose use of murder, beatings, intimidation, and destruction swept aside all opposition." Trump's nods and winks to the Proud Boys and other militant groups do not come close to this kind of armed assault on democracy. Thus far his use of the military has been more a publicity stunt than a violent power grab.[29]

As Trump's government "floods the zone" with executive orders, lawsuits, layoffs among the bureaucracy, mass deportations, troop deployments, and other disruptions to the system, many critics have been drawn into making the most extreme comparisons. I don't believe the F-word is a good fit for Trump. Focusing on the ways in which he could theoretically impose a fascist dictatorship takes attention away from what he is already doing. Even today we can see how Trump is using the state as a vehicle for personal enrichment. During his first term, he made millions of dollars from the patronage of his network of hotels by domestic and international lobbyists. In the first six months since his reelection, he has used his office to bilk more than $700 million from supplicants through various crypto schemes and scams.[30]

In trying to predict where Trump's reign is going, Argentina's Cristina Fernandes de Kirchner, Croatia's Ivo Sanader, or South Africa's Jacob Zuma, who used office to accumulate tens or even hundreds of millions of dollars in kickbacks, are likely useful guides. At the very least, there is a good chance that Trump will emulate the nepotism of India's Indira Gandhi, who conferred wealth and power on her sons, Sanjay and Rajiv; ominously, the Nehru–Gandhi family is now in its fifth generation of leadership of the Indian National Congress party. Even if Trump further curtailed political competition, the institutionalization of kleptocracy like that of the Philippines' populist-cum-dictator, Ferdinand Marcos, seems a more probable outcome than the genocidal schemes of Hitler or the brutal corporatism of Mussolini. Corruption, rather than totalitarianism, seems the more likely destination for populist leaders.[31]

These distinctions are not merely academic wordplay. Populists allow opponents to exist and to mobilize politically; fascists do not. Populism seeks to tilt the electoral playing field, fascism to end the game of politics altogether. Populism needs an institutionalized opposition to justify its existence; fascism is characterized by the violent demobilization, if not elimination, of its opponents. Labeling populism an "authoritarian form of democracy," as Finchelstein does in his popular recent books on populism and fascism, adds far more confusion than clarity. It is like labeling something a wet form of dry.

To say that Trump is a "Wannabe Fascist" minimizes the vast gap between words and deeds. Whatever the sins of populists like Trump, recourse to the systematic violent repression of the opposition is not an option for them. Today, such violence is deployed only by handful of the most secretive regimes in the world: North Korea, Myanmar, Turkmenistan. Populism is not simply fascism-lite. Populism's dependence on mass support—on the people—marks it off as something categorically different from fascism. Populism is a species of democracy, fascism a species of authoritarianism.[32]

Notes

1. "Ratfucker-in-Chief," in Gary Wills, "The Kingdom of Heaven," *New York Review of Books*, June 13, 1974; Richard Nixon, *The Memoirs of Richard Nixon* (Arrow, 1978).
2. On the connections between Chennault, Ellsberg, and the Watergate break-in, see Garrett M. Graff, *Watergate: A New History* (Avid Reader Press, 2022).
3. "the most ruthless," Mark Feldstein, "JFK's Own Dirty Trick on Nixon," *Pioneer Press*, November 11, 2015, https://www.twincities.com/2011/01/14/mark-feldstein-jfks-own-dirty-trick-on-nixon/.
4. The 10–20 percent figure is from Alexander Baturo, Paul Kenny, and Evren Balta, "Leaders' Experience and the Transition from Populism to Dictatorship," *Democratization*, August 28, 2024, 1–24, https://doi.org/10.1080/13510347.2024.2391482.
5. Paul Kenny, Kirk Hawkins and Saskia Ruth, "Populist Leaders Undermine Democracy in These 4 Ways. Would a President Trump?" *The Washington Post*, August 18, 2016, https://www.washingtonpost.com/news/monkey-cage/wp/2016/08/18/populists-undermine-democracy-in-these-4-ways-would-president-trump/.
6. "Statement by Press Secretary Sean Spicer, January 21, 2017, https://trumpwhitehouse.archives.gov/briefings-statements/statement-press-secretary-sean-spicer/.
7. "among the most dishonest human beings on earth," Michael M. Grynbaum. "Trump Strategist Stephen Bannon Says Media

Should 'Keep Its Mouth Shut,'" *New York Times*, January 26, 2017, https://www.nytimes.com/2017/01/26/business/media/stephen-bannon-trumpnews-media.html; "a running war with the media," Julie Hirschfeld Davis and Matthew Rosenberg, "With False Claims, Trump Attacks Media on Turnout and Intelligence Rift," *The New York Times*, January 21, 2017, https://www.nytimes.com/2017/01/21/us/politics/trump-white-house-briefing-inauguration-crowd-size.html; "the enemy of the people" David Remnick, "Trump and the Enemies of the People," *The New Yorker*, August 15, 2018. https://www.newyorker.com/news/daily-comment/trump-and-the-enemies-of-the-people.

8. *The January 6th Report* (Celadon Books, 2017), 376–377; 430–431.
9. Megan Brenan, "Americans' Trust in Media Remains at Trend Low," *Gallup*, October 14, 2024, https://news.gallup.com/poll/651977/americans-trust-media-remains-trend-low.aspx.
10. Simon Shuster, *The Showman: The Inside Story of the Invasion that Shook the World and Made a Leader of Volodymyr Zelensky* (HarperCollins, 2024).
11. Benedict Minder, "Chávez Closes Down Opposition Media Outlets," *Financial Times*, January 25, 2010, https://www.ft.com/content/5b28989a-0905-11df-ba88-00144feabdc0; Roy Carroll, *Comandante: Hugo Chávez's Venezuela* (Penguin, 2013), 186–187.
12. "direct manipulation," quoted in Tom Ginsburg and Aziz Z. Huq, *How to Save a Constitutional Democracy* (University of Chicago Press, 2020), 70.
13. Paul D. Kenny, "'The Enemy of the People': Populists and Press Freedom," *Political Research Quarterly* 73, no. 2 (2020): 261–275.
14. "Our propaganda," Ian Kershaw, "How Effective Was Nazi Propaganda?" in *Nazi Propaganda: The Power and the Limitations*, edited by David Welch (Routledge, 1983 [2016]), 199.
15. "a fraud on the American public," "dumps of votes," "This is total fraud," "This election was rigged," quoted in *The January 6th Report* (Celadon Books, 2017), 376–377.
16. Lawrence Lessig and Matthew Seligman, *How to Steal a Presidential Election* (Yale University Press, 2024).
17. *The Economist*, "A Wild Gerrymander Makes Hungary's Fidesz Party Hard to Dislodge," April 2, 2022, https://www.economist.com/graphic-detail/2022/04/02/a-wild-gerrymander-makes-hungarys-fidesz-party-hard-to-dislodge.

18. Nic Cheeseman and Brian Klass, *How to Rig an Election* (Yale University Press, 2019), 169–170.
19. Results available on request.
20. This is one of the *Federalist Papers* whose authorship remains unsure. Alexander Hamilton or James Madison [Publius], *Federalist Papers*, 51, February 8, 1788, https://guides.loc.gov/federalist-papers/text-51-60#s-lg-box-wrapper-25493427.
21. Christian Houle and Paul D. Kenny, "The Political and Economic Consequences of Populist Rule in Latin America," *Government and Opposition* 53, no. 2 (2018): 256–287; Andreas Kyriacou and Pedro Trivin, "Populism and the Rule of Law: The Importance of Institutional Legacies," *American Journal of Political Science* 59, no. 2 (2024): 495–510.
22. "guardrails," Daniel Ziblatt and Steven Levitsky, *How Democracies Die: What History Reveals about our Future* (Penguin, 2019); for the argument that strong institutions inhibit authoritarian power grabs, see Kurt Weyland, *Democracy's Resilience to Populism's Threat: Countering Global Alarmism* (Cambridge University Press, 2024); on the challenge of measuring institutional weakness, see Daniel M. Brinks, Steven Levitsky and Maria Victoria Murillo, *Understanding Institutional Weakness*, (Cambridge University Press, 2019), 15; Steven Levitsky and María Victoria Murillo, "Variation in Institutional Strength," *Annual Review of Political Science* 12, no. 1 (2009): 115–133.
23. "institutions are not" K. S. Komireddi, *Malevolent Republic: A Short History of the New India*, rev. ed. (Hurst, 2024), 182; Zsuzsanna Szelény, *Tainted Democracy: Viktor Orbán and the Subversion of Hungary* (Hurst, 2023), 56.
24. Robert A. Caro, *The Years of Lyndon Johnson: Volume I: The Path to Power* (Vintage, 1982); Robert A. Caro, *The Years of Lyndon Johnson: Volume II: Means of Ascent.* (Random House, 1992); Robert A. Caro, *The Years of Lyndon Johnson: Volume III: Master of the Senate.* (Vintage, 2002). Robert A. Caro. *The Years of Lyndon Johnson: Volume IV: The Passage of Power* (Random House, 2012).
25. Scholarship is divided on how much institutional damage Trump wrought during his first term; see John L. Campbell, *Institutions under Siege: Donald Trump's Attack on the Deep State* (Cambridge University Press, 2022);"Trump learned," Peter Baker, "Trump

Takes on the Pillars of the 'Deep State,'" *New York Times*, November 14, 2024.

26. "fitted the general," quoted in Michael S. Schmidt, "As Election Nears, Kelly Warns Trump Would Rule Like a Dictator," *The New York Times*, November 6, 2024, https://www.nytimes.com/2024/10/22/us/politics/john-kelly-trump-fitness-character.html; "Trump is a fascist," quoted in Matt Rothschild, "Trump and the Fascist Threat,' *Civic Media*, October 23, 2024, https://civicmedia.us/news/2024/10/23/trump-and-the-fascist-threat; Federico Finchelstein, *The Wannabe Fascists: A Guide to Understanding the Greatest Threat to Democracy* (University of California Press, 2024).
27. "a genus," Roger Griffin, *The Nature of Fascism* (Routledge, 1993), 26; Emma Bowman, "Harris Called Trump a 'Fascist.' Experts Debate What Fascism is—and Isn't," *NPR*, October 29, 2024, https://www.npr.org/2024/10/29/nx-s1-5164488/harris-trump-fascist-explained; Dylan Matthews, "Is Trump a Fascist? 8 Experts Weigh In," *Vox,* October 23, 2020, https://www.vox.com/policy-and-politics/21521958/what-is-fascism-signs-donald-trump; for examples of the conflation of populism and fascism, see Juan Linz, "Some Notes Towards a Comparative Study of Fascism in Sociological Historical Perspective," in Walter Laqueur, ed., *Fascism: A Reader's Guide* (University of California Press, 1979), 12; Umberto Eco, "Ur-Fascism," *New York Review of Books* 42, no. 11 (1995): 2.
28. "Trump is undermining," Matthews, "Is Trump a Fascist?"; "characterized by," "no clear programme," Christopher Duggan, *Fascist Voices: An Intimate History of Mussolini's Italy* (The Bodley Head, 2012), 103, 63; on Fascism's lack of an ideological doctrine, see Stanley G. Payne, *Fascism, Comparison and Definition* (University of Wisconsin Press, 1980), 4
29. "Hitler's place," Matthews, "Is Trump a Fascist?"; "Having taken power," "Without violence," "a militia party," John Foot, *Blood and Power: The Rise and Fall of Italian Fascism* (Bloomsbury, 2022), 1, 3, 108.
30. On the estimate of $700m: "The Growing Scandal of $TRUMP", *The Ezra Klein Show*, May 28, 2005, https://www.youtube.com/watch?v=JNJD-vKtrPc.
31. Ezra Klein, "The Growing Scandal of $Trump," *The New York Times*, May 28, 2025, https://www.nytimes.com/2025/05/28/opinion/ezra-klein-podcast-zeke-faux.html; David Frum, "The

Trump Presidency's World Historical Heist," *The Atlantic*, May 28, 2025, https://www.theatlantic.com/ideas/archive/2025/05/trump-golden-age-corruption/682935/. For comparative evidence, see Dong Zhang, "Draining the Swamp? Populist Leadership and Corruption," *Governance* 37, no. 4 (2024): 1141–1161; Julio F. Carrión and James G. Korman, "Populism and State Capture: Evidence from Latin America," *European Review of Latin American and Caribbean Studies / Revista Europea de Estudios Latinoamericanos y Del Caribe*, no. 116 (2023): 1–21; Andreas Kyriacou and Pedro Trivin. "Populism and the Rule of Law: The Importance of Institutional Legacies." *American Journal of Political Science* (2024), https://doi.org/10.1111/ajps.12935.

32. "authoritarian form of democracy," Federico Finchelstein, *From Fascism to Populism in History* (University of California Press, 2017), xvi; Finchelstein, *The Wannabe Fascists.*

8

AFTER POPULISM

What comes after populism?

This book goes to press as Donald Trump has begun the second of two non-consecutive terms in office. Before he re-entered the White House, Trump, in his characteristic "does he mean it, does he not?" fashion—an ambiguity that has long served as both his shield and his cudgel—floated the idea of a seeking a third term in 2028. His supporters tittered with the knowing air of those in on a private joke. His opponents, meanwhile, shuddered, knowing that in the age of Trump, yesterday's taunt has a way of becoming tomorrow's executive order.

As it stands, a third term would be unconstitutional. Indeed, for many Americans, a third term would signify nothing less than the complete collapse of democracy. Of course, a third term didn't always have such significance. The Twenty-Second Amendment, which prohibits it, was only ratified in 1951. Before that, FDR was in his fourth term when he died in 1945. Democracy survived his life and death. Theodore Roosevelt narrowly lost his bid for a third term in 1912. Few fretted that democracy was on the brink. The nation's first president, George Washington, was implored to run for a third term in 1796. Democracy would likely have survived a third Washington term if it had come to pass. A third Trump term in 2028 seems unlikely at this point; but Trump will nevertheless bequeath a legacy that bodes ill for American democracy.

When George Washington did step down, he left Americans with a "farewell address" that has become required reading in civics courses ever since. Ever conscious of his reputation, Washington observed the convention that a man did not seek office; he was chosen for it. He duly thanked the American people for selecting him twice as president. But now, he felt, his duty was done. Also on Washington's mind was the growing polarization of American politics. He bemoaned the "combinations and associations" that placed the "will of a party" above the "will of a nation." After the War of Independence—itself partly a civil war—Washington was the only man who seemed to stand above the fray. He was the obvious choice to be the nation's inaugural president, with the office, in many ways, designed to fit the man. So ill-defined were the prerogatives of the executive branch that Washington could have used his authority to clamp down on the fractious parties that plagued his presidency.

Yet he made a different choice, tolerating, even if not embracing, political parties. The Federalists, in effect Washington's party, held on to power for another term. John Adams was a profound thinker and an honest man, but not a good politician. It was he, rather than Washington, who repressed the opposition with the Alien and Sedition Acts of 1798. In 1802, he lost the presidency to Thomas Jefferson and the latter's new Democratic-Republican party. Then, by accident, if not design, with the vigorous Alexander Hamilton replacing Adams as the effective leader of the Federalists, America looked to have stumbled on one of the essential instruments of democracy: a competitive party system.

The great advantage of a competitive party system is that it doesn't take a big swing in popular sentiment to change the government every few years. In this way, governments are held accountable. If they perform well, they may be retained. If they do not, they will be removed. However, without a competitive party system, the government knows it cannot lose.

This lack of accountability is a recipe for misgovernance, corruption, populism, and ultimately, the erosion of democracy.

Although America would eventually develop such a competitive party system, alas, it didn't quite happen in the early decades of the nineteenth century. If you haven't seen the musical *Hamilton*, spoiler alert—the hero dies in a duel with his long-time New York political rival, Aaron Burr, in 1804. The Federalists went into disarray and the Democratic-Republican party consolidated its hold on power—controlling government until 1828. This elitist status quo—known as the Era of Good Feelings—was eventually blown up by a groundswell of resentment and the election of the nation's first populist president, Andrew Jackson.

Interestingly, for our purposes, the Age of Jackson saw the emergence of a competitive party system that lasted for decades. Jackson's Democrats exchanged power with the Whig Party, whose main plank was opposition to the party of "King Andrew." The Whigs were then replaced by the Republican Party on the eve of the Civil War, giving rise to the two-party system that has persisted until today. Over recent electoral cycles, the Republican and Democratic parties have become increasingly polarized, with voters seemingly sorting themselves along a coherent highly educated/liberal/globalist versus uncredentialed/conservative/nationalist cleavage. The question thus arises: Could today's populist age—the Age of Trump—signal the consolidation of a novel political realignment, one that could invigorate American democracy in the years to come? What about beyond America? Could we also see the consolidation of stable party systems formed along these lines around the world?

This is unlikely. Returning to the Jackson case, a few things have to be kept in mind. First, whatever his regime did to entrench democracy as a way of government for white men, it brought disaster upon America's Indigenous peoples, while also postponing the nation's necessary reckoning with racial slavery. Second, the kind of party system it introduced was one based on clientelism, or vote buying. As a result, it institutionalized an unprecedented level of corruption. The spoils system, which turned government into a vast patronage machine, did not merely entrench inefficiency and graft; it set in motion a political cycle that would, time and again, produce sudden eruptions of populist fervor. The People's Party of the 1890s, the meteoric rise of Theodore Roosevelt in the early twentieth century—both were, in their own way, reactions against a system that had become too comfortable in its own corruption. As I noted in Chapter 7, one of the most notable features of Trump's presidencies has been the scale of their corruption.

Indeed, this oscillation between populism and clientelism has hardly been unique to the United States. In the later democratizing nations of Latin America, southern Europe, and Asia, it has been less a cycle than a permanent condition, a political seesaw with no equilibrium. Populists like Perón and Indira Gandhi have used patronage as a way to consolidate their rule, transforming themselves, at least partially, from populists to machine party bosses. But as we saw in Chapter 5, clientelistic political systems of this sort are prone to further periodic crises. The party machines of Perón and Gandhi were themselves outflanked by a new generation of populists. In places like Peru and Pakistan, Guatemala and Greece, power has swung between populist insurgents and corrupt, patronage-driven machines, each feeding on the failures of the other, each promising an end to instability while ensuring its continuation.

For years—decades, even—this fate was kept at bay in the programmatic party-controlled states of Western Europe and its far-flung settler outposts. The machinery of organized politics, creaking though it often was, held together. But the transformations wrought by technology in recent decades—the way it has reordered social life, remapping professional and private human relationships—have corroded these parties to the point that their restoration now seems impossible. As we saw in Chapter 5, people no longer inhabit the dense, face-to-face political networks that once stitched civil society together. The church pews are vacant, the unions memberless. We live in an era of direct communion between mass audiences and their political celebrities, an age where connection is instantaneous but community is elusive. Alienation has not prevented the rise of sudden, dramatic social movements—indeed, it may fuel them—but it has left the steady, disciplined work of party organization harder than ever to sustain. For now, the populists of Old Europe remain in a state of partial triumph, their power real but incomplete. They have taken cities, parliaments, ministries, but only rarely have they claimed the whole edifice of government for themselves.

If—perhaps when—they do, it is difficult to imagine them repairing this fractured system, for the simple reason that they have no interest in doing so. Populists thrive where parties fail. I am unaware of a populist who has made the transformation to a more programmatic form of rule. This would, of course, require building institutions and obeying their rules—anathema to populists.

In Chapter 7, we examined what happens in the rare instances when populism becomes a permanent dictatorship. The aim of this chapter is to look at what happens *after populism* in the other eight or nine out of ten cases. In most instances, the result is a kind of serial, or intermittent populism as the foregoing discussion suggests. This is the state in which much of the world finds itself today—a place of instability and anxiety. In the final part of this book, I'll ask how we might escape the populist trap. Before we get there, though, one other question needs to be asked.

Is populism ever good for democracy?

If you've been paying attention so far, this question might seem redundant. I've documented myriad ways in which populist governments seek to erode the competitiveness of democracy—in a minority of cases, to the point of crossing the threshold into dictatorship. Yet many scholars argue that populism may be "a corrective" to democracy, as well as a threat. How is this possible? Scholarship advancing this view usually comes from the ideational approach. In this sense, populism's effect depends on the "host ideology" with which it is paired. So-called inclusive populists stress socioeconomic policies that favor the lower classes, thereby potentially enhancing democracy, while "exclusionary" populists instead define the people in terms of identity, with more perilous consequences for minorities.

Yet this approach is not especially convincing. There are multiple examples of populists on the left also undermining democracy. Hugo Chávez brought about a short-term reduction in Venezuelan inequality through massive social spending programs financed by a boom in oil prices; yet his methods—including cracking down on the media and packing the supreme court with his supporters—changed Venezuela from democracy to dictatorship. Indira Gandhi, despite her turn to the left in the late 1960s, dramatically prorogued India's parliament from 1975. More broadly, populists on the left might even be *more* likely to erode press freedom because of their willingness to nationalize private industries. Whatever being "inclusionary" does, it does not protect democracy. A rejoinder to this criticism is that what matters is not whether populism's host ideology is right or left in economic terms, but whether it is right or left in the sense of authoritarian or not. Yet this approach doesn't solve the problem. It defines it away. Declaring that authoritarians are bad for democracy is about as insightful as pointing out that fire is hot—technically true, but not exactly a breakthrough in political analysis.[1]

An alternative argument is that populism can be democratizing out of power but rarely in it. We've seen that once in power, populism's defining traits—its lack of institutionalization, its instinctive hostility to constraints—make it a dangerous force for democracy. Dispensing with the rules entirely may seem like a bold stroke against corruption or elitism, but in practice, it means dismantling the very framework that allows for pluralism. In opposition, however, populism thrives on exposing the failures of the status quo, challenging institutions that have grown complacent, and giving voice to grievances that the political establishment would rather ignore. Populism draws its energy not from abstract demagoguery, but from a real and often justified sense that the system is failing. By shining a light on these inequities, populism has the potential—at least in theory—to push democracy toward reform rather than decay. Populism could, then, improve the quality of democracy.

This possibility is clearest in moments when the institutions populists attack are themselves manifestly unjust. Including non-democracies as the starting point, populism's opposition to the status quo takes on a more constructive character. In most authoritarian regimes, mass mobilization is strictly prohibited. During the Cold War, demonstrations against Communist Party rule in Hungary, Czechoslovakia, and China were brutally put down. Less ideological military dictators like Iraq's Saddam Hussein and Uganda's Idi Amin were just as quick to violently choke off any threat to their rule. Authoritarian leaders who fail to prevent or quickly suppress popular mobilization are at great risk of being removed from power, and violently at that.

There have been moments—rare, but significant—when populists, rather than eroding democracy, have become its unlikely champions. Periods of opening, or partial liberalization, are often most auspicious for democratizing populist movements to develop. In a handful of non-democratic states where a degree of political liberalization was allowed to persist, populists have rallied the masses against the entrenched order, turning popular resentment into a force for enhancing rather than subverting democracy. The O'Connells, the Gandhis, the Mandelas—these figures exist, but they are the exception, not the rule. For every one of them, history has given us a dozen

Trumps, Orbáns, and Putins, leaders who have mastered the art of wielding populism not to build democracy but to dismantle it. And yet, if we are to understand populism, we cannot cherry-pick the cases that fit our anxieties while ignoring those that complicate them. We need a theory that accounts for both the norm—the steady democratic erosion that populism so often brings—and the anomaly—the rare instances where it has done the opposite. If the direst predictions of democratic backsliding prove true, these history lessons will be ignored at our peril.

If any case has equal claim to have given rise to the term populism as that of the Populist Party in the United States, it is that of Russia's nearly contemporaneous *narodnik* movement. It is worth exploring why it failed so ignominiously. Although the term *narod* does not have an exact equivalent in English, it is usually translated as "people" or "common people." *Narodnichestvo*—literally people-ism or populism—was then both a set of revolutionary ideas and a disparate movement that sought to liberate an impoverished peasant population held in a state of near slavery in late tsarist Russia. Although Russian serfs were not strictly property in the same way as American slaves, they were tied to the land and could be transferred from one aristocratic landowner to another against their will. They were even characterized as being ethnically distinct from Russia's numerically small and Europeanized elite. Although formally emancipated in 1861, Russia's peasants continued to live in appalling conditions.

The Russian populist movement was led by members of the educated and Westernized elite, who idolized the uncorrupted and thoroughly native Russian peasants. Perhaps for their own ends, the bourgeois elite saw in the peasants the possibility of forcing democratic reforms on the absolutist tsar. In the Russian case, populism was a movement for the people, not of them. Populist intellectuals urged middle-class students to "go to the people" and mobilize them. But the people turned out to be much more conservative toward institutions than the populists imagined. Populists bemoaned the peasant's religiosity and misogyny; as one historian of the movement writes, the "peasants themselves remained impervious to the intelligentsia's revolutionary plans for them." A true populist movement in which the masses mobilize in opposition to the institutional status quo was especially unlikely to take off in late imperial Russia. For sure, despite the apparent apathy of the peasantry, there was obvious dissatisfaction with the status quo. But Russian populism failed, because the state and its elite had the means and the will to repress it. The revolutionary ideas of the *narodnik* movement were pushed underground and taken up by anarchists like the People's Will. The rupture in state authority caused by World War I made the revolution of 1917 possible, but the triumphant Bolsheviks were anything but populist.[2]

Populism, by its nature, thrives by giving voice to popular opposition to the entrenched order. Freedom of expression is not just a feature of populism; it is its oxygen. Deng Xiaoping, China's reformist premier, learned this the hard way during the Tiananmen Square protests of 1989. As the demonstrations dragged on, their demands grew bolder, shifting from calls for reform to demands for outright political change. In the end, the uprising was crushed with brutal force, a spectacle of repression that served as a lasting warning. Ever since, Chinese leaders have worked tirelessly to prevent such mass mobilizations from taking root again. In fully authoritarian systems like tsarist Russia and Communist China—where dissent is snuffed out before it can gather momentum—populism has little room to breathe. Yet it does not require a fully liberal democracy to take hold. Where there is even a glimmer of political openness—where the press retains some freedom; where elections, however flawed, still matter—populism can force its way through.

Early nineteenth-century Ireland was hardly a place of freedom and equality for Irish Catholics. By then, various movements—ranging from the peaceful to the violent—to shake off British rule had failed, the most recent being Wolfe Tone's United Irishmen revolt of 1798. With the Act of Union of 1801, which removed the separate Irish parliament in favor of providing seats directly at Westminster, Britain appeared to be settled in for the long haul. Catholics in Ireland had been given the right to vote in 1793 and could run for office after 1801, but the status quo was hardly fair as far as Catholics were concerned. Even though most Catholics could vote, this was still done in public, which meant that Protestant landlords exerted considerable control over their tenants' ballots. Moreover, Catholics remained effectively barred from office by the Test Acts, which would have required them to disavow their religion to take their seats.

Daniel O'Connell was from a prosperous landed Catholic family, which had retained its status during the years of British colonial rule. Although a brilliant lawyer, O'Connell was prevented from acquiring a lucrative position as King's Counsel because of his religion. Catholic Emancipation was narrowly about allowing well-to-do Catholics like himself access to parliament and political office, but to get there, O'Connell needed to mobilize the masses. O'Connell faced exactly the problem of apathy we've discussed with reference to the present day. There was mass resignation rather than resistance to the 1801 elimination of the Dublin parliament. O'Connell would privately describe his fellow Catholics as "crawling slaves" for their failure to act.[3]

By the 1810s, however, tenants were spontaneously defying their landlords. O'Connell reacted to this democratic potential to outflank the old Protestant order. He promised farmers an improvement in living standards and freedom from the everyday oppressions of British rule. In 1823, O'Connell created a broad membership organization called the Catholic Association, which he used as a means of disseminating his message. He was a gifted speaker—one peasant said of O'Connell's sonorous voice, "You'd hear it a mile off as if it was coming through honey"—and he attracted enormous crowds to his speeches. At one later "monster meeting" in Tara in 1843, more than half a million people were said to be in attendance. O'Connell stood for and won a seat in County Clare in 1828 as "Man of the People." He was barred from taking office, but when elections for the vacant seat were held again in 1829, O'Connell repeated his success.

The end result of O'Connell's mass mobilization was mixed. The Roman Catholic Relief Act of 1829 finally removed most of the Penal Laws, which had limited Catholic advancement. However, even though the Relief Act allowed O'Connell and other Catholics to take up office, it raised the franchise from forty shillings to ten pounds, effectively disenfranchising 80 percent of Irish voters. O'Connell continued his agitation, but this time along with the movement for more fundamental democratic reforms in mainland Britain.

Across the Irish Sea, the allocation of parliamentary seats along historic lines meant that the Westminster parliament was utterly unrepresentative of an increasingly urbanized British population. Many "rotten boroughs" of just a few hundred dependent peasants had the same representation at Westminster as cities of millions like Leeds and Manchester. After 1829, the pressure for reform reached a crescendo, with millions of British workers pressing to widen the franchise. The result was the Reform Act of 1832, which introduced a series of democratizing amendments, including the introduction of new seats for urban constituencies.

Important as it was, the act increased the proportion entitled to vote only from 1 to 7 percent. As a result, most workers felt themselves still denied the gains that should have come from their participation in the pressure for reform prior to 1832. Another charismatic Irishman, Feargus O'Connor, became the frontman of a vast new movement known as Chartism, whose aim was to expand the franchise still further; 3,317,752 people signed the 1842 petition for the People's Charter—this was about a third of the adult population and over three-and-a-half times the size of the actual electorate in 1841. The people, working-class people, wanted to reform a set of institutions that excluded them. As one Chartist put it, "The pulpit, the press, the stage, the universities and public seminaries, the literature of the country, in short, every avenue to knowledge and every channel of information . . . are all preoccupied and conducted in the interests of the upper and middle classes." In short, the system was rigged.[4]

Parliament's rejection of the People's Charter in 1848 was not just a defeat; it was a statement of intent. The ruling class would not yield, not to petitions, not to protests, not to the sheer weight of public demand. O'Connor's health began to fail soon after, and with it, the movement itself faded. By decade's end, Chartism was little more than a memory. Daniel O'Connell, the great champion of Catholic emancipation, had died the previous year. Their causes—democratic rights for the working class, self-rule for Ireland—remained unfinished business. It was the labor unions, in the end, that would push Britain toward fuller democracy and social reform. It was a combination of above-ground and clandestine nationalist political organization that won Irish independence.

But to dismiss the populists of this earlier era as mere failures would be to miss the point. Before mass labor parties, before disciplined nationalist movements, there were individuals—millions of them—who, in isolation, had little power, but who, when mobilized by populist leaders, forced their grievances onto the national stage. These populist movements did not complete the work, but they set the terms of the (mostly successful) struggles that followed. If Chartism did not win democracy, it made the working classes impossible to ignore. If O'Connell did not win Irish freedom, he ensured that subsequent nationalists would have a more sympathetic audience. Populism would provide the spark to democratic and liberation movements elsewhere.

If by the turn of the twentieth century, Britain was a liberal democracy, the same was not true of its colonies. The Irish might have been first in and first out, becoming independent in 1921, but they weren't the last. Taking an entirely different path to the Irish revolutionaries, Indians largely eschewed the use of terrorism. No one took this non-violence to extremes more than Mohandas Gandhi. An English-educated lawyer from a middle-class background, Gandhi was dismayed by the state of Indian migrant laborers he observed while working in South Africa. Forcibly removed from the whites-only section of a train in what was then Natal Province, Gandhi's humiliation drove him to mobilize for the rights of his fellow Indian expats.

When he returned home, he took up the job of securing equal rights for all Indians. By the end of World War I, British rule in India was even less democratic than in Ireland. Although more or less free to conduct their private affairs, the Indian masses were essentially afforded no role in governing the colony. The British were not entirely averse to repression—as the massacre at Amritsar in 1919 illustrated—but their preferred strategy was to placate the elite, while keeping the masses passive. Prominent Indian nationalists like Motilal Nehru, Mohammad Jinnah, and others worked for reform from within colonial institutions. Gandhi, in contrast, took resistance out of doors, mobilizing the masses in resistance campaigns that appealed to their material interests—rent strikes, opposition to salt taxes, and so on. Gandhi was far from universally supported by India's political leadership; but his worship by the masses provided a focal point for the nationalist movement that may have been otherwise lacking. India gained independence in 1947, and democracy survived Gandhi's assassination in 1948.

The fact that neither Gandhi nor O'Connell nor O'Connor actually led governments may be revealing. It's far from clear that populist anti-colonial movements that gain power necessarily enhance democracy. Sukarno in Indonesia, Kwame Nkrumah in Ghana, Julius Nyerere in Tanzania, and Jomo Kenyatta in Kenya are among those who cultivated personalistic movements that succeeded in overthrowing colonial rule. However, in each case, once they had attained power, they curtailed the rights of the opposition and sooner or later became dictators. It seems to be, in short, that populist movements have the potential to be democratizing when they are opposing an unrepresentative status quo. Once they come to power, however, they revert to form. Their demands for pluralism last only as long as they are in the minority.

The exception that proves the rule is South Africa. Apartheid-era South Africa was the quintessential minority-run political system. White Afrikaners, mostly descendants of Dutch colonial settlers, dominated both the country's economy and its political system. Over the first half of the twentieth century, the African National Congress (ANC) became the primary opposition to the regime, but its initially peaceful mobilization was brutally repressed. As in the other cases where there was no option of peaceful mass politics, the ANC turned to sabotage and terrorism. While some of the ANC leadership went into exile, Nelson Mandela stayed on to lead the insurgency. Arrested and convicted in 1962, Mandela spent most of the next three decades at the notorious detention center on Robben Island. Yet he remained a leader to those in the movement who passed in and out of prison and he retained his status as figurehead of the movement. As a Justice Department memo described Mandela around 1980, "He now has acquired the characteristic prison-charisma of the contemporary liberation leader."[5]

As Western sanctions against South Africa began to bite and the possibility of an alternate economic sponsor was eliminated with the collapse of the Soviet Union—and China not yet having assumed this role in Africa—the Apartheid regime was forced into concessions. Mandela was released in 1990 and began negotiating with President F. W. de Klerk. Even the latter acknowledged that Mandela "had an exceptional ability to make everyone with whom he came into contact feel special." The primary non-negotiable for Mandela and the ANC was a unitary, majoritarian electoral system. Given South Africa's demographics, this virtually guaranteed the

ANC power, something that a power-sharing executive like that adopted in Northern Ireland would not have done.[6]

De Klerk accepted the inevitable, but he secured in the transition agreement a high level of protection for whites in the bureaucracy, the judiciary, and the military. He also obtained agreement that there would be no major expropriations of private land or wealth. The 1994 constitution ensured protection for white dominance of the economy, while ceding control over the political realm to the black majority. Mandela too accepted the bargain. He appreciated that at least in the short term, the public and private sector needed the expertise of white South Africans. After his overwhleming victory in the general elections in 1994 he declared, "We have to be careful not to create the fear that the majority is going to be used for the purpose of coercing the minority."[7]

As in the case of any populist in power, formal institutional provisions were no guarantee that Mandela would not use his political power to renege on the deal. However, unlike other cases where democratically elected populists have used their control over the executive and legislative branches to erect legal impediments to the opposition, Mandela had no such need. With a massive majority and a weak and divided opposition, Mandela was virtually certain of keeping power as long as he wanted, so he had little incentive to risk his international reputation by hampering the opposition's capacity to mobilize. It turned out, moreover, that the aging Mandela was far more interested in using, and burnishing, his celebrity abroad than in governing at home. He had no intention of personally holding on to power.

This was quite unlike the sitution in places like Hungary or Türkiye, where young populist leaders had a clear interest in retaining office. Orbán and Erdoğan faced an opposition that posed a credible political threat to their rule, which incentivized them to erode press freedoms and judicial autonomy. Mandela was also institutionally well-placed to be able to keep his own coaliation together. The fact that a sizable segment of the growing South African economy was in state, or para-state, hands at the time of transition also meant that the government was able to cultivate a black economic elite without having to expropriate white-owned firms or land held by the private sector as the contemporaneous Mugabe regime did in Zimbabwe. The ANC had the ready means to quickly transition into a clientelistic party—distributing patronage in return for political support. Control over South Africa's public television network also provided a ready instrument for disseminating the party message without interfering with the private media.

The conditions faced by Mandela are in many ways sui generis. Given the unusual domestic and geopolitical context in which Mandela came to power, it would be rash to generalize too broadly from this experience. Few populists emerge with such overwhelming majorities grounded on clear demographic lines. Although other populists have won substantial electoral victories, as we've seen previously, popularity can ebb quickly given the general lack of institutionalized party ties between populists and their supporters. Commanding a national liberation movement (NLM) as much as a party, Mandela had a very different inheritance from other populist leaders. At the same time, South Africa's well-endowed state sector provided the ANC the means to consolidate its hold on power through patronage, another asset that many incoming populists lack.

What's more, as the ANC's margin of victory fell over the years, the willingness of its leaders, especially Jacob Zuma, to resort to repression of the opposition increased. The public broadcaster became increasingly politicized, while editors and journalists were pressured to support the ANC regime in the name of defending the "national interest." Now the ANC—the new face of the corrupt status quo—faces the prospect of being undone by new populist challengers like Julius Malema—one-time leader of the ANC's young wing, and now head of his own party, the Economic Freedom Fighters (EFF).[8]

So, can populism be good for democracy? When majorities of the population are kept out of power, as in oligarchic, colonial, or apartheid-like contexts, populism may be democracy-enhancing. In these contexts, it is in the strategic interests of the populist to push for reforms that give more people more political rights. Populism, as a weakly institutionalized political movement, may be the best hope of pushing for such reforms when formal opposition parties are heavily constrained, if not outlawed. Populism's democratizing potential, then, seems to be limited to relatively few situations: non-democratic, but somewhat liberal. Our definition of populism should account for these unuusal cases. Yet the implications of populist rule for democracy should also be clear. In office, all populists, whatever their original goals, face the same temptation to erode the ability of the opposition to challenge them for power—to undermine, rather than strengthen, democracy.

Does populism beget populism?

If populism in power seems unlikely to precipitate a deep renewal of party-based democracy, the question naturally arises: What does come after it? Commonly, what follows populism is more populism. To see how and why, let's examine the Italian case. Superficially, the postwar Italian party system resembled that of the bureaucratic German or British ones. On the left was the Italian Socialist Party (PSI), led by Pietro Nenni, and the more radical Italian Communist Party (PCI), led by Palmiro Togliatti. The PSI's support base was in the unionized working class, while the communists were stronger among the peasantry. On the center right was the Christian Democratic Party (DC), which drew primarily on the organizational capacity of the church, promising a conservative but democratic counterpoint to the feared radicalism of the PCI. At the political level, voters' attachment to these (nominally) ideologically distinct parties—the DC and the PSI/PCI—has sometimes been identified as electoral support through *voto di appartenza*—a vote based on loyalty and affection. In the early years, the status of the free market, and especially of Italy's dependent relationship with the United States, loomed large in political choice. Yet as the DC became the party of government, the more important source of electoral support was clientelism or the *voto di scambio*—vote-buying.

Italian politics, with its murky relationship with organized crime, would become notoriously corrupt. This system came to a calamitous end in the early 1990s as revelations of bribery and extortion were uncovered by activist public prosecutors. The collapse of support for all of the traditional parties left a void in the political space that allowed a new political force led by media magnate Silvio Berlusconi to enter politics. A man of modest origins but great ambition, Berlusconi made his initial fortune in a number of major real estate deals in Milan in the 1970s. Through the 1980s, his fortune grew and his business empire diversified, most notably into television. As municipal elections approached in November 1993, Berlusconi endorsed Rome's Gianfranco Fini, leader of the neo-fascist Italian Social Movement (MSI), but by the turn of the new year, it was clear that Berlusconi wanted power for himself. Presaging the rise of Trump some two decades later, Berlusconi exploited his media resources for all they were worth. Although a well-connected tycoon himself, he was sufficiently distant from the old elite to adopt the image of an outsider, declaring "enough of these politicians."[9]

Berlusconi called for a "free organization of voters" rather than "the umpteenth party faction." As owner of the famous AC Milan football club, and piggybacking on Italians' love of football, he christened his new non-party movement Forza Italia. His "non-party" quickly expanded across the country, establishing local "clubs" to provide some organizational footing, but it lacked formal branches, members, party congresses, or internal elections. Berlusconi himself chose the candidates and the movement's imagery, while Forza's appeal remained very much focused on the charisma of the former crooner himself. Berlusconi's networks bombarded viewers with Forza Italia advertisements, and unsurprisingly, viewership of his channels was strongly positively associated with voting for his movement. Forza captured 21 percent of the vote in the March 1994 elections, making a party that hadn't existed just six months previously the largest in parliament.[10]

With his coalition partners, the nationalist and xenophobic Alleanza Nationale and the Northern League, and a few nominal independents, Berlusconi became the Second Republic's first prime minister. However, Berlusconi's first cabinet didn't last long. Deserted by the League, Berlusconi was forced to cede power to the economist, Lamberto Dini, who was then serving as Berlusconi's treasury minister. In 1996, Berlusconi finished as runner-up to the leftist Olive Tree coalition (the former communist Democratic Party of the Left, or PDS, being the largest party), which backed former European Commission bureaucrat Romano Prodi as prime minister. Just two years later, however, Berlusconi was back in the prime minister's office, this time with a larger majority.

Although his third term lasted for five years, a lifetime in Italian politics, his legacy was not to introduce any newfound political stability. Berlusconi's rule was characterized by rampant abuse of power, corruption, and sleaze. Indeed, much of his party's legislative efforts appear to have been dedicated to ensuring that Berlusconi's business interests continued to thrive and that Berlusconi and his allies remained out of prison. So disgraced had the Italian political establishment become after the scandals of the prior Christian Democratic party era and the two decades of Berlusconi predominance that the country was forced to turn to a sequence of essentially unelected and minority technocratic leaders to deal with the economic crisis of the late 2000s.

In 2018, with not much place left for voters to go, a plurality of Italians turned to the Five Star Movement (M5S) of celebrity satirist Beppe Grillo. With a conviction for manslaughter on his record, Grillo ruled himself out of taking parliamentary leadership, but he remained the charismatic face of the party through the election. Propelled to first place by a groundswell of resentment toward the domestic and international status quo, M5S, under the nominal leadership of Giuseppe Conte, led successive populist governing coalitions. Its primary partner in these years, the Northern League, is also often classified as being populist. Although this would be true in later years, at first, the League developed under Umberto Bossi as a more traditional party with strong social roots in Lombardy and a mass membership. Even membership itself required some degree of activism and participation. Yet the League's organization subsequently declined so that by the time Matteo Salvini burst onto the scene in 2018, defeating its disgraced leader, Bossi, it was more recognizably a populist party. Even as its number of party branches had fallen to a third of the level just seven years before, it was growing its vote share through Salvini's charismatic leadership.

By 2021, Italy appeared to be done with parties altogether. M5S's Conte was replaced in 2021 by the economist, Mario Draghi, who led a government of national unity. However competent, and that is a matter of debate I can't resolve here, the lack of political party building inherent in his technocratic government left Italy susceptible to further populist mobilization. The year 2022 saw the rise of yet another populist movement, the Brothers of Italy (Fratelli d'Italia). For years little more than the hardcore remnants of Italy's neo-fascist MSI, the Brothers' popularity grew exponentially with the selection of Giorgia Meloni as leader. Meloni, now Italy's first female prime minister, was a direct draw for many, one former Berlusconi voter describing her as "smart, very determined and charismatic."[11]

Italy is often cast in the role of quaint traditionalism, if not, in the words of political scientist, Edward Banfield, "amoral familism." But Italy's predicament has much less to do with national culture than it does with the total collapse of its historical political party organizations. Populism did not cause the collapse of the Italian party system; rather, populism was and remains a political strategy that is successful in a context devoid of deeply institutionalized parties. In this sense, "backward" Italy may offer us a glimpse of the future, arriving at its post-party state earlier than everyone else.[12]

Although the parties established in the first half of the twentieth century in places like the Netherlands and Sweden have held on to power, their dominant positions have been deeply eroded. In France, where, with the exception of the communists, parties were never as organizationally integrated in society, populism has been a recurrent presence. Emanuel Macron's defeat of the socialists and the center right created a huge political void that the populist far right—under Marine Le Pen—and far left—under Jean Luc Mélanchon—have rushed to fill.

Even where the old party brands remain ascendant, as in Britain and the United States, party organizations are increasingly "hollow," with little by way of social connection to those who vote for them. With each populist like Trump or the UK's Boris Johnson chipping away at this already degraded edifice, the prospect of further successful populist campaigns in the near future remains likely. Because populists are unlikely to remedy the conditions that led to their election in the first place, their exit from power often simply produces a further round of mobilization against the institutional status quo.[13]

Democratic politics with parties is no idyll. But without them, the situation tends to be far worse. The reason is not that non-populist parties and their politicians are pure of heart. Rather, simply by each party member following her own primary interests of obtaining re-election and promotion to ever more powerful positions in government, she constrains her party leader from doing his worst. A sequence of populist rule—serial populism—is likely to result in a more institutionally degraded form of democracy. As we saw over the last two chapters, populists hamper the ability of minorities to organize politically, and often the result is discriminatory and harmful economic and social policies. With parties in deep decline and unlikely to return to their former health, the preservation of the pluralist institutions needed for democracy to work is a major challenge.

What is to be done?

Populism is not inherently undemocratic, but in practice, it wears away the institutional safeguards that protect pluralism and uphold the division of power. These institutions are often frustrating—they slow policymaking, force compromise, and produce half-measures that satisfy no one entirely. But in a diverse society, this is not a flaw; it is a necessity. In a world of conflicting interests, we face a choice: Either impose total homogeneity or accept a system that gives as many people as possible most of what they want most of the time. Compromise is not a weakness; it is the price of living together in a free society.

This is the great insight of classical liberalism—one that deserves preservation. Populism's promise is seductive: Sweep away the procedures, the delays, the bureaucracy, and finally, the people's will shall be done. But this is an illusion. There is no single "people." The moment we dispense with institutions that mediate between competing interests, we do not achieve unity—we usher in the tyranny of the momentary majority.

One response to populism is to call for stronger institutional safeguards. Central banks must be independent. All executive actions should be subject to judicial review. There should be autonomous bureaucratic czars in charge of policy areas from immigration to public health. Scientific communities and expert quangos should control the policymaking process. I am unconvinced that technocracy is the answer. There is surely a valid case for expertise and technology to play a role in some areas of government. But these areas should be the exception, and political leaders need to do a better job of justifying why they should be excluded from the purview of voters.

The majority of policy areas—from immigration to crime to trans rights—are surely political ones; that is, there is no simple technocratic solution to them. Even public health may benefit from more open political debate. Recent research reveals that the social distancing measures advocated by scientific experts during the COVID-19 pandemic may have done more harm than good. Political parties, advocacy groups, and citizens should be free to debate these issues and come up with policies that meet the approval of a majority without imposing excessively on minorities. To choke off these areas from public oversight is only to invite populist opposition to an institutionally closed status quo. Ultimately, in many policy realms, our disagreements are political and legitimate. There are no right answers, only agreeable ones.[14]

This means that non-populists should genuinely engage with the demands that motivate populist opposition to the status quo. In other words, non-populists need to do a better job of listening to voters rather than simply shutting down voter concerns over cultural issues, calling them illegitimate. This doesn't mean caving to majoritarian demands to expropriate or abuse minorities; but it would imply taking seriously demands to reduce *further* immigration, to strictly police crime, or to cater to conservative majorities on other cultural issues.

Some will object here that this is to let populism win. Even if populists don't come to power, their policies become the law of the land. For me, this is to mistake the nature of populism. As we've seen, populism is not a distinctively dangerous or illiberal set of policies. It is, rather, a challenge to the institutional status quo. Sometimes these challenges can be a good thing—when mainstream parties take them up, the result can be an improvement of democracy. While the original Populist Party fizzled out, the Democratic and Republican parties each adopted parts of its radical platform—breaking up monopolies, direct election of senators—taking many of its supporters with them, too.

Populism is hazardous not for its *ideas* but because of the *form* it takes. Public opinion, even on issues as contentious as immigration and identity politics, may not be nearly as dangerous as many of populism's opponents think. Sensible immigration reforms can be introduced without threatening the welfare of current immigrants. The same, I believe, is true of other culture war issues. But when people feel that democratic institutions are no longer responsive to popular opinion, they are willing to risk more radical alternatives. Populists come along and say they'll do without those institutions. Populist supporters don't typically want dictatorship, but by weakening the institutions that preserve pluralism, this can be what they get.

In the short term, non-populists need to be better politicians. Counterintuitively, part of the political short-term response might be to ignore the problem—the populist per se. At the height of his anti-communist campaign in the early 1950s, Joseph McCarthy was one of the most popular politicians in the country. During the 1950 midterm elections for Congress, McCarthy had more invitations to speak than the rest of the Senate combined. There's no doubt he was eyeing higher office. What should have been the response? One option was to meet McCarthy head-on as President Harry Truman had done. The problem with this, as one contemporary pointed out, was that for McCarthy, any publicity was good publicity. "That damn fool Truman *created* that monster. [McCarthy] didn't exist until Truman went eyeball-to-eyeball with him," a critic noted.[15]

The approach of Truman's successor, Dwight Eisenhower, was the complete opposite. Ike's strategy was to avoid any mention of McCarthy and wait for him to slip up. Eisenhower was one of the only politicians with greater popularity than McCarthy, and some believed that he should have used his political capital to stand up to him. In his biography of McCarthy,

Larry Tye praises Senator Herbert Lehman of New York for criticizing McCarthy. Yet McCarthy never even bothered to engage. Tye misses the logic of the troll completely. You don't troll someone less famous than you. When, running out of enemies to purge, McCarthy extended his attacks to the widely admired US Army, he went too far. The Army hired Joseph Welch, a Boston attorney, to respond to McCarthy. Speaking at a hearing, Welch said what everyone was thinking: "Have you no sense of decency, sir?" McCarthy's hubris was laid bare. His popularity rapidly declined and his career was effectively finished when the Senate issued him a formal censure.[16]

There is a lesson here. Those who oppose populism would do well to listen—not to populists themselves but to the grievances that fuel their rise. Populist mobilization reveals the raw nerves of public resentment, the frustrations of those who feel unheard and unrepresented. Ignoring these discontented voters, or worse, dismissing them outright, only strengthens populism's appeal. The wiser course is to engage them, to offer alternatives that speak to their concerns without capitulating to the populists who exploit them.

The instinctive response to populism's assault on institutions has been to defend those institutions wholesale. But not all institutions are equally worth defending. Those that preserve pluralism—that safeguard the right to vote, to organize, to dissent—should be strengthened, not weakened. Yet institutions that serve narrow policy goals or entrenched interests should not be placed beyond the reach of democratic debate. As public choice theorists long ago noted, those who hold power within institutions will always fight to protect their turf, to expand their influence, regardless of whether it serves the public good. Some institutions outlive their usefulness. Some need to be reformed—or removed. A democracy that recognizes this, that adapts rather than calcifies, is a democracy that more people can believe in.

Notes

1. Paul D. Kenny, "'Inclusionary' Populism and Democracy in India," in *The Routledge Handbook of Populism in the Asia Pacific* edited by D. B. Subedi, Howard Brasted, Karin von Strokirch, and Alan Scott, (Routledge, 2024), 163–175.
2. "go to the people," "the peasants," in Christopher Ely, *Russian Populism: A History* (Bloomsbury, 2022), 47, 95.
3. "crawling slaves," quoted in Patrick M. Geoghegan, *King Dan: The Rise of Daniel O'Connell, 1775–1829* (Gill & Macmillan Ltd., 2008), 102.
4. "The pulpit," quoted in Malcolm Chase, *Chartism: A New History* (Manchester University Press, 2007), 145.
5. "He now has," quoted in Anthony Sampson, *Mandela: The Authorized Biography* (HarperCollins, 2011), 299.
6. "had an exceptional," quoted in Sampson, *Mandela*, 497.
7. "We have to," quoted in Sampson, *Mandela*, 491.
8. Sean Jacobs, "Tensions of a Free Press: South Africa after Apartheid," The Joan Shorenstein Center (Research Paper R-22), June 1999, https://shorensteincenter.org/wp-content/uploads/2012/03/r22_jacobs.pdf.
9. "enough of these politicians," in Stanton H. Burnett and Luca Mantovani, *The Italian Guillotine: Operation Clean Hands and the Overthrow of Italy's First Republic* (Rowman and Littlefield, 1998), 160.
10. "free organization," quoted in Broder, *First They Took Rome: How the Populist Right Conquered Italy* (Verso, 2020), 23.
11. "smart," Angelo Amante and Rodolfo Fabbri, "Self-Employed, Catholics Drive Meloni's Italian Electoral Triumph," *Reuters*, September 27, 2022, https://www.reuters.com/world/europe/self-employed-catholics-drive-melonis-italian-electoral-triumph-2022-09-27/.
12. "amoral familism," Edward Banfield, *The Moral Basis of a Backward Society* (Free Press, 1967).
13. "hollow," Daniel Schlozman and Sam Rosenfeld, *The Hollow Parties: The Many Pasts and Disordered Present of American Party Politics* (Princeton University Press, 2024).

14. On COVID-19, see Stephen Macedo and Francis Lee, *In COVID's Wake: How Our Politics Failed US* (Princeton University Press, 2025).
15. "That damn fool Truman," in Larry Tye, *Demagogue: The Life and Long Shadow of Senator Joe McCarthy* (HarperCollins, 2020), 342.
16. "Have you," quoted in Tye, *Demagogue*, 3.

FURTHER READING

Defining populism

Cristobal Rovira Kaltwasser et al., eds., *The Oxford Handbook of Populism* (Oxford, 2017), provides useful introductions to different definitional approaches. Benjamin Moffitt, *Populism* (Polity, 2020), also gives a concise review of the main approaches, ultimately advancing a cultural-stylistic approach.

On the ideational approach to populism, see Cas Mudde, "The Populist Zeitgeist," *Government and Opposition* 39, no. 4 (2004): 541–563; Cas Mudde and Cristobal Rovira Katlwasser, *Populism: A Very Short Introduction* (Oxford University Press, 2017); and Matthijs Rooduijn, "The Nucleus of Populism: In Search of the Lowest Common Denominator," *Government and Opposition* 49, no. 4 (2014): 573–599; on the cultural-stylistic approach, which sits somewhere between the ideational and strategic versions, see Benjamin Moffitt, *The Global Rise of Populism: Performance, Political Style, and Representation* (Stanford University Press, 2017).

On the strategic approach, see Kurt Weyland, "Clarifying a Contested Concept: Populism in the Study of Latin American Politics," *Comparative Politics* 34, no. 1 (2001): 1–22; Robert R. Barr, "Populists, Outsiders and Anti-Establishment Politics," *Party Politics* 15, no. 1 (2009): 29–48; and Paul D. Kenny, "The Strategic Approach to Populism," in *The Routledge Handbook of Populism in the Asia Pacific*, edited by D. B. Subedi, Howard Brasted, Karin von Strokirch, and Alan Scott (Routledge, 2023), 37–48.

On the constitutional approach, see Jan-Werner Muller, *What Is Populism?* (University of Pennsylvania Press, 2016); William

Galston, *Anti-Pluralism: The Populist Threat to Liberal Democracy* (Yale, 2018) and Takis Pappas, *Populism and Liberal Democracy: A Comparative and Theoretical Analysis* (Oxford University Press, 2019). Each essentially argues that populism is defined by its opposition to pluralism. See also Rogers Brubaker, "Why Populism?" *Theory and Society* 46 (2017): 357–385.

Measuring populism

On measurement in the discursive approach, see Kirk A. Hawkins, "Is Chávez Populist? Measuring Populist Discourse in Comparative Perspective," *Comparative Political Studies* 42, no. 8 (2009): 1040–1067; AgnesAkkerman, Cas Mudde, and Andrej Zaslove, "How Populist Are the People? Measuring Populist Attitudes in Voters," *Comparative Political Studies* 47, no. 9 (2014): 1324–1353; Teun Pauwels, "Measuring Populism: A Review of Current Approaches," *Political Populism* (2017): 123–136.

On measurement in the strategic approach, see Paul D. Kenny, "The Strategic Approach to Populism," in *The Routledge Handbook of Populism in the Asia Pacific*, pp. 37–48 (Routledge, 2021); Kurt Weyland, *Democracy's Resilience to Populism's Threat: Countering Global Alarmism* (Cambridge University Press, 2024).

On measuring populist attitudes, see Anne Schulz, Philipp Müller, Christian Schemer, Dominique Stefanie Wirz, Martin Wettstein, and Werner Wirth, "Measuring Populist Attitudes on Three Dimensions," *International Journal of Public Opinion Research* 30, no. 2 (2018): 316–326, and Alexander Wuttke, Christian Schimpf, and Harald Schoen, "When the Whole Is Greater Than the Sum of Its Parts: On the Conceptualization and Measurement of Populist Attitudes and Other Multidimensional Constructs," *American Political Science Review* 114, no. 2 (2020): 356–374; for critiques, see Paul D. Kenny and Boris Bizumic, "Is There a Populist Personality? Populist Attitudes, Personality, and Voter Preference in Australian Public Opinion," *Journal of Elections, Public Opinion and Parties* (2023): 1–26; Bruno Castanho Silva, Mario Fuks, and Eduardo Ryô Tamaki, "So Thin It's Almost Invisible: Populist Attitudes and Voting Behavior in Brazil," *Electoral Studies* 75 (2022): 102434.

The demand side

For an overview of the demand side, I highly recommend Sergei Guriev and Elias Papaioannou, "The Political Economy of Populism," *Journal of Economic Literature* 60, no. 3 (2022): 753–832.

On economic causes specifically, Walter Bossert, Andrew E Clark, Conchita D'Ambrosio and Anthony Lepinteur, "Economic Insecurity and Political Preferences," *Oxford Economic Papers* 75, no. 3 (2023): 802–825; L. Guiso, H. Herrera, M. Morelli and T. Sonno, "Economic Insecurity and the Demand for Populism," *Economica* 91, no. 362 (2024): 588–620. See Dani Rodrik, "Why Does Globalization Fuel Populism? Economics, Culture, and the Rise of Right-Wing Populism," *Annual Review of Economics* 13, no. 1 (2021): 133–170 and Barry Eichengreen, *The Populist Temptation: Economic Grievance and Political Reaction in the Modern Era* (Oxford University Press, 2018).

For research on the role of identity politics and nationalism, see Roger Eatwell and Matthew Goodwin, *National Populism: The Revolt Against Liberal Democracy* (Penguin, 2018); Bart Bonikowski, "Ethnonationalist Populism and the Mobilization of Collective Resentment," *The British Journal of Sociology* 68 (2017): S181–S213; Eric Kaufmann, *Whiteshift: Populism, Immigration and the Future of White Majorities* (Penguin, 2018). Pippa Norris and Ronald Inglehart, *Cultural Backlash: Trump, Brexit, and Authoritarian Populism* (Cambridge University Press, 2019), argue that populists register highly on the culturally authoritarian–libertarian dimension. On the United States, see John Sides, Michael Tesler, and Lynn Vavreck, *Identity Crisis: The 2016 Presidential Campaign and the Battle for the Meaning of America* (Princeton University Press, 2019); for Britain, see Geoffrey Evans and James Tilley, *The New Politics of Class: The Political Exclusion of the British Working Class* (Oxford University Press, 2017).

On religion as a kind of identity politics, see Tobias Cremer, *The Godless Crusade: Religion, Populism and Right-wing Identity Politics in the West* (Cambridge University Press, 2023).

On the interrelationships between the economic and cultural sides: Yotam Margalit, "Economic Insecurity and the Causes of Populism Reconsidered," *Journal of Economic Perspectives* 33, no. 4 (2019): 152–170; Petar Stankov, *The Political Economy of Populism* (Routledge, 2021).

On the role of economic geography in the turn to populism, see I. Colantone and P. Stanig, "The Economic Determinants of the 'Cultural Backlash': Globalization and Attitudes in Western Europe," BAFFI CAREFIN Centre Research Paper No. 91, 2018, http://ssrn.com/abstract=3267139; David Autor, David Dorn, Gordon Hanson and Kaveh Majlesi, "Importing Political

Polarization? The Electoral Consequences of Rising Trade Exposure," *American Economic Review* 110, no. 10 (2020): 3139–3183; Lawrence J. Broz, Jeffry Frieden, and Stephen Weymouth, "Populism in Place: The Economic Geography of the Globalization Backlash," *International Organization* 75, no. 2 (2021): 464–494;

On the role of rural and post-industrial resentment in the rise of Trump: Stephanie Ternullo, *How the Heartland Went Red: Why Local Forces Matter in an Age of Nationalized Politics* (Princeton University Press, 2023; Stephanie Muravchik and Jon A. Shields, *Trump's Democrats* (Brookings Institution Press, 2020); and Nicholas Jacobs and Daniel Shea, *The Rural Voter: The Politics of Place and the Disuniting of America* (Columbia University Press, 2023); Kathrine Cramer, *The Politics of Resentment: Rural Consciousness in Wisconsin and the Rise of Scott Walker* (Chicago University Press, 2016); Arlie Russell Hochschild, *Strangers in Their Own Land: Anger and Mourning on the American Right* (New Press, 2018); Farah Stockman, *American Made: What Happens to People When Work Disappears* (Random House, 2021).

For overviews of the original Populist movement: McMath, Robert Carroll, *American Populism: A Social History, 1877–1898* (Macmillan, 1993); Charles Postel, *The Populist Vision* (Oxford University Press, 2007). For a historical interpretation of populism in America, see Michael Kazin, *The Populist Persuasion: An American History* (Cornell University Press, 1998).

For a notable memoir of post-industrial decline and the rise of populism, see: J. D. Vance, *Hillbilly Elegy: A Memoir of Family and Culture in Crisis* (HarperCollins, 2018).

The supply side

On the importance of the "supply side," see Paul D. Kenny, *Why Populism? Political Strategy from Ancient Greece to the Present* (Cambridge University Press, 2023). For an alternative approach to understanding the supply side, see Luigi Guiso, Helios Herrera, Massimo Morelli and Tommaso Sonno, "Demand and Supply of Populism," EIEF Working Paper 17/03, February 2017, https://www.eief.it/files/2017/02/wp-173.pdf.

On the importance of the prior decline of political parties, see Peter Mair, *Ruling the Void: The Hollowing of Western Democracy* (Verso, 2023), and John B. Judis, *The Populist Explosion: How the Great Recession Transformed American and European Politics* (Columbia

Global Reports, 2016); Carles Boix, *Democratic Capitalism at the Crossroads: Technological Change and the Future of Politics* (Princeton University Press, 2019), provides a compelling argument that populists are essentially political entrepreneurs who exploit unmet policy demands in the marketplace. For an especially insightful analysis of the Italian case, see David Broder, *First They Took Rome: How the Populist Right Conquered Italy* (Verso Books, 2020). On the European left, see Anton Jager and Arthur Borriello, *The Populist Moment: The Left After the Great Recession* (Verso Books, 2023).

Comparing populism to clientelism, see Nicos Mouzelis, "On the Concept of Populism: Populist and Clientelist Modes of Incorporation in Semiperipheral Polities," *Politics & Society* 14, no. 3 (1985): 329–348. See also Paul Kenny, *Populism in Southeast Asia* (Cambridge University Press, 2019).

Institutions

On the importance of institutions to understanding populism, see Samuel Issacharoff, *Democracy Unmoored: Populism and the Corruption of Popular Sovereignty* (Oxford University Press, 2023); Nadia Urbinati, "A Revolt Against Intermediary Bodies," *Constellations* 22, no. 4 (2015): 477–486.

On fairness, see Lixing Sun, *The Fairness Instinct: The Robin Hood Mentality and Our Biological Nature* (Prometheus Books, 2013).

On charisma, see Mark Van Vugt and Anjana Ahuja, *Naturally Selected: The Evolutionary Science of Leadership* (HarperBusiness, 2011); Takis S. Pappas, "Are Populist Leaders 'Charismatic'? The Evidence from Europe," *Constellations: An International Journal of Critical & Democratic Theory* 23, no. 3 (2016).

Populist policy under democracy

On the idea that the main appeal of populism is left-wing economic policy, see Rudiger Dornbusch and Sebastian Edwards, *The Macroeconomics of Populism* (Chicago, 1992). On the reality of populist economic policy, see Manuel Funke, Moritz Schularick, and Christoph Trebesch, "Populist Leaders and the Economy," *American Economic Review* 113, no. 12 (2023): 3249–3288.

On the effect of populism on inequality, see Martin Strobl, Andrea Sáenz de Viteri, Martin Rode, and Christian Bjørnskov, "Populism and Inequality: Does Reality Match the Populist Rhetoric?" *Journal of Economic Behavior & Organization* 207 (2023): 1–17.

On populism and the global economy: Kent Jones, *Populism and Trade: The Challenge to the Global Trading System* (Oxford University Press, 2021); Manuel Funke, Moritz Schularick, and Christoph Trebesch, "Populist Leaders and the Economy," *American Economic Review* 113, no. 12 (2023): 3249–3288.

On the adaptation of non-populist parties: Gijs Schumacher and Kees Van Kersbergen, "Do Mainstream Parties Adapt to the Welfare Chauvinism of Populist Parties?" *Party Politics* 22, no. 3 (2016): 300–312.

Populism and dictatorship

On populism and press freedom, see Paul D. Kenny, "'The Enemy of the People': Populists and Press Freedom," *Political Research Quarterly* 73, no. 2 (2020): 261–275.

On populist assaults on the law, see David Landau, "Populist Constitutions," *University of Chicago Law Review* 85 (2018): 521; Wojciech Sadurski, *A Pandemic of Populists* (Cambridge University Press, 2022); ; Eric A. Posner, *The demagogue's Playbook: The Battle for American Democracy from the Founders to Trump* (St. Martin's Griffin, 2020). Allan R. Brewer-Carías, *Dismantling Democracy in Venezuela: The Chávez Authoritarian Experiment* (Cambridge University Press, 2010); Tom Gingburg and Aziz Z. Huq, *How to Save a Constitutional Democracy* (University of Chicago Press, 2020); For comparative evidence, see Christian Houle and Paul D. Kenny, "The Political and Economic Consequences of Populist Rule in Latin America," *Government and Opposition* 53, no. 2 (2018): 256–287; and Andreas Kyriacou and Pedro Trivin, "Populism and the Rule of Law: The Importance of Institutional Legacies," *American Journal of Political Science* 59, no. 2 (2024): 495–510.

On the full breakdown of democracy under populism, see Daniel Ziblatt and Steven Levitsky, *How Democracies Die* (Penguin, 2019); Julio F. Carrión, *A Dynamic Theory of Populism in Power: The Andes in Comparative Perspective* (Oxford University Press, 2022); Kurt Weyland, *Democracy's Resilience to Populism's Threat: Countering Global Alarmism* (Cambridge University Press, 2024); Armin Schäfer and Michael Zürn, *The Democratic Regression: The Political Causes of Authoritarian Populism* (Polity, 2024); Larry M. Bartels, *Democracy Erodes from the Top: Leaders, Citizens, and the Challenge of Populism in Europe* (Princeton University Press, 2023); Alexander Baturo, Paul Kenny, and Evren Balta, "Leaders' Experience and the Transition from Populism to Dictatorship," *Democratization* 85 (August 2024): 1–24

After populism

On populism and technocratic government: Jacob Hale Russell and Dennis Patterson, *The Weaponization of Expertise: How Elites Fuel Populism* (MIT Press, 2025); Daniele Caramani, "Will vs. Reason: The Populist and Technocratic Forms of Political Representation and Their Critique to Party Government," *American Political Science Review* 111, no. 1 (2017): 54–67.

INDEX

For the benefit of digital users, indexed terms that span two pages (e.g., 52–53) may, on occasion, appear on only one of those pages.